The Opening of the West

DOCUMENTARY HISTORY OF THE UNITED STATES
Edited by Richard B. Morris

Chronological Volumes:

The Opening of
the West

Edited by
JACK M. SOSIN

Harper & Row, Publishers
New York, Evanston, and London

THE OPENING OF THE WEST

Introduction, notes, and compilation copyright ©
1969 by Jack M. Sosin.

Printed in the United States of America.

First edition: HARPER PAPERBACK, 1969, Harper & Row,
Publishers, Incorporated, 49 East 33rd Street, New York,
N.Y. 10016.

A clothbound edition of this title is
published by the University of
South Carolina Press.

Library of Congress Catalog Card Number: 79–625501.

Contents

The Opening of the West

Introduction

FOR nearly a century and a half after Englishmen first settled in North America, population was confined to the narrow continental shelf. First clustered about the coastal bays and estuaries, settlements were gradually extended up the navigable rivers onto the Piedmont and toward the mountain barrier where the rugged mountains, plateaus, and valleys of the Appalachian highlands stretched in a great arc from northern New England to central Georgia and Alabama. These peaks, called the Allegheny Mountains in the north and the Cumberland Mountains in the south, ran almost unbroken except for a few natural gaps cut by wind and rivers. Beyond them lay the West, the great Ohio and Mississippi valleys.

Powerful Indian tribes also lay in the path of the settlers. By the middle of the eighteenth century an estimated twelve thousand warriors lived in the North. In central and western New York and Pennsylvania were the remnants of the once dominant Iroquois; almost a century of prolonged conflict had reduced them to about two thousand braves, divided into six tribes or nations. Some five hundred Delaware warriors and three hundred Shawnee braves were to evacuate their lands along the Susquehanna River and move west to the Muskingum and Scioto valleys of Ohio. North along the Sandusky River were several hundred Huron or Wyandot, while west to the Mississippi resided the Miami, Potawatomi, and the Wabash and Illinois confederacies. Thousands of Chippewa, Ottawa, and Huron resided around the Great Lakes. South of the Ohio River and east of the Mississippi were some fourteen thousand warriors divided into four main groups. In the valleys and mountains of eastern Tennessee and northern Alabama were the Cherokee, reduced by war and disease to twenty-eight hundred braves. More than thirty-six hundred Creek warriors occupied the region extending from the Alabama River to the Ogeechee and the Florida peninsula. West of the Big Tombigbee River lived at least five thousand Choctaw fighting men and beyond them along the Yazoo were five hundred fierce Chickasaw warriors. Fortunately for the pioneers, the Indians were not united in the face of encroachments on their lands; indeed the whites were able to use one tribe against another. At times the red men grudgingly withdrew, but often the land had to be taken by force.

Despite almost a century and a half of sporadic warfare, neither the frontiersmen nor the militia had evolved effective tactics against the Indians. Short of a constant watch there was no adequate defense against Indian harassment. With every cabin vulnerable, forts and blockhouses simply could not shelter all of the families on the frontiers. And against a static defense such as this, the Indian raiders easily slipped around the posts and, by evading patrolling rangers, devastated the surrounding areas. The ill-equipped and ill-trained militia, at best, could operate only for short distances and for limited periods in the Indian country. Often they were caught in bloody ambushes and decisively defeated. Attempts by frontiersmen to fight in Indian fashion, as individuals or in loosely organized bodies behind cover, most often resulted in indecisive encounters or in disaster for the whites. Successful war against the Indians required perceptive leaders who understood native warfare, commanders who could discipline and train men to act in co-ordinated units and who would employ mobility and firepower the Indians could not match. Perhaps the first such commander, an officer who properly evaluated and counteracted Indian tactics, was Colonel Henry Bouquet, who won the Battle of Bushy Run (1763). But General John Sullivan at Newtown (1779) against the Iroquois, Anthony Wayne at Fallen Timbers (1793) against the Ohio tribes, and Andrew Jackson at Horseshoe Bend (1814) against the Creeks employed comparable tactics.

The long, often hazardous journey over rugged mountains and wilderness traces was another major obstacle for the emigrants. There were few transportation improvements before the nineteenth century, and until the adaptation of steam to water and land traffic, men relied on human and animal muscle and on river currents. The earliest emigrants to the Ohio Valley came through Pennsylvania and Virginia. During the French and Indian War British troops under Generals Forbes and Braddock had built two roads over the rugged Allegheny Mountains to Redstone (Brownsville) on a tributary of the Monongahela and to Fort Pitt (Pittsburgh). Afterwards pioneers used these roads and later were able to float rafts or flatboats down the Ohio. On both banks of the river were established the early towns: Limestone (Maysville), Louisville, Marietta, and Cincinnati. Further down the river, towns were later settled in Indiana and Illinois. The earliest southern route used in the eighteenth century lay along the Great Wagon Road through the Valley of Virginia between the Blue Ridge and Appalachian Mountains. From Fort Chiswell on the Holston River, a single wagon road led to the Cumberland Gap, where travelers picked up the Wilderness Road, cut by Daniel Boone before the Revolutionary War north to the Kentucky Basin. A branch trace west from the Wilderness Road led to Knoxville. An extension was later cut to Nashville on the Cumberland River and, following the War of 1812, one fork was extended to Memphis, another southwest to Huntsville in the Tennessee Valley of northern Alabama. Emigrants from New England by the 1790's could cross New York by the Mohawk and Catskill turnpikes to Lake Erie, where boats were available for passage to northern Ohio and later to northern Indiana and Michigan. By the turn of the century, settlers could follow Zane's Trace from Wheeling on the Ohio west and then south in an arc through Zanesville and Chillicothe to Maysville, Kentucky. By 1818 a road from Cumberland, Maryland, across the mountains had reached Wheeling, and by 1833, it had been extended to Columbus.

The future was to witness the construction of canals and railroads linking the East and the West. The Erie Canal had already been completed to Buffalo by 1825, but no canals or railroads in the West were finished before 1830. Steamboat traffic was already established, however. The first steamboat built at Pittsburgh, *The New Orleans*, was sent downstream in 1811. Four years later *The Enterprise* ascended the Mississippi and the Ohio as far as the falls at Louisville. By 1819 there were thirty-one steamboats in operation, and by 1825, seventy-five had joined the hundreds of rafts, flatboats, and keelboats hauling people, goods, and produce on the western waters.

Along the sources of these western streams at the crest of the Appalachian Mountains the first settlements were founded shortly before the American Revolution. Leading the vanguard were speculators and groups of families, the Harrod brothers along the Monongahela and Redstone Creek, the Zanes at Wheeling, the Harrods again in Kentucky, along with the McAfee brothers, Richard Henderson, and the Logans. And on the Holston,

Watauga, and Nolichucky rivers in southwestern Virginia and eastern Tennessee, the Campbells, Seviers, Shelbys, Donelsons, and Robertsons led the early pioneers. In the decade before the outbreak of the Revolution, a flood of emigrants from the British Isles had added to the population of North America and to the pressure for westward expansion. Then, because of conditions in Britain and in Europe, emigration was limited until the end of the Napoleonic Wars. Between 1775 and 1815, therefore, the western settlements were to be populated in the main by people born in the United States, Americans who poured out of the eastern states in astonishing numbers. As the result of a phenomenal birth rate among native Americans, the population of the country, and with it emigration to the West, mushroomed. Kentucky had only about twelve thousand settlers, the Knoxville and Nashville settlements even fewer, at the close of the Revolutionary War, but by 1790 over a hundred thousand lived there, with Kentucky claiming seventy thousand. North of the Ohio had been a thin line of settlements, but in ten years they boasted a population of fifty thousand. In another decade almost a quarter of a million people lived in Ohio alone, while Indiana, Illinois, and Michigan had over forty thousand. By 1815, with the population of the country totaling almost eight and a half million, fifteen out of every hundred Americans lived in the West. The population of Ohio had doubled, while Indiana had one hundred and fifty thousand, Illinois fifty-five thousand, and Michigan almost nine thousand souls. In the Southwest, the population of Alabama and Mississippi had stood at ten thousand at the turn of the century. Because of heavy migration from the states of the Old South it increased four times in the next decade and by 1820 had again more than quadrupled.

With the flood of people came organized government. Before 1820 the United States organized ten territorial governments in the West. The area of the initial Northwest Territory later included Indiana Territory (1800), Michigan Territory (1805), and Illinois Territory (1809). The region south of Kentucky included Southwest Territory (1790), Mississippi Territory (1798), and Alabama Territory (1817). Following the Louisiana Purchase in 1803, Congress created Orleans Territory (1804), Louisiana Territory (1805), Missouri Territory (1812), and Arkansas Territory (1819). Territories were created or renamed as portions of existing territories were advanced to a higher governmental stage or admitted into the Union as states. Indeed, so heavy was the flow of people west that by 1821 nine new states west of the Appalachian Mountains had been added, seven east and two west of the Mississippi River— Kentucky (1792), Tennessee (1796), Ohio (1803), Louisiana (1812), Indiana (1816), Mississippi (1817), Illinois (1818), Alabama (1819), and Missouri (1821). Five of the nine were added in the years following the War of 1812. The power of the Indians had been broken and prices for agricultural produce had boomed.

The earliest governments for the transappalachian communities, in some instances, were set up independent of outside control. Settlers along the Watauga in 1774 and the Cumberland in 1780, believing themselves outside the jurisdiction of Virginia or North Carolina, established government by popularly ratified compacts. In Kentucky, Richard Henderson, other speculators from North Carolina, and the settlers also set up an independent government. In these instances the documents reveal few, if any, innovations. At the outbreak of the American Revolution, Pennsylvania, Virginia, and North Carolina brought all of the western settlements under their jurisdiction and established county governments for them. These units were then further divided into smaller counties as population increased. Kentucky passed directly from Virginia County government to statehood in 1792. The governmental arrangement for all of the other western regions was determined by Congress once it was given jurisdiction by the states in the 1780's.

The basic structure of government in the West was set down in the Northwest Ordinance of 1787. The document reflected not only the political values of the time, but also existing political practices. As conditions changed, modifications were made in the territorial governments for later western communities. Many of these alterations reflected the wishes of the western populace, but often westerners were not agreed among themselves as to the desirability of political reform, self-government, or the advantage of statehood over territorial status.

The ability of settlers to obtain land contributed largely to the flow of people west. Under the British and colonial regimes individuals received land from governments by a variety of means: purchase, gift, or grant for service, especially military service, or for settling the back country. Laxness in administering the land policy, the need for revenue, and the desire to placate the Indians led the royal government in the last years before the Revolution to systematize procedures by prohibiting purchases by individuals from the Indians, establishing boundaries between white and Indian land, and regularizing the sale of land cleared of Indian title. A comparison of the provisions of this policy with those adopted by the Continental Congress shows great similarity.

The later years of the colonial period also witnessed an upsurge in land speculation, the time-proven method of acquiring wealth in America. Securing land cheaply, not for cultivation, but for later sale at a profit, was practiced by resident and nonresident speculators, by the rich and those of moderate means, by individuals and organized groups. By the middle of the eighteenth century Virginians had organized several syndicates, the Greenbriar Company, the Loyal Company, and the Ohio Company, to exploit hundreds of thousands of acres of western lands. Imitating the Virginians, speculators in other colonies organized the Louisa (Transylvania) Associates, the Susquehanna Company, the United Wabash and Illinois Company, and the Walpole Associates, which laid claim, on the basis of purchase from some Indians, to portions respectively of Pennsylvania, West Virginia, Kentucky, Illinois, and Indiana. Following the Revolution, speculators continued to operate in companies or syndicates, as witnessed by the efforts of the Ohio Associates of Massachusetts, the promoters associated with John Cleves Symmes of New Jersey, and William Blount of North Carolina, to exploit the Ohio and Tennessee river valleys. In 1795 four Yazoo or Mississippi land companies, by fraudulent means, obtained thirty-five million acres of land from Georgia for a mere half million dollars. Not all speculators were successful, and by no means were they all easterners. Many resided in the West and engaged in small-scale operations which did not tie up capital for long periods. Indeed, almost any farmer who held more land than he used, hoping to sell part of his holdings to later arrivals, was a speculator. Choice sections of Kentucky, Tennessee, Ohio, and Indiana were picked up at an early date by speculators.

In the eighteenth century land speculators were aided, at times, by the confusion created by conflicts between governments over jurisdiction. Georgia, North and South Carolina, Virginia, Connecticut, and Massachusetts claimed large portions of the transappalachian region on the basis of their colonial charters. New York, claiming to have succeeded to the suzerainty exercised by the

Iroquois Indians over the western tribesmen, contested with Virginia for much of the Old Northwest. A hot struggle was waged in Congress during the Revolution. Delegates from states with fixed western boundaries, such as Maryland and New Jersey, were particularly determined that the West, the common treasure won by the efforts of all, should be a national public domain, under the jurisdiction of Congress, not Virginia. In part, the struggle reflected a conflict between competing land speculators, those supported by the government of Virginia and others from Pennsylvania, New Jersey, and Maryland, who hoped Congress would honor their purchases from the Indians. All of the delegates were interested in securing territory to fulfill promises of land bounties made to Continental troops. During the war some states, asserting jurisdiction in the West, put up for sale lands located there. Virginia, claiming Kentucky and the Old Northwest by the Land Act of 1779, sold land at the rate of £40 per 100 acres. North Carolina, with territory available in Tennessee, allowed settlers to buy 640 acres at two shillings an acre, while Georgia almost gave land away—two shillings would buy 100 acres. Both Virginia and North Carolina recognized the rights of squatters—those who had occupied unclaimed lands—and awarded military bounties for land.

To the states and the Confederation government the West proved a source of revenue. The need for money and the pressing demands of the unpaid officers of the Continental Army finally led in 1784 to a resolution of the conflict between Congress and Virginia. After New York had given up her nebulous claims, Virginia, in return for congressional recognition of the right of the Old Dominion to Kentucky, and other minor concessions, ceded to the Confederation the region north and west of the Ohio River. Other states ceded their claims to the West in the years following: Massachusetts in 1785, Connecticut in 1786, South Carolina in 1787, North Carolina in 1790, and Georgia in 1802. Connecticut reserved for her citizens a tract of almost four million acres extending 120 miles west of Pennsylvania between Lake Erie and the forty-first parallel, north latitude.

After the cession of the Old Northwest by Virginia, Congress adopted a land ordinance in 1785 which became the basic law for disposing of the public domain. After 1785 private purchases from the Indians were not recognized and no land could be sold until the Indians had ceded title to the federal government. Nor could land be sold to individuals or legally occupied until surveyed. Until the turn of the century the federal government officially gave no preference to squatters. The Ordinance of 1785 was a compromise between two systems of locating and surveying lands: the indiscriminate, haphazard system practiced in the South whereby an individual received a warrant and then located where he desired; and the system prevalent in New England of locating by groups on specifically designated land surveyed prior to settlement. In the statute adopted in 1785 the minimum unit was the lot or section of 640 acres, to be sold at public auction at no less than one dollar per acre. Townships six miles square, divided into thirty-six sections, were to be sold alternately as a whole township and by separate sections. The provisions for townships and for survey prior to sale were to remain in subsequent congressional land laws. But the price and minimum unit for purchase in the Ordinance of 1785 reflected more the need of the Confederation government for money than the requirements and conditions of prospective settlers in the West. Later legislation rectified the situation. By the Land Act of 1796 townships were to be sold alternately in tracts of eight sections and single, 640-acre lots. The price was raised to a minimum of two dollars an acre. These terms were equally unrealistic, and only 48,566 acres were sold. William Henry Harrison, delegate to Congress from the Northwest Territory, sponsored a land act adopted four years later. It introduced a credit system and allowed sale of a half section (320 acres) at two dollars an acre with one quarter payment after forty days and the remainder in quarterly installments after two, three, and four years. Land offices were set up in the major Ohio towns—Cincinnati, Marietta, and Steubenville. The minimum purchase was dropped to 160 acres in 1804 and to 80 acres in 1817. Following the Panic of 1819, the credit system was abandoned. In 1812 Congress created the General Land Office, a bureau of the Treasury Department. It had the responsibility of surveying and selling the public domain, collecting money, and granting patents. Branches of the General Land Office, local offices, were opened in the territories and the states; twenty-one were operating in 1817 and thirty-six in 1832. In each local office, registers of tracts, surveyors' plats, and entry books were maintained. Under the general legislation, squatters who occupied land before it was surveyed or sold had no rights, but from 1799 to 1830 Congress passed special pre-emption laws, limited in application to those occupying lands at the time the laws were enacted.

The heavy migration into both the Northwest and the Southwest, along with the frenzied speculation in public land in the years 1815 to 1819, was stimulated by the credit system in the land legislation, the expansion of private bank credit, and also by the high prices paid for western agricultural produce. This last fact alone indicated that western farmers, as farmers in the colonial period before them, were engaged in commercial, export agriculture. As early as 1782 farmers from the Monongahela country were shipping wheat and flour to the infant settlements in Kentucky and down the Ohio and Mississippi rivers to be exported from New Orleans. On both sides of the Ohio subsistence farming soon gave way to the raising of cash crops: in Kentucky they were tobacco, hemp, and grains. In 1810 Kentucky had two thousand stills, one for every two hundred persons, producing more than 2.2 million gallons of whisky, over five gallons for every man, woman, and child in the state. These distilleries consumed large quantities of locally produced grains. In the Ohio and Cumberland river valleys corn and hogs early became the basis of the farm economy. Further north, wheat was harvested and livestock raised for sale in Philadelphia and Baltimore. Shipment to market was a problem, but by the turn of the century various types of water craft were carrying an ever-increasing volume of produce down the Ohio and Mississippi rivers.

The opening of the Old Southwest brought a further market for the produce of the upper Ohio and Mississippi valleys. Some cotton was raised in middle Tennessee by the early 1780's, but with the invention of the cotton gin in the 1790's, the production of staple cotton boomed. By 1811 the virgin lands of Alabama, Mississippi, Tennessee, and Louisiana produced more than ten million pounds. The expansion of cotton planting stimulated the growth of the West, directly where new fields were opened by planters from the Old South and indirectly by providing a market for the foodstuffs produced in the Northwest. And yet the upper Mississippi Valley was not entirely dependent on the cotton domain of the Southwest as a market, for a large portion of the meat and grain which came down river was exported from New Orleans to the growing urban centers of the East and to the traditional markets for American agricultural produce, southern Europe and the

West Indies. By 1820, New Orleans, the port of the West, was the fifth ranking city in the country, behind New York, Philadelphia, Baltimore, and Boston. The opening of the Erie Canal in 1825 and the construction of other canals and railroads after 1830 connecting the West with the coastal cities did not initiate commercial agriculture in the West. They merely routed shipment of some western produce, especially wheat and flour, from the more northern sections of the Northwest, from south to east. Corn, pork, whisky, produced in the southern sections of the Ohio Valley, continued to flow down the Mississippi. Much of this was consumed in the South, but much was transhipped elsewhere.[1]

In return for produce the West received manufactured goods carried over the mountains, brought up the Mississippi, or carried overland along the Natchez Trace to Nashville and the other western towns. As the documents reveal, the merchants in these small commercial centers depended on their eastern counterparts for credit and marketing services. They also indicate that the region before 1830 had developed industry and was enjoying a mixed economy.

Life in the West during the initial years of settlement was cruder and more violent than in the older sections of the country, but even during these early years it is apparent from the documents that in culture, education, and manners the pioneers tended to retain the values and practices, the social and class distinctions, they had known in New England, the Old South, and the Middle Atlantic states. Indeed, some westerners continued to think of themselves as Jerseyites, Marylanders, Virginians, or Yorkers. Change there was, to be sure, but change affecting the country as a whole and not merely those moving to the West. By the second third of the nineteenth century it was evident that the transappalachian West had been socially, politically, and economically integrated into the nation.

1. On this point see Paul W. Gates, *The Farmer's Age: Agriculture 1815–1860*, Vol. III of *The Economic History of the United States* (New York, 1960), p. 174.

I

Clearing the Indian Barrier

1. Origin of Dunmore's War

CLEARING western land of Indian title involved purchase from the natives; but in case of disputed title, or where more than one group was involved, it required the pressure of military force. In 1768 the British government purchased the left bank of the upper Ohio from the Six Nations of New York, but the Shawnee and Delaware residing on the lands in question refused to recognize the cession. By exerting pressure, speculators and frontiersmen from Virginia and Maryland forced the Indians into open conflict. The immediate causes of Dunmore's War are here described by a Pennsylvania official in the West. His letter is reprinted from the Pennsylvania Archives (Harrisburg, Pa., 1853), 1st series, IV, 511–513.

Devereux Smith to Dr. William Smith, 1774

Pittsburgh, June 10th, 1774

SIR,

I returned to this place the 11th of May, and found my Family in the greatest confusion, owing to the appearance of an Indian War, and the Tyrannical treatment they received from Doctor [John] Connolly in my absence.

. . . I understood from some of the Shawneese Chiefs at a Council with Mr. McKee, the Indian Agent under Sir William Johnson, that they were much dissatisfied at the Rapid Progress the Virginians had made down the Ohio, in Settleing the Lands below the purchase, viz., below Siota [Scioto] river, which they looked upon as a great Encroachment on their liberties and Properties. They also expressed their Surprize to see a number of armed men assembled at this place, with their colours at different times, making a Warlike appearance, and said, that after the first Muster of the 25th of January, some of the Militia fired on them at their camps near the mouth of the Sawmill Run.

These Shawneese Chiefs were sent for by Mr. [George] Crog-han, last Summer, and came here about the 25th of December, and remained till the first of April, during which time they often com-plained to the Inhabitants of this Place, that Mr. Croghan had sent for them to do business, and kept them in great distress for want of Provision and Clothing. Upon which the Inhabitants were at some expence Supplying them during their stay, and when they were going Home, made a Collection of Goods for them, in order to send them off Satisfied.

On the 15th of April, Mr. Wm. Butler sent off a Canoe loaded with Goods for the Shawny Towns, and on the 16th it was at-tacked about forty miles from here, by three Cherokee Indians, who had waylaid them on the river Bank; they killed one White man, and wounded another, and a third made his Escape. They plundered the Canoe of the most valuable part of the Cargo, and made off, but as they were Cherekees, we were sure they did this for sake of Plunder alone, therefore thought no more of it than the Loss. As Mr. Butler was under the necessity of sending People to assist in bringing his Peltry from the Shawny Towns, he sent off another Canoe on the 24th of April, in care of two Indians who were well known to be good men, and two White men; on the 27th, about 90 miles from here, they were fired upon from Shore, and both the Indians were killed by Michael Cresap and a party he had with him, they also scalped the Indians. Mr. Cresap then immediately followed the above mentioned Shawneese Chiefs some small distance down, where they were encamped, and fired upon them, killed one and wounded two more. The Indians fled to the Delaware Towns, which were the nearest, and are greatly Exasperated at this treatment, as they did not expect any such thing from the English. About that same time a party headed by one Gratehouse [Michael Greathouse], barbarously Murthered and Scalped nine Indians at the House of one Baker, near Yellow Creek, about 55 miles down the river. Owing to these cruelties committed by Cresap and Gratehouse, the Inhabitants of Racoon and Weiling [Wheeling] fled from that Settlement, and are chiefly gone to Virginia. After Cresop had been guilty of these cruelties, he returned to Maryland, but has since come back with a Party of men. Cresop wrote to Connolly and Mr. [Alexander] McKee, threatening that if they did not give him security, that the Indians would not do any mischief for six months, that he Cresop, would immediately proceed to commit further Hostilities against the Indians. About the 21st of April, Connolly wrote a Letter to the Inhabitants of Weiling, telling them that he had been informed by good authority, that the Shawneese were ill disposed towards the White men, and that he therefore required and Commanded them to hold themselves in readiness to repell any Insults that might be offered by them. This letter fell into the hands of Cresop, and he says that it was in consequence of this letter and the murther committed by the Cherokees on Mr. Butler's People, that he committed the Hostilities above mentioned. I am informed that the 6th of May Mr. Croghan sent Capt. White-Eyes, (one of the Indian Chiefs,) in company with some of our Traders, to acquaint the Shawneese & Delawares, that the outrages which had been committed, was done by some of our ill disposed People, and without the least Countenance from Government, this Indian promised to use his best endeavours to accommodate matters, and returned here the 24th of May, and brought with him ten White men, who had been protected by the Delawares eight days in their Towns, and guarded safe to this Place; he also brought a Speech from the Delawares, from which we have great reason to believe they are not inclined for war; we also believe that they will endeavour to Preserve the lives of the Traders that are now amongst the Shawneese: he also brought from the Shawneese Chief, (called the hard man,) an answer to a Speech sent to them by Mr. Croghan, upon this occasion, in which he signifies that the Shawneese are all Warriors, and will not listen to us untill they have satisfaction of us, for what Injuries they have received from the Virginians, &c.

White-Eyes informs us that a Mingo man called Logan, (whose Family has been murthered in the number,) had raised a Party to cut off the Shawny Town Traders, at the Canoe Bottom on Hawkhawkin Creek, where they were Pressing their Peltry, but we have heard since that the Shawneese have taken them under their Care untill matters are further settled, but God knows what fate they have met with; we hope they are still alive, and if it be so, they have a chance to come in, if the outrageous behaviour of the Virginians do not prevent them. The 6th of this month we had account from Muddy Creek, (empties into the river Monongahela near Cheat river,) that the Indians had killed and scalped one man, his wife and three children, and that three more of the same man's children were missing, and has since been confirmed; we suppose this to be Logan's party, and that they will do more mischief before they return. About the 20th of May, one Campbell, lately from Lanc^r, was killed and scalped near Newcomer's Town, and one Proctor at Weiling, by a party of Shawneese and Mingoes.

2. The Battle of Bushy Run

THE DECISIVE battles by which the Indians were defeated and the West effectively opened for settlement were won by disciplined, trained troops —sometimes regulars. Perhaps the first to understand and properly counteract Indian fighting tactics was Colonel Henry Bouquet, a Swiss officer serving in the British Army. In 1763, during Pontiac's Uprising, Bouquet led a force of British regulars to the relief of the besieged garrison at Fort Pitt. While still a short distance from their objective, they were attacked by the Indians. Bouquet's account, taken from his papers in the British Museum (Additional Manuscripts, 21653, f.203) is reprinted from Sylvester K. Stevens, Donald H. Kent, and Leo J. Roland (eds.), The Papers of Col. Henry Bouquet (16 vols., Harrisburg, Pa., 1940), series 21653, 209–211.

Colonel Henry Bouquet to General Sir Jeffery Amherst

Camp at Bushy Run, 6th Augt 1763

SIR

. . . We took Post last Night on the Hill where our Convoy halted when the Front was attacked (a comodious Piece of Ground & just spacious enough for our Purpose)[.] There we encircled the whole & covered our wounded with the Flour Bags:

In the Morning the Savages surrounded our Camp at the Distance of about 500 Yards; & by shouting and yelping quite round that extensive Circumference thought to have terrified us with their Numbers: They attacked us early, & under Favour of an incessant Fire, made several bold Efforts to penetrate our Camp & although they failed in the Attempt our Situation was not the less perplexing, having experienced that brisk Attacks had little Effect upon an Enemy who always gave way when pressed, & appeared again immediately in another quarter Our Troops were besides extremely fatigued with the long March, and as long Action, of the preceding Day, & distress'd to the last Degree by a total Want of

Water, much more intolerable than the Enemy's Fire. Tied to our Convoy we could not lose Sight of it without exposing it & our wounded to fall a Prey to the Savages, who pressed upon us on every Side; & to move it was impracticable; having lost Many Horses & most of the Drivers, stupified by Fear hid themselves in the Bushes, or were incapable of hearing or obeying any Orders.

The Savages growing every Moment more audacious it was thought proper still to increase their Confidence by the Means, if possible, to intice them to come close upon us, or to stand their Ground when attacked. With this View two Companies of Light Infantry were ordered within the Circle; & the Troops on their Right & left opened their Files & filled up the Space; that it might seem they were intended to cover the Retreat. The third Light Infantry Company & the Grenadiers of the 42^d. were ordered to support the two first Companies. This Manoeuvre succeded to our Wish, for the few Troops who took Possession of the Ground lately occupied by the two Light Infantry Companies, being brought in nearer to the Center of the Circle, the Barbarians mistaking these Motions for a Retreat hurried head long on, & advancing upon us with the most daring intrepidity galled us excessively with their heavy Fire; but as the very Moment that certain of Success, they thought themselves Masters of the Camp, Major Campbell at the Head of the two first Companies, sallied out, from a Part of the Hill they could not observe, & fell upon their right Flank. They resolutely returned the Fire, but could not stand the irresistable Shock of our Men, who, rushing in among them killed many of them & put the rest to Flight. The Orders sent to the other two Companies were delivered so timely by Captain Basset, & executed with such celerity and Spirit that the routed Savages, who happened to run that Moment before their Front, received their full Fire when uncovered by the Trees. The four Companies did not give them Time to load a second Time nor even to look behind them, but pursued them, till they were totally dispersed. The left of the Savages, which had not been attacked, was kept in Awe by the Remains of our Troops posted on the Brow of the Hill for that Purpose; nor durst they attempt to support, or assist, their Right, but, being witness to their Defeat, followed their Example and fled. Our brave Men disdained so much to touch the dead Body of a vanquished Enemy that scarce a Scalp was taken, except by the Rangers & Packhorse Drivers.

3. Anthony Wayne at Fallen Timbers

THE SPIRIT *of the Ohio tribes was broken by General Anthony Wayne in a decisive victory on August 20, 1794, at the Battle of Fallen Timbrs. The Kentucky militia under George Rogers Clark had proved incapable of defending the frontier settlements, and two expeditions of border militiamen, one under General Josiah Harmar and the other under Arthur St. Clair, governor of the Northwest Territory, had ended in disastrous defeats. But a new commander, Wayne, drilled and disciplined his troops before pushing into the Indian country up along the Auglaize River until he reached the Maumee. Here the British from Canada had built a fort to encourage the tribesmen. Wayne's account of the battle is taken from his letter to Secretary of War Henry Knox, in the Wayne Papers, Historical Society of Pennsylvania, and is printed in Richard C. Knopf (ed.), Anthony Wayne . . . The Wayne-Knox-Pickering-McHenry Correspondence (Pittsburgh, Pa., 1960), pp. 351–354.*

Wayne to Knox

Head Quarters
Grand Glaize, 28th Augt. 1794

SIR

It's with infinite pleasure that I now announce to you the brilliant success of the Federal army under my Command in a General action with the combined force of the Hostile Indians & a considerable number of the Volunteers & Militia of Detroit on the 20th Instant, on the banks of the Miamis [Maumee] in the vicinity of the British post & Garrison at the foot of the rapids. . . .

. . . on the morning of the 20th the army again advanced in Columns agreeably to the standing order of March—the Legion on the right, its right flank cover'd by the Miamis, One Brigade of Mounted Volunteers on the left, under [General Robert] Todd, & the other in the rear under [General Thomas] Barbee, a select Battalion of Mounted Volunteers moved in front of the Legion commanded by Major [William] Price, who was directed to keep sufficiently advanced, so as to give timely notice for the troops to form in case of Action. . . .

After advancing about Five miles, Major Price's corps received so severe a fire from the enemy, who were secreted in the woods & high grass, as to compel them to retreat.

The Legion was immediately formed in two lines principally in a close thick wood which extended for miles on our left & for very considerable distance in front, the ground being cover'd with old fallen timber probably occasioned by a tornado, which render'd it impracticable for the Cavalry to act with effect, & afforded the enemy the most favorable covert for their mode of warfare these savages were formed in three lines within supporting distance of each other & extending near two miles at right angles with the River. I soon discover'd from the weight of the fire, & extent of their Lines that the enemy were in full force in front in possession of their favorite ground & endeavoring to turn our left flank, I therefore gave orders for the second line to advance to support the first, & directed Major Genl [Charles] Scott to gain & turn the right flank of the savages with the whole of the Mounted Volunteers by a circuitous route, at the same time I ordered the front line to advance & charge with trailed arms & rouse the Indians from their coverts at the point of the bayonet, & when up to deliver a close & well directed fire on their backs followed by a br[i]sk charge, so as not to give time to load again I also order'd Capt [Robert] Mis Campbell who commanded the Legionary Cavalry to turn the left flank of the Enemy next the river & which afforded a favorable field for that Corps to act in,

All those orders were obeyed with spirit & promptitude, but such was the impetuosity of the charge by the first line of Infantry —that the Indians & Canadian Militia & Volunteers were drove from all their Coverts in so short a time, that altho every possible exertion was used by the Officers of the second line of the Legion & by Generals Scott, Todd & Barbee of the Mounted Volunteers, to gain their proper positions but part of each cou'd get up in season to participate in the Action, the enemy being drove in the course of One hour more than two miles thro' the thick woods already mentioned, by less than one half their Numbers, from Every account the Enemy amounted to two thousand combatants, the troops actually engaged against them were short of nine hundred; [illegible] Savages with their allies abandoned themselves to flight & dispersed with terror & dismay, leaving our victorious army in full & quiet possession of the field of battle, which terminated under the influence of the Guns of the British Garrison. . . .

After remaining three days & nights on the banks of the Miamis in front of the Field of battle during which time all the Houses & Corn fields were consumed & destroyed for a considerable distance both above & below Fort Miamis as well as within pistol shot of the Garrison who were compeled to remain tacit spectators to this general devestation & Conflagration; among which were the Houses stores & property of Colo[nel Alexander] McKee, the British Indian Agent & principal stimulator of the War now existing between the United States & the savages

The army returned to this place on the 27th by easy marches laying waste the Villages & Corn fields for about Fifty miles on each side of the Miamis—

4. Andrew Jackson Against the Creeks

THE INDIANS east of the Mississippi were not decisively eliminated until the War of 1812, when in two battles their power was finally broken. On October 5, 1813, a picked force of 3000 men, under William Henry Harrison, defeated 400 British under Colonel Henry Proctor and 600 Indians led by Tecumseh. The following year an equal number of troops and some friendly Indians, under Andrew Jackson, crushed the Creeks at the bloody Battle of Horseshoe Bend. This report of the engagement by Jackson to Governor Willie Blount of Tennessee is in the archives of the Tennessee Historical Society and is printed in John Spencer Bassett (ed.), Correspondence of Andrew Jackson (7 vols., Washington, D.C., 1924), I, 490–492.

Fort Williams, March 31, 1814

I took up the line of march from this place on the morning of the 24th instant and . . . I reached the bend of the Tallapoosa . . . on the morning of the 27th. This bend resembles in its curvature that of a horse shoe, and is thence called by that name among the whites. Nature furnishes few situations so eligible for defence; and barbarians have never rendered one more secure by art. Across the neck of land which leads into it from the North, they had erected a breast-work, of greatest compactness and strength—from five to eight feet high, and prepared with double rows of port-holes very artfully arranged. The figure of this wall, manifested no less skill in the projectors of it, than its construction: an army could not approach it without being exposed to a double and cross fire from the enemy who lay in perfect security behind it. The area of this peninsular, thus bounded by the breastworks includes, I conjecture eighty or a hundred acres.

In this bend the warriors from Oakfuskee, Oakchaya, New Youka, Hillabees, the Fish ponds, and Eufaula towns, apprised of our approach, had collected their strength. Their exact number cannot be ascertained; but it is said, by the prisoners we have taken, to have been a thousand. It is certain they were very numerous; and that relying with the utmost confidence upon their strength—their situation, and the assurances of their prophets, they calculated on repulsing us with great ease.

Early on the morning of the 27th having encamped the preceding night at the distance of six miles from them—I detailed General Coffee with the mounted men and nearly the whole of the Indian force, to pass the river at a ford about three miles below their encampment, and to surround the bend in such a manner that none of them should escape by attempting to cross the river. With the remainder of the forces I proceeded along the point of land which leads to the front of the breast-work; and at half past ten oclock A.M. I had planted my artillery on a small eminence, distant from its nearest point about eighty yards, and from its farthest, about two hundred and fifty; from whence I immediately opened a brisk fire upon its centre. With the musquetry and rifles I kept up a galling fire whenever the enemy shewed themselves behind their works, or ventured to approach them. This was continued with occasional intermissions, for about two hours, when Captain Russell's company of spies and a part of the Cherokee force . . . crossed over to the extremity of the peninsular in canoes, and set fire to a few of their buildings which were there situated. They then advanced with great gallantry towards the breast-work, and commenced firing upon the enemy who lay behind it.

Finding that this force notwithstanding the d[e]termined bravery they displayed, was wholly insufficient to dislodge the enemy and that General Coffee had secured the opposite banks of the river, I now determined upon taking possession of their works by storm. Never were men better disposed for such an undertaking than those by whom it was to be effected. They had entreated to be lead to the charge with the most pressing importunity, and received the order which was now given, with the strongest demonstration of joy. The effect was such, as this temper of mind foretold. The regular troops, led on by their intrepid and skillful commander Colonel Williams, and by the gallant Major Montgomery were presently in possession of the nearer side of the breast-work; and the militia accompanied them in the charge with a vivacity and firmness which could not have been exceeded and has seldom been equalled by troops of any description. . . .

Having maintained for a few minutes a very obstinate contest, muzzle to muzzle, through the port-holes, in which many of the enemy's balls were welded to the bayonets of our musquets, our troops succeeded in gaining possession of the opposite side of the works. The event could no longer be doubtful. The enemy altho many of them fought to the last with that kind of bravery which desperation inspires, were at length entirely routed and cut to pieces. The whole margin of the river which surroun[d]ed the peninsular was strewed with the slain. Five hundred and fi[f]ty seven were found by officers of great respec[t]ability whom I had ordered to count them; besides a very great number who were thrown into the river by their surviving friends, and killed in attempting to pass by General Coffee's men stationed on the opposite banks. . . .

Both officers and men who had the best opportunities of judging, believe the loss of the enemy in killed, not to fall short of eight hundred and if their number was as great as it is represented to have been by the prisoners . . . their loss must even have been more considerable—as it is quite certain that not more than twenty can have escaped. Among the dead was found their famous prophet Monahoee—shot in the mouth by a grape shot; as if Heaven designed to chastise his impostures by an appropriate punishment. Two other prophets were also killed—leaving no others, as I learn, on the Tallapoosa. I lament that two or three women and children were killed by accident. I do not know the exact number of prisoners taken; but it must exceed three hundred, all women and children except three or four.

The battle may be said to have continued with severity for about five hours; but the firing and the slaughter continued until it was suspended by the darkness of the night. The next morning it was resumed and sixteen of the enemy slain who had concealed themselves under the banks.

Our loss was twenty six white men killed and one hundred and seven wounded—Cherokees, eighteen killed, and thirty six wounded, friendly Creeks Five killed and eleven wounded.

II

Early Settlements

5. The Kentucky and Tennessee Stations

PIONEERS in the early movement west followed several courses. In the North they had to traverse the mountains of Pennsylvania to the Allegheny or Monongahela rivers and then move down the Ohio to their settlements, first south of the river in Kentucky and then in the 1780's and 1790's on the right bank. In the South, once the pioneers were beyond the Blue Ridge, they followed the Great Appalachian Valley southwest to the Holston, Watauga, and Nolichucky rivers, the headwaters of the great Tennessee and Cumberland river systems. The Wilderness Trail, cut by Daniel Boone and a company of axmen, led through the Cumberland Gap and into Kentucky. Other traces led to the Cumberland Valley, which could also be reached by the rivers.

Thomas Hanson's Journal

Many types were involved in the early westward movement—settlers, hunters, militia officers, and, most important, speculators. The journal of Thomas Hanson illustrates the diversity of men who laid out the first surveys in Kentucky despite the dangers of hostile Indians. Several of these men are noteworthy. James Knox, an Irishman by birth, was the leader of the "long hunters" in Kentucky and Tennessee, while John Floyd and Isaac Hite were to become prominent settlers and speculators. William Christian and William Preston, among the most prominent men in western Virginia, were frontier gentry. James Harrod and his brothers from the Monongahela country were much lower on the social scale. In 1774 they were in Kentucky staking "tomahawk" claims to land, but were forced to abandon their settlements until the following year. Hanson's journal, which is among the papers in the Draper Collection 14558–84, The State Historical Society of Wisconsin, is printed in Reuben Gold Thwaites and Louise P. Kellogg (eds.), Documentary History of Dunmore's War 1774 (Madison, Wis., 1905), pp. 110–133.

April 7th [1774]. We left Col. Wm Preston's in Fincastle County . . . eight of us being in company, viz Mr. John Floyd assistant surveyor, Mr. [James] Douglas, D[itt]o, Mr. [Isaac] Hite, Mr. [Alexander] Dandridge, Thos Hanson, James Nocks [Knox]— Roderick McCra & Mordecai Batson. . . .

18th. We surveyed 2000 acres of Land for Col. Washington, bordered by Coal River & the Canawagh. . . .

20th. We proceeded to the mouth of the Kanawha, 26 miles. At our arrival we found 26 People there on different designs—Some to cultivate land, others to attend the surveyors, They confirm the same story of the Indians [being hostile]. . . .

21st. Mr. Floyd wrote to Coln. Preston [chief surveyor of Fincastle County] letting him know how affairs are at present & what happened on the journey. Mr. Floyd and the rest of the People are in high Spirits, and determined to go down the river, to do the business they came on & try the consequences unless a superior Force should attack them,

22nd. The Company consisting of 18 men with 4 Canoes proceeded down the Ohio River, Messrs. Floyd & Taylor going on foot down the other side about 10 miles to a Creek. On the East Side, the Bottoms are narrow, but on the West side of the Ohio they appear broader. . . .

[May] 2nd. We made a survey of this Bottom for Paterick [sic] Henry. It contains 4 or 500 acres, of very good land, including the Fort & Town. . . . The River here is 494½ yards wide. At 9 o'clock we embarked, and went down 7 miles, then landed and Surveyed a Bottom, which Contains 5 or 600 acres for Wm. Henry. The land is excessive good. From there we proceeded 13 miles lower down the River, passed Shot Pouch Creek, five miles below the last Bottom we surveyed. The Bottoms here are but small & not very good. We had rain this night which gave us wet skins, as we were ill provided.

3rd. We proceeded 4 miles lower to Salt Lick Creek, and made a survey of 200 acres, the Bottoms narrow & beachey, We had a hard frost this night, which killed almost every thing that was green.

4th. We proceeded 5 miles lower, and then Mr. Floyd made a survey of 2000 acres on a large Bottom which runs 5 miles down the River, and ends opposite to an Island, whereon we lodged. This night the Frost was very severe, the Island is called Oppony Island.

5th. We proceeded 5 miles lower and then landed on a bottom, which Mr. Floyd surveyed for Mr. John May. It contains about

700 acres, very good land. There was frost again this night. We lay on a very large Island opposite our Survey.

6th. We proceeded 3 miles and then landed on a Bottom, which Mr. Floyd surveyed It runs on the River 3 miles, but is narrow, he finished the survey at a small Creek, which he called Nashes creek from his valiant behaviour on the following occurrence. While we are surveying, Nash hunted thro' the Bottom & at the Creek met with two Indians, who called him Brother, but attempted to change Guns with him, which Nash refused. When they found he would not change, They would have killed him for her, but he was much on his guard, and they had but one Gun between them. Therefore by his Quickness & Alertness, he got Clear. Soon after the Indian that had no Gun overtook one Mc Culloch and took his double barriled Rifel from him. This alarmed us, and 12 men went in search of the Indians, 6 of them one Way & 6 another. The first 6 men saw the Indian, that had taken the Gun & one of the men fired at him but missed him, we kept under arms until evening. . . .

8th. We proceeded 19 miles down the river then encamped, The Bottoms narrow & broken.

9th. We proceeded to Locust Creek 12 miles, & there began a Survey on the Bottom which extended 7 miles, & Contains 3000 acres. We lay all night at the end of the bottom. The land very good.

10th. We proceeded down the River, passed Little Miamia at 2 miles went from thence to Licking Creek 8 miles. A survey was made on the upper side of this Creek, good land & there is part of the bottom on the lower side not Surveyed very good, we proceeded 11 miles lower & then encampt; It Thundered & rained this night.

11th. We rose early in the morning, & proceeded down 6 miles, which brought us to a Bottom of good land. We made a survey of the same for Doct[or] Hugh Mercer, containing 1000 acres. 4 miles below this Bottom, is great Miamia coming in on the Western side of it. There is a fine Bottom on the Eastern side of the Ohio, not surveyed. We proceeded 12 miles lower down to an Island & there encamped.

12th. We proceeded down to a Creek 8 miles which lies within 3 miles of the big Bone Lick. There was 1000 acres surveyed for William Christian, about the Lick. The Land is not so good as the other Bottoms, likewise a little broken. There is a number of large Teeth to [be] seen about this Lick, which the People imagined to be Elephants, There is one Seven Feet & three Inches long. It is nine inches in Diameter at one End and five inches at the other.

13th. Mr. Douglass made a Survey of 2000 acres on the upper side of the Creek for Mr. William Christian, good land. At Mr Douglasses return, we embarked & floated down the River to Kentucky, 47 miles & by daybreak landed. In our passage we came to an Indian Camp, landed & found two Delewares, & a Squaw, we gave them Some Corn & Salt.

14th. Our Company divided, eleven men went up to Harrod's Company one hundred miles up the Kentucky on Louisa River. (n. b. Capt Harrod has been there many months [really a few days] building a kind of Town &c.) in order to make improvements. This day a quarrel arose between Mr. [Hancock] Lee and Mr. Hyte. Lee cut a stick and gave Hite a whipping with it, upon which Mr. Floyd demanded the Kings Peace, which stopt it sooner than it would have ended if he had not been there. . . .

16th. Mr. Floyd and Mr. Taylor surveyed eight miles & a quarter up the side of the Ohio, but the land is not so good as the other Bottoms we passed, for it is Beachy & of a more sour nature.

17th. Mr. Floyd and Mr. Hite & 5 men with them went 20 miles up Kentucky to a Salt Spring, where we saw about 300 Buffaloes collected together. The Bottoms were broken & Beachy all the way we went up. Mr. Floyd landed several times to look at the land, But found none to please him.

18th. We looked over the land & examined the spring of salt water—The land is worth nothing but the springs if collected together would afford a very good salt work. Mr. Floyd offered Mr. Hite his men to assist him to make his Survey there; but Mr. Hite neglected it.

19th. Went into the country for 8 or 10 miles & find it something better than at the springs; but seemed rather of a sour nature. Mr. Floyd with three men went by land to see the country Mr. Hite & 2 men returned to the Canoes & floated down the River.

20th. We found Mr. Floyd & his 3 men within 9 miles of the mouth of the Kentucky at a creek which we called Bear Creek. We all embarked & went down to the mouth of the Kentucky.

21st. Mr. Floyd surveyed 600 acres of land on the lower side of the mouth of Kentucky which takes in little Kentucky for Col[n]. Preston. The land is very good, but I think some of it overflows.

22nd. In the evening we embarked and went down the river three miles & half, leaving a letter at the mouth of Kentucky to direct any Person or Persons that followed the line how to find us.

23[d]. As we were on a bottom, Mr Taylor surveyed 1000 acres & then Mr Douglas began at his line, & Surveyed another 1000 acres, which took in the Bottom, except a small point at the lower end. It is 7 miles long. We campt at the lower end, Good land.

24th. Mr. Floyd went on the top of the hill from the River & surveyed a tract of land which is good and well Timbered & watered. We encampt 5 miles below on a small bottom, where it rained in the time.

25th. Mr Floyd surveyed the Bottom and some upland to the Quantity of 1000 acres. It was Showery weather.

26th. We embarked & at the same time saw a canoe coming down the river with a Red flag flying. We hailed them but they would not come to us, therefore we went to them and found them to be 2 Indians. One of them was called Dickirson who had a pass from the Commandant at Fort Pitt, to go down the River in order to collect their Hunters, and cause them to go home, as they expected a war between the white people & the Shawnese. They told us that the people on the river near Fort Pitt had left their Habitations and were gone to the fort, But expected they were returning again to their homes. That they thought it would be made up again. They said the white people & the Indians had a skirmish & that the white people had killed 16 Indians viz. 13 Shawnees 2 Mingoes & 1 Deleware. We parted with them but were afraid that they would follow us. Therefore Mr. Floyd Mr. Toylor Mr. Douglas & and an other man got into a canoe by themselves thinking to have a further conference with the Indians, but they being fearful would not come nigh us any more. This put our people into different opinions as to what to do. Some were for going down the river by way of the Mississippi But Mr. Floyd and the rest of the surveyors were determined to do the business they came on, If not repulsed by a greater force than themselves.

A Letter from Evan Shelby

THE SHELBY family of Maryland was among the first to settle in Tennessee. It was to provide military and political leadership in the western country for years. Evan Shelby, who settled initially in the Holston-Watauga settlements of southwestern Virginia and eastern Tennessee, hoped—as did many officers who had served in the provincial militia during the French and Indian War—to claim land under the terms of the royal proclamation of October 7, 1763. This letter to John Shelby, written from the Holston River, is in the Draper Collection (16DD4), The State Historical Society of Wisconsin. Shelby's orthography and values are both revealing.

[Holston River, January 3, 1774]

This is Too Lett you know that we are all Saffe ar[r]ived at our habitation on Halson [Holston] after a J[o]urney of three Days apon the Road wher[e] wee found all things In good order and wee Seeme satisfyd with the C[o]untry[.] Wee sent all our Stock To the Bain, we have Just come hom[e] from Salting them and they are now in Bet[t]er order then when wee Came from [the] Partomack [Potomac] River So that our Stock will be Lit[t]le Cost to us more than salting of them Except half a Duzon Cows wee Ceep for milk and four horses wee Ceep To work. . . . Wee have no news hear . . . Except that it is certain the officers is To have their [manuscript illegible] of Land upon these waters which will I hop[e] be the means of Satling of this C[o]untry with a much Better Sort of People then it wou[l]d [have] been Settled with[.] But I always thought if the officers had their Choice they wou[l]d Sooner Chews [choose] it hear than on the Ohio. . . .

I wou[l]d Recommend it To you Both to Pinchis [purchase] all officers and Soldiers Right you Can Pos[s]ible Get. . . .

Collonell Gaitts [Gates] was amentioning To me as I was Coming out, if I Cou[l]d Git him proper Locations for a Large quantidy of Land he Cou[l]d procure a Grant forit[.] I have Sent you the Locations if he will Enter into a proper article of agreement with me that I Shall have one third of the Land if the Said grants Sh[o]uld be optained. . . . Ther[e] has Sume Gentlemen from north Carolina wrot to apon the Same action but Mr[.] Gaitts spacking to me at Berkeley Court as I was a coming up I have not answer[ed] thier Latters Till I heare from him or you on this account. . . .

. . . As ther[e] has been such Disturbances in the Gover[n]-ment of north Carollina of Late [the Regulator Movement] I Sh[o]u[l]d think if wee was to sett forth that wee wood undertake to satle it with men of Property and of them of the astablisht [established] church of Ingland it wood be a Great indusment To obtain the grants and To al[l]ow us a Countty To be Struck off Immediatle [sic] to Supress vellanse [violence] for I believe his Lordship [Lord Dunmore, governor of Virginia] has felt the affects of the Last Disasters in that Province. . . .

John Donelson's Journal

THE FIRST frontier stations in the Cumberland Basin (present Nashville) were founded in the winter of 1779–80 by North Carolinians and Virginians. The migration was carried out in two parts. James Robertson led most of the men and the livestock by circuitous traces overland from the Holston River settlements. Soon after their departure, John Donelson, the projector of the enterprise, set out with several boats bearing the families and property of emigrants from Fort Patrick Henry, near Long Island. They floated down the Holston and Tennessee rivers and then poled up the Ohio and the Cumberland. When they arrived, they found that the Robertson party had already gotten there and started the stations. The journal of the Donelson voyage is in the Draper Collection (11ZZ13–23) and is printed in James G. M. Ramsey, The Annals of Tennessee . . . (Charleston, S.C., 1853), pp, 197–202.

December 22, 1779.—Took our departure from the fort and fell down the river to the mouth of Reedy Creek, where we were stopped by the fall of water, and most excessive hard frost; and after much delay and many difficulties we arrived at the mouth of Cloud's Creek, on Sunday evening, the 20th February, 1780, where we lay by until Sunday, 27th, when we took our departure with sundry other vessels bound for the same voyage, and on the same day struck the Poor Valley Shoal, together with Mr. Boyd and Mr. Rounsifer, on which shoal we lay that afternoon and succeeding night in much distress.

Monday, February 28th, 1780.—In the morning the water rising, we got off the shoal, after landing thirty persons to lighten our boat. In attempting to land on an island, received some damage and lost sundry articles, and came to camp on the south shore, where we joined sundry other vessels also bound down.

Tuesday, 29th.—Proceeded down the river and camped on the north shore, the afternoon and following day proving rainy.

Wednesday, March 1st.—Proceeded on and camped on the south shore, nothing happening that day remarkable.

March 2d.—Rain about half the day; passed the mouth of French

Broad River, and about 12 o'clock, Mr. Henry's boat being driven on the point of an island by the force of the current was sunk, the whole cargo much damaged and the crew's lives much endangered, which occasioned the whole fleet to put on shore and go to their assistance, but with much difficulty bailed her, in order to take in her cargo again. The same afternoon Reuben Harrison went out a hunting and did not return that night, though many guns were fired to fetch him in.

Friday, 3ᵈ.—Early in the morning fired a four-pounder for the lost man, sent out sundry persons to search the woods for him, firing many guns that day and the succeeding night, but all without success, to the great grief of his parents and fellow travellers.

Saturday, 4ᵗʰ.—Proceeded on our voyage, leaving old Mr. Harrison with some other vessels to make further search for his lost son; about ten o'clock the same day found him a considerable distance down the river, where Mr. Ben. Belew took him on board his boat. At 3 o'clock, P.M., passed the mouth of Tennessee River, and camped on the south shore about ten miles below the mouth of Tennessee.

Sunday, 5ᵗʰ.—Cast off and got under way before sunrise; 12 o'clock passed the mouth of Clinch; at 12 o'clock, M. came up with the Clinch River Company, whom we joined and camped, the evening proving rainy.

Monday, 6ᵗʰ.—Got under way before sunrise; the morning proving very foggy, many of the fleet were much bogged—about 10 o'clock lay by for them; when collected, proceeded down. Camped on the north shore, where Capt. Hutching's negro man died, being much frosted in his feet and legs, of which he died.

Tuesday, 7ᵗʰ.—Got under way very early, the day proving very windy, a S.S.W., and the river being wide occasioned a high sea, insomuch that some of the smaller crafts were in danger; therefore came to, at the uppermost Chiccamauga Town, which was then evacuated where we lay by that afternoon and camped that night. The wife of Ephraim Peyton was here delivered of a child. Mr. Peyton has gone through by land with Capt. Robertson.

Wednesday, 8ᵗʰ.—Cast off at 10 o'clock, and proceed down to an Indian village, which was inhabited, on the south side of the river; they insisted on us to "come ashore," called us brothers, and showed other signs of friendship, insomuch that Mr. John Caffrey and my son then on board took a canoe which I had in tow, and were crossing over to them, the rest of the fleet having landed on the opposite shore. After they had gone some distance, a half-breed, who called himself Archy Coody, with several other Indians, jumped into a canoe, met them, and advised them to return to the boat, which they did, together with Coody and several canoes which left the shore and followed directly after him. They appeared to be friendly. After distributing some presents among them, with which they seemed much pleased, we observed a number of Indians on the other side embarking in their canoes, armed and painted with red and black. Coody immediately made signs to his companions, ordering them to quit the boat, which they did, himself and another Indian remaining with us and telling us to move off instantly. We had not gone far before we discovered a number of Indians armed and painted proceeding down the river, as it were, to intercept us. Coody, the half-breed, and his companion, sailed with us for some time, and telling us that we had passed all the towns and were out of danger, left us. But we had not gone far until we had come in sight of another town, situated likewise on the south side of the river, nearly opposite a small island. Here they again invited us to come on shore, called us brothers, and observing the boats standing off for the opposite channel, told us that "their side of the river was better for boats to pass." And here we must regret the unfortunate death of young Mr. Payne, on board Capt. Blackemore's boat, who was mortally wounded by reason of the boat running too near the northern shore opposite the town, where some of the enemy lay concealed, and the more tragical misfortune of poor Stuart, his family and friends to the number of twenty-eight persons. This man had embarked with us for the Western country, but his family being diseased with the small pox, it was agreed upon between him and the company that he should keep at some distance in the rear, for fear of the infection spreading, and he was warned each night when the encampment should take place by the sound of a horn. After we had passed the town, the Indians having now collected to a considerable number, observing his helpless situation, singled off from the rest of the fleet, intercepted him and killed and took prisoners the whole crew, to the great grief of the whole company, uncertain how soon they might share the same fate; their cries were distinctly heard by those boats in the rear.

We still perceived them marching down the river in considerable bodies, keeping pace with us until the Cumberland Mountain withdrew them from our sight, when we were in hopes we had escaped them. We were now arrived at the place called the Whirl or Suck, where the river is compressed within less than half its common width above, by the Cumberland Mountain, which juts in on both sides. In passing through the upper part of these narrows, at a place described by Coody, which he termed the "boiling pot," a trivial accident had nearly ruined the expedition. One of the company, John Cotton, who was moving down in a large canoe, had attached it to Robert Cartwright's boat, into which he and his family had gone for safety. The canoe was here overturned, and the little cargo lost. The company pitying his distress, concluded to halt and assist him in recovering his property. They had landed on the northern shore at a level spot, and were going up to the place, when the Indians, to our astonishment, appeared immediately over us on the opposite cliffs, and commenced firing down upon us, which occasioned a precipitate retreat to the boats. We immediately moved off, the Indians lining the bluffs along continued their fire from the heights on our boats below, without doing any other injury than wounding four slightly. Jenning's boat is missing.

We have now passed through the Whirl. The river widens with a placid and gentle current; and all the company appear to be in safety except the family of Jonathan Jennings, whose boat ran on a large rock, projecting out from the northern shore, and partly immersed in water immediately at the Whirl, where we were compelled to leave them, perhaps to be slaughtered by their merciless enemies. Continued to sail on that day and floated throughout the following night.

Thursday, 9th.—Proceeded on our journey, nothing happening worthy attention to-day; floated till about midnight, and encamped on the northern shore.

Friday, 10th.—This morning about 4 o'clock we were surprised by the cries of "help poor Jennings," at some distance in the rear. He had discovered us by our fires, and came up in the most wretched condition. He states, that as soon as the Indians discovered his situation they turned their whole attention to him, and kept up a most galling fire at his boat. He ordered his wife, a son nearly grown, a young man who accompanied them, and his negro man and woman, to throw all his goods into the river, to lighten their

boat for the purpose of getting her off, himself returning their fire
as well as he could, being a good soldier and an excellent marks-
man. But before they had accomplished their object, his son, the
young man and the negro, jumped out of the boat and left them.
He thinks the young man and the negro were wounded before
they left the boat. Mrs. Jennings, however, and the negro woman,
succeeded in unloading the boat, but chiefly by the exertions of
Mrs. Jennings, who got out of the boat and shoved her off, but
was near falling a victim to her own intrepidity on account of the
boat starting so suddenly as soon as loosened from the rock. Upon
examination, he appears to have made a wonderful escape, for his
boat is pierced in numberless places with bullets. It is to be remarked, that Mrs. Peyton, who was the night before delivered of
an infant, which was unfortunately killed upon the hurry and confusion consequent upon such a disaster, assisted them, being frequently exposed to wet and cold then and afterwards, and that her
health appears to be good at this time, and I think and hope she
will do well. Their clothes were very much cut with bullets, especially Mrs. Jennings's.

Saturday, 11th.—Got under way after having distributed the
family of Mrs. Jennings in the other boats. Rowed on quietly that
day, and encamped for the night on the north shore.

Sunday, 12th.—Set out, and after a few hours' sailing we heard
the crowing of cocks, and soon came within view of the town;
here they fired on us again without any injury.

After running until about 10 o'clock, came in sight of the
Muscle Shoals. Halted on the northern shore at the appearance
of the shoals, in order to search for the signs Capt. James Robertson was to make for us at that place. He set out from Holston early
in the fall of 1779, was to proceed by the way of Kentucky to the
Big Salt Lick on Cumberland River, with several others in company, was to come across from the Big Salt Lick to the upper end
of the shoals, there to make such signs that we might know he had
been there, and that it was practicable for us to go across by land.
But to our great mortification we can find none—from which we
conclude that it would not be prudent to make the attempt, and
are determined, knowing ourselves to be in such imminent danger,
to pursue our journey down the river. After trimming our boats in
the best manner possible, we ran through the shoals before night.
When we approached them they had a dreadful appearance to

those who had never seen them before. The water being high made a terrible roaring, which could be heard at some distance among the drift-wood heaped frightfully upon the points of the islands, the current running in every possible direction. Here we did not know how soon we should be dashed to pieces, and all our troubles ended at once. Our boats frequently dragged on the bottom, and appeared constantly in danger of striking. They warped as much as in a rough sea. But by the hand of Providence we are now preserved from this danger also. I know not the length of this wonderful shoal; it had been represented to me to be 25 or 30 miles. If so, we must have descended very rapidly, as indeed we did, for we passed it in about three hours. Came to, and camped on the northern shore, not far below the shoals, for the night.

Monday, 13th.—Got under way early in the morning, and made a good run that day.

Tuesday, 14th.—Set out early. On this day two boats approaching too near the shore, were fired on by the Indians. Five of the crews were wounded, but not dangerously. Came to camp at night near the mouth of a creek. After kindling fires and preparing for rest, the company were alarmed, on account of the incessant barking our dogs kept up; taking it for granted that the Indians were attempting to surprise us, we retreated precipitately to the boats; fell down the river about a mile and encamped on the other shore. In the morning I prevailed on Mr. Caffrey and my son to cross below in a canoe, and return to the place; which they did, and found an African negro we had left in the hurry, asleep by one of the fires. The voyagers returned and collected their utensils which had been left.

Wednesday, 15th.—Got under way and moved on peaceably the five following days, when we arrived at the mouth of the Tennessee on Monday, the 20th, and landed on the lower point immediately on the bank of the Ohio. Our situation here is truly disagreeable. The river is very high, and the current rapid, our boats not constructed for the purpose of stemming a rapid stream, our provision exhausted, the crews almost worn down with hunger and fatigue, and know not what distance we have to go, or what time it will take us to our place of destination. The scene is rendered still more melancholy, as several boats will not attempt to ascend the rapid current. Some intend to descend the Mississippi to Natchez; others are bound for the Illinois—among the rest my son-in-law and daughter. We now part, perhaps to meet no more, for I am determined to pursue my course, happen what will.

Tuesday, 21st.—Set out, and on this day laboured very hard and got but a little way; camped on the south bank of the Ohio. Passed the two following days as the former, suffering much from hunger and fatigue.

Friday 24th.—About 3 o'clock came to the mouth of a river which I thought was the Cumberland. Some of the company declared it could not be—it was so much smaller than was expected. But I never heard of any river running in between the Cumberland and Tennessee. It appeared to flow with a gentle current. We determined, however, to make the trial, pushed up some distance and encamped for the night.

Saturday, 25th.—To-day we are much encouraged; the river grows wider; the current is very gentle, and we are now convinced it is the Cumberland. I have derived great assistance from a small square sail which was fixed up on the day we left the mouth of the river; and to prevent any ill-effects from sudden flaws of wind, a man was stationed at each of the lower corners of the sheet with, directions to give way whenever it was necessary.

Sunday, 26th.—Got under way early; procured some buffalo-meat; though poor it was palatable.

Monday, 27th.—Set out again; killed a swan, which was very delicious.

Tuesday, 28th.—Set out very early this morning; killed some buffalo.

Wednesday, 29th.—Proceeded up the river; gathered some herbs on the bottoms of Cumberland, which some of the company called Shawnee salad.

Thursday, 30th.—Proceeded on our voyage. This day we killed some more buffalo.

Friday, 31st.—Set out this day, and after running some distance, met with Col. Richard Henderson, who was running the line between Virginia and North-Carolina. At this meeting we were much rejoiced. He gave us every information we wished, and further informed us that he had purchased a quantity of corn in Kentucky, to be shipped at the Falls of Ohio for the use of the Cumberland settlement. We are now without bread, and are compelled to hunt the buffalo to preserve life. Worn out with fatigue, our progress at present is slow. Camped at night near the mouth of a little river, at which place and below there is a handsome bottom of rich land. Here we found a pair of hand-mill stones set up for grinding, but appeared not to have been used for a great length of time.

Proceeded on quietly until the 12th of April, at which time we came to the mouth of a little river running in on the north side, by Moses Renfoe and his company called Red River, up which they intend to settle. Here they took leave of us. We proceeded up Cumberland, nothing happening material until the 23d, when we reached the first settlement on the north side of the river, one mile and a half below the Big Salt Lick and called Eaton's Station, after a man of that name, who with several other families, came through Kentucky and settled there.

Monday, April 24th.—This day we arrived at our journey's end at the Big Salt Lick, where we have the pleasure of finding Capt. Robertson and his company. It is a source of satisfaction to us to be enabled to restore to him and others their families and friends, who were entrusted to our care, and who, sometimes since, perhaps, despaired of ever meeting again. Though our prospects at present are dreary, we have found a few log cabins which have been built on a cedar bluff above the Lick, by Capt. Robertson and his company.

6. Migration to the Southwest

THE RICH lands of the Southwest, soon to be exploited by cotton planters, were opened in the years immediately following the War of 1812. The following narrative by Gideon Lincecum illustrates both the importance of family units in the western movement and the almost compulsive migrating habits of some Americans. The "Autobiography" of Lincecum, printed in the Publications of the Mississippi Historical Society VIII (Oxford, Miss., 1904), 470–473, was actually compiled from a series of letters written by Lincecum.

Gideon Lincecum

The Alabama, Black Warrior, Tombecbee, and Chatahoochie countries had all been acquired by conquest, and I was determined to seek a home in the wilderness. My father had made up his mind to go to the new country with his large family and he had been insinuating to me the propriety of breaking up to go with him. There was another little thing that increased my restlessness. My wife's relations were all wealthy and my wife said they had been mean enough to cast little slurs at her and her poverty. She also persuaded me to sell out and go with my father to the new country. All these influences confirmed me in the resolution to get ready and bid adieu to my native State.

Father and I sold out our possessions and were soon on the road to the new country. We had proceeded about forty-five miles when we came to the Ocmulgee river, which at that time was a dividing line between the Georgians and the Creek Indians. A man by the name of Ferguson came to our camp and getting a little "tight" with my father, in a kind of frolic, sold my father his land and cattle. All along the river the people owned herds of cattle which they kept in the range on the Indian side of it. There was plenty of deer over there, too; and being satisfied that my father would not remain more than a year, I concluded to stop also and . . . idle away the time until he got tired of his bargain and made ready to move again. . . .

My father loved a border life, and the place he had purchased on the Ocmulgee, as the people had already commenced settling on the opposite side of the river, was no longer looked upon as a border country. He sold his place and was soon equipped and geared up for the road, and so was I. I had been reared to a belief and faith in the pleasure of frequent change of country, and I looked upon the long journey, through the wilderness with much pleasure.

Our company consisted of my father and mother and eight children, with six negroes; Joseph Bryan, my brother-in-law, and his wife and two negroes; my wife and me and two small sons and two negroes. We had good horses and wagons and guns and big dogs. We set out on the 10th of March, 1818. I felt as if I was on a big camp hunt.

The journey, the way we traveled, was about 500 miles, all wilderness; full of deer and turkeys, and the streams were full of fish. We were six weeks on the road; and altogether it was, as I thought and felt, the most delightful time I had ever spent in my life. My brother Garland and I "flanked it" as the wagons rolled along and killed deer, turkeys, wild pigeons; and at nights, with pine torches, we fished and killed a great many with my bow and arrows, whenever we camped on my water course. Little creeks were full of fish at that season.

At length we reached Tuscaloosa, Ala. It was at that time a small log cabin village; but people from Tennessee were arriving daily, and in the course of that year it grew to be a considerable town.

I concluded to stop there, and my father and his family and Bryan and his family continued their journey to a small improvement eight miles below Tuscaloosa, on the river, where they settled, and, cutting down a canebrake, made corn; and killed bear, venison, and fish enough to supply the family. . . .

I built a little clapboard house on the river side of the town, which had not yet been surveyed. The land hunters from Georgia found us and continued their friendly calls on us until what money I had left from the long journey was eaten up. This was a circumstance for which I had made no provisions. . . . [That fall he removed his family to the Tombigby River.]

Our wagons being the first that had ever traversed that unhacked forest, we of course, had to make a sufficient road for them to pass. It fell to my lot to go in advance and blaze the way, and by taking advantage of the open spaces amongst the trees, I saved a great deal of time. The woods having been burnt every year by the Indian hunters, there were but few logs remaining, and we got along very nicely. Except when we came to the water courses, we had but little difficulty. There are three little rivers and several creeks that crossed our path. We were forced to dig down the banks of these streams before crossing them.

In the afternoon of the twelfth day we landed on the banks of the Tombecbee river, three miles by land above where Columbus, Miss., now stands.

Soon all the families had houses, and all the hands went to work, cutting down and clearing the maiden forest to make fields to plant corn in. I cut down six acres of cane brake that jammed itself almost down to the place where I built my house. I burnt off the cane on the 5th of May, and planted it with a sharp stick on the 6th. Twice while it was growing I cut and beat down the young cane that sprouted up from the old cane stumps. That was all the work the crop got. The bear and raccoons ate and destroyed a good deal of it, and yet I gathered 150 Bushels of good corn. . . .

Maryland Planters Move West

THE FOLLOWING extracts of letters from Colonel L. Covington and D. Rawlings, planters in Maryland, to their friends A. Covington and J. T. Magruder, in Washington, Mississippi Territory, show the problems of moving west. The letters are printed in Ulrich B. Phillips (ed.), The Documentary History of American Industrial Society, Plantation and Frontier (Cleveland, Ohio, 1910), II, 208–211. Reprinted by permission of the publishers, Arthur H. Clark Company.

D. RAWLINGS TO J. T. MAGRUDER

All difficulties are now surmounted and with the indulgence of Heaven a part of our families will be off for the Mississippi Territory the 1st week in April, to be followed by ourselves, dear wives and children in June, or the latter part of the summer, if the Col[onel] can make terms with the God of War, so as to secure delay until the hot months shall have passed away. Rich[ar]d Skinner, John Steele and Thos. Rawlings will descend the Ohio with our people from Redstone, whither we shall attend them in person. We are now in this place together on a purchase of goods, and arrangements pertaining to the solemn task before us.

Regarding your friendship and judgment, we submit to you for preparation and arrangements for the reception of our negroes at a time which your own calculations may indicate, reckoning from the period intimated for out set out from our doors, and for their engagements, your experience will point out a mode far better than any plans we would possibly advise. That on this score the acts of our friends will be conclusive. L. Covington being obliged to continue on to Orleans, will perhaps leave Mrs. C. for awhile in Washington, where D. R. will certainly take residence till purchase and improvements can be made to advantage. If houses are not to be obtained in Washington with care and certainty at any time, it will be subject of consideration for you to determine the propriety of availing yourself of the first you can obtain, to commence a rent say in September; or, perhaps, one may be gotten immediately and a tenant put in it, subject to removal on our arrival. One house can contain us for a short period.

L. COVINGTON, GEORGETOWN, APRIL 25, 1809,
TO A. COVINGTON, WASHINGTON, MISS.

This will reach you but a little while before our friend D. Rawlings, who is 12 days on his journey to the waters of the Ohio. In a very few more, by the blessings of Providence he will have embarked at Brownsville (Redstone old fort) for the Natchez, where we hope for your preparation to receive him and family, together with about 50 black people. In my flock there are 35, two of whom are yours, as I have before apprized you, viz. Dick, a lad received in exchange for your Sam, and a negro girl, Ally, bought for you of Mr. Watson, 13 years of age. She cost 240 dollars, of which particular I know not that I have apprized you. One other of my gang, Charles, belongs to General Joseph Wilkinson, and with whom I wish you to act as with one of my own. Negro Rachel and two children (wife and children to my man Watt) I wish to be kept in employment as my own until a better disposition can be made of them, so that they may refund to me the expenses consequent upon their outfit and journey to that country. I have so repeatedly of late apprized you of our wishes, intentions and movements in relation to this enterprise, that it would be unnecessary to press you with particulars. Let us hope that you will not find so much trouble in making such arrangements and disposition for and with my people as may render them in such way and degree profitable as may reimburse and compensate me for my sacrifices here and my trouble and expense in conducting them to that land of promise. In truth I have fondly flattered myself that my estate in your country (should it please God the people arrive safe) will be far more profitable and more considerable than that I leave in Maryland; but I have to regret that so much of the trouble in the first stages of preparation should be imposed upon my friends. I am however in some degree consoled that should you need assistance, our friends Magruder and perhaps Wailes will be at hand and will willingly give their aid. Dr. R. cannot fail to be most welcome and useful to your society, yet he too, will no doubt need your friendly advice and assistance. B. Ellis who goes with my people will be entitled to my consideration, and I pray you give to him thy patronage; if possible find him employment, and let my old man Isaac work with him at his trade, if you shall think it advisable to do so. Ellis will be indebted to me about $80 or $90 and employment will be my only chance for remuneration. To our mutual and worthy friend I shall owe a heavy debt of gratitude for his care and attention to my people on so long and so fatiguing a journey; let it therefore be your first care to make such means as I may have in your protection, subservient to his convenience. He may want waiters about his house, or nurses for his dear family of infants. We have sent only one trunk, the key of which Mrs. R. will deliver to his sister Harriet, in which some furniture for beds, &c., &c., will be found. Use all and everything to thy and our friend's wishes until we unite with thee. At present my going is uncertain. Becca is still in a state of expectation at Galilee, and my dependence upon public men still adds to the uncertainty.

Through the Cumberland Gap

PERMANENT settlements were first made in Kentucky in 1775. That year four communities were independently formed; one called Boonesborough was founded by Richard Henderson of North Carolina. In 1775 Henderson and his associates purchased the Kentucky and Cumberland river basins from some Cherokee Indians and attempted to form an independent colony. William Calk, whose journal was later printed in the Mississippi Valley Historical Review, VII (March, 1921), 365–369, accompanied Henderson over the trail cut by Boone through Cumberland Gap and shared in the laying out of Boonesborough. Calk and his companions left Prince William County, Virginia, on March 13, 1775. By the twenty-third they had reached the Holston River.

Fryday ye 24th we Start early & turn out of the wagon Road to go across the mountains to go by Danil Smiths. we lose Drive [Calk's negro slave]. Come to a turabel [terrible] mountain that tried us all almost to death to git over it & we lodge this night on the Lawrel fork of holston under a grait mountain & Roast a fine fat turkey for our Suppers & Eat it without aney Bread

Satrd 25 we Start Early travel over Some more very Bad mountains one that is caled Clinch mountain & we git this night to Danil Smiths on clinch and there we Staid till thursday morning[.] on tuesday night & wednesday morning it Snowed Very hard and was very colad & we hunted a good deal there while we Staid in Rough mountains & Kild three Deer & one turkey[.] Eanock ABram & I got lost tuesday night & it asnowing & Should a lam in the mountains had not I had a pocket Compas By which I

Got in a littel in the night and fired guns and they heard them and caim in By the Repoart

Thursd 30th we Set out again & went down to Elk gardin and there Suplid our Selves With Seed Corn & irish tators then we went on alittel way I turnd my hors to drive afore me & he got Scard Ran away threw Down the Saddel Bags & Broke three of our powder goards & ABrams flask Burst open a walet of corn & lost a good Deal & made aturrabel flustration amongst the Reast of the horses[.] Drakes mair ran against a sapling & noct [knocked] it down we cacht [catched] them all agin & went on & lodgd at John Duncans[.]

fryd 31st we suplayd our Selves at Dunkans with a 108 pounds of Bacon & went on again to Brileys mill & suployd our Selves with meal & lodged this night at clinch By a large cainbrake & cuckt [cooked] our Suppers.

April satd first this morning there is ice at our camp half inch thick we Start Early & travel this Day along a verey Bad hilley way cross one creek whear the horses almost got Mired Some fell in & all wet their loads we cross Clinch River & travell till late in the Night & camp on cove creek having two men with us that wair pilates

Sund 2d this morning is avery hard frost we Start Early travel over powels mountain and camp on the head of Powels valey whear there is verey good food

mond 3d we Start Early travel down the valey cross powels River go some throw the woods with out aney track cross some Bad hils Git into hendersons Road camp on a creek in powels valey; tuesday 4th Raney we Start about 10 oclock and git down to capt [John] martins in the valey where we over take Coln. henderson & his companey Bound for Caintuck & there we camp this Night there they were Broiling & Eating Beef without Bread; Wednesday ye 5th Breaks away fair & we go on down the valey & camp on indian Creek we had this creek to cross maney times & very Bad Banks ABrams Saddel turned & the load all fell in we go out this Eavening & Kill two Deer

thurd 6th this morning is ahard frost & we wait at camp for Coln. henderson & companey to come up they come up about 12 oclock & we Join with them and camp there Still this night waiting for Some part of the companey that had their horses Ran away with their packs; fryday ye 7th this morning is avery hard Snowey morning & we Still continue at camp Being in number about 40 men & Some Neagros this Eaevening Comes aletter from Capt Boon at caintuck of the indians doing mischief and Some turns back

William Calk His Jurnal April ye 8th 1775 Satterday

Satrd 8th We all pact up & Started Crost Cumberland gap about one oclock this Day we Met a great maney peopel turnd Back for fear of the indians but our Company goes on Still with good courage we come to a very ugly Creek With Steep Banks & have it to Cross Several times on this Creek we camp this night

Sunday 9th this morning We wait at camp for the cattel to Be drove up to Kill a Beef tis late Before they come & peopel makes out alittel snack & agree to go on till till Night we git to cumberland River & there we camp meet 2 more men turn Back

Monday 10th this is alowry morning & very like for Rain & we keep at camp this day and Some goes out ahunting I & two more goes up avery large mountain Near the top we Saw the track of two indians & whear they had lain unter Some Rocks Some of the companey went over the River a bofelo hunting But found None at night[.] Capt. hart comes up with his packs & there they hide Some of thier lead to lighten their packs that they may travel faster

tuesday 11th this is a very loury morning & like for Rain But we all agree to Start Early we Cross Cumberland River & travel Down it about 10 miles through Some turrabel Cainbrakes as we went down abrams mair Ran into the River with Her load & Swam over he follow[e]d her & got on her & made her Swim Back agin it is a very Raney Eaevening we take up camp near Richland Creek they Kill a Beef Mr Drake Bakes Bread with out Washing his hands we Keep Sentry this Night for fear of the indians—

Wednesday 12th this is a Raney morning But we pack up & go on we come to Richland creek it is high we toat our packs over on a tree & swim our horses over & there We meet another Companey going Back they tell Such News ABram & Drake is afraid to go aney further there we camp this night—

thursday 13th this morning the weather Seems to Brake & Be fair ABram & Drake turn Back we go on & git to loral [Laurel] River we come to a creek before wheare we are obliged to unload & to toate our packs over on alog this day we meet about 20 more turning Back we are obligd to toat our packs over loral River & Swim our Horses one hors Ran in with his pack and lost it in the River & they got it [again]

fryday 14th this is a clear morning with a Smart frost we go on & have avery mirey Road and camp this Night on a creek of loral River & are Surprisd at camp By a wolf—

Satterday 15th clear with a Small frost we Start Early we meet Some men that turns & goes With us we travel this Day through the plais Cald the Bressh & cross Rockcase River & camp ther this Night & have fine food for our horses—

Sunday 16th cloudy & warm we Start Early & go on about 2 mile down the River and then turn up a creek that we crost about 50 times Some very Bad foards with a great Deal of very good land on it the Eavening we git over to the Waters of Caintuck & go alittel Down the creek & there we camp keep Sentry the forepart of the night it Rains very har[d] all night—

monday 17th this is a very Rany morning But Breaks about 11 oclock & we go on and Camp this Night in Several companeys on Some of the creeks of caintuck

tuesday 18th fair & cool and we go on about 11 oclock we meet 4 men from Boons Camp that Caim to cunduck [conduct] us on we camp this night Just on the Beginning of the Good land near the Blue lick they kill 2 Bofelos this Eavening—

Wednesd 19th Smart frost this morning they kill 3 Bofelos about 11 oclock we come to where the indians fired on Boons Companey & Kild 2 men & a dog & wounded one man in the thigh we campt this night on oter creek—

thursday 20th this morning is Clear & cool We Start Early & git Down to Caintuck to Boons [Boonesborough] foart about 12 oclock wheare we stop they Come out to meet us & welcom us in with a voley of guns

fryday 21st Warm this Day they Begin laying off lots in the town and pre[p]aring for peopel to go to worek to make corn—

Satterday 22d they finish laying out lots this Eavening I went afishing and Cacht 3 cats they meet in the night to Draw for choise of lots But Refer it till morning—

William Calk his Jurnal April ye 23d 1775.

April Sunday 23d this morning the peopel meets & Draws for Chois of loots this is avery warm day

monday 24th We all view our loots & Some Dont like them

about 12 oclock the Combsses come to town & Next morning they make them abark canew and Set off down the River to meet thier Companey—

tuesday 25th in the Eavening we git us a plaise at the mouth of the creek & Begin clearing this day we Begin to live with out Bread

Wednesday 26th We Begin Building us a house & a plaise of Defence to keep the indians off

thursday 27th Raney all Day But We Still keep about our house—

Satterday 29th We git our house kivered with Bark & move our things into it at Night and Begin houskeeping Eanock Smith Robert Whitledge & my Self. . . .

John Floyd Moves to Kentucky

IN CONTRAST to William Calk, whose journal reveals him to have been a rustic, unlettered man, John Floyd belonged to the gentry of the Virginia-Kentucky frontier. He was one of the early surveyors on the Ohio waters in 1774, and finally moved to Kentucky with his family five years later. He writes here to his friend, William Preston, first from Harrodsburg, and then from Beargrass Creek. The commissioners referred to are land commissioners appointed under the Virginia Land Act of 1779. Both letters are in the Draper Collection (17CC184–186), The State Historical Society of Wisconsin.

[Harrodsburg, October 30, 1779]

MY DEAR FRIEND.

We arrived here in six weeks, all safe and hearty: but fatigue, perplexity, &c. has almost made a skeleton of me.

My wife brought out the little boy without any of my assistance, and neither of them were any trouble on the way. I lost neither horse nor cow, but my trouble in driving them here was too much. I am this morning gathering up my affairs to set out for Beargrass in high spirits.

The commissioners [for land claims] are here, and I procured my certificate yesterday for 1400 acres at Woodstock, and was immediately offered six fine young Virginia born negroes for it. You never saw such keenness as is here about land. I am vexed that I am forced to send your warrants back to be renewed before I can get them surveyed—do send them out again as soon as possible. My surveyor's commissions are at Mr. Trigg's, and Col. Robinson informes us Mr. Madison could not procure me a commission for this county without the old one. I wish it could be sent down. I am now very anxious to have a place, & I find all your observations about it very just.

The [land] court moves to the falls [of the Ohio, Louisville] next week, and I am desirous to be there in order to get places for Capt. Madison & Mr. Johnson. I see many selling their claims here and I think they will do the same there. I hear nothing from Capt. Smith; I fear he has gave out coming, and if so his opportunity in getting lands will soon be over. Col. Robinson left Capt. Rowland Madison about Cumberland with a tired horse—he has not yet got out. Corn is 30 dollars per bushel. I wish I had my crop from Arcadia. I want to hear how my brother Charles goes on, I directed him to bring me 10 cows in the spring; if he can I shall be quite safe for that article, and I believe there is no doubt of Buffalo beef plenty.

Beargrass [Creek], 26 Nov. 1779

My dear sir.

I arrived here the 8th instant with all my family and stock, safe and hearty. I have this day got a fine cabbin raised, and hope in a few days to have a shelter something better than a tent which we have laid in almost ten weeks. I should not have been quite so tedious in building, but the first tree Bob cut down on the place lodged and slipped back on the stump and tore off his right foot, or at least all the skin and flesh from his ancle down. I have nothing to dress it, and am persuaded it must rot off what is left. I have no view now but to grub and maul, which I think I can do with the greatest cheerfulness on so fine a tract of land. Had I not better take the six negroes for Woodstock to work this?

I am writing by firelight and I fear you cannot read it. The commissioners are sitting at the falls; when I hear how they settle preemptions I shall try to purchase for Capt. Madison. I have no bread provided yet, but I hope to get some corn from Boonsborough by water. It cant be bought here for 50 dollars per bushel. Salt 200 dollars or 10 days work. £300 was given for Knox's 1400 acres on this creek, which he claimed by settlement &c. and the land really poor. Poplar Grove pleases one as well as before. Many are the cabins on it, and I found 11 on mine. Send out the Little warrants I enclosed to be renewed as soon as you can. Numerous will be the crowd at Harrodsburg [at the land office] the first of May. Numbers are going from here down the Ohio, 15 miles below the mouth to a place called the Iron Banks, in order to settle a garrison. The falls is sickly, and the land act drives them off by hundreds. I have had no time to attend the commissioners here, and I am told they have granted a settlement & preemption to Capt. Wm. Lynn on your salt spring by mistake; and on Drummon's Lick to Col. Clark.

I am in a dangerous situation—only five men, and the Indians killed or took a man from Bullitt's Lick and wounded another since I came here. My company all disappointed me in coming out, but I have no doubt of settlers enough from the falls as many are preparing to join me here.

An Ohio Settlement

UNLIKE EARLY Louisville, where because of the provisions of the Virginia Land Act of 1779 settlers often found the land pre-empted by surveys taken for absentee speculators, was Marietta, across the Ohio River. Here the soil was granted by Congress to a company from New England formed by Benjamin Tupper, Rufus Putnam, and other Revolutionary War officers. The following letters from Samuel Holden Parsons to the Reverend Manasseh Cutler, printed in Charles S. Hall, Life and Letters of Samuel Holden Parsons (Binghamton, N.Y., 1905), pp. 542–543, 544, illustrate how the company, after donating land for Marietta, created a New England town in the West.

Marietta, Dec. 11, 1788

DEAR SIR.

I cannot longer neglect to inform you of the occurrences which have taken place here since you left us. . . .

The time of the meeting of the Proprietors having arrived, a number sufficient to proceed did not appear; an adjournment took place, at which time 14 shares only appeared personally, and by special authority, Col. Crary not having then arrived. We then proceeded to take the opinion of the Proprietors present on the subject of granting lands to settlers, and altering the former mode of dividing our lands agreed upon by the agents at Boston. They (five shares only dissenting) gave it as their opinion that it was a matter well within the authority of the general agents, and requested them to take up the matter and to grant lands to settlers, not exceeding one hundred acres out of each share, and to divide the common estate in such manner as would be most conducive to the common interest without respect to former votes. The agents have taken up the subject, 957 shares being represented, and Col. Crary being Chairman, voted (214 shares represented by Col. Crary excepted), unanimously to make grants of lands to encourage settlement . . . and appointed a committee to reconnoitre the country and affix the proper places for that purpose, repealed the votes ordering the mode of division, and directed the committee to examine where are the proper places to divide farms to the Proprietors. . . .

The settlers here appear highly satisfied with the measures we have taken, and very many will go out to those lands. As they must be settled in the spring or early next summer, it will be necessary for as many as wish to receive the donations to be out as soon as possible. We have had an addition of about one hundred within two weeks, and more are expected. We are constantly putting up buildings, but arrivals are faster than we can provide convenient covering. Between forty and fifty houses are so far done as to receive families, and ten more are in building, about one-half of which I expect will be able to receive families next week.

[Marietta], 23d January 1789

. . . We have ordered a division to the Proprietors of 160 acres to each right, to be drawn the third Tuesday of March, within the settling rights. We have voted to give 200 settling rights to nonproprietors before the first of October, and those Proprietors who by that time will agree to settle their own rights by themselves or others, shall have the right to do so—if any more vacant rights at that time, they shall also be given to settlers. The duties are five years residence on the donation lands, within that time to build a house at least 24 by 18 feet, a stone or brick chimney, a cellar, and to clear twenty acres within three years, to set out fifty apple trees and twenty peach trees, and obey all militia laws.

7. West by River and Trace

THE MOVE west involved a long, arduous journey. For the pioneers from the New England and Middle Atlantic states, there were initially the rugged Allegheny Mountains to be crossed. A good description of this route was written in 1789 by Abraham Steiner, a Moravian missionary, telling of his journey with Johann Heckewelder. The journal, now in the archives of the Moravian Church at Bethlehem, Pa., was translated from the German and edited by Paul A. W. Wallace in Thirty Thousand Miles with John Heckewelder (Pittsburgh, Pa., 1958), pp. 236–243.

Across the Allegheny Mountains

On the 22nd [of April] we rode to Shippensburg, where we had breakfast. . . . We saw . . . our first packhorses. They put packs on them which they have to carry over the mountains. The drivers do not set off before 8 or 9 o'clock in the morning, but they drive all day till late in the evening. There are often 40 or 50 horses together. From here it is 10 miles to the foot of the Blue Mountain[s]. . . . From this point on we had mountains to climb. There are 3 high ones here, one right after the other, which they call the Blue Mountains. A few years ago there was only a path over them, but now there is as good a road as can be expected on such mountains. The tops of these 3 mountains are not wide. No sooner are you up than you start down again. The road has been cut to a good width out of the mountain-side, & on the lower side, most of the way, there is a wall, sometimes pretty high, and every 20 rods there is a place for wagons to pass. On the first mountain the road up and down is neither stony nor steep. Between the first and second mountain there is a mile-wide valley [Horse Valley] through which a creek [Conodoguinet] runs north, and there are plantations and mills. . . . The second mountain is somewhat higher & the road, especially on the far side, is steeper & more stony, but on the west side it loops about so much that one can get down without danger. Between this and the third mountain is a valley several miles wide through which Canagotshik [Conococheague] Creek flows south. It is called Path Valley. . . . The third mountain is rather stony, but otherwise not so bad. Among the rocks is a house whose inhabitants have neither a garden nor the least bit of field. They make their living solely by selling whiskey to travellers. . . .

The 23rd. We passed the place where Fort Littleton formerly stood. It is now a fine plantation & a very good inn. It lies between the Blue Mountains and Sidelinghill. Now the soil becomes poorer. There are many small hills, with bigger ones seen in the distance. The soil has more gravel and there is a lot of pitch pine. 13 miles from our last night's lodging we came to the foot of Sideling Hill, a pretty high mountain. Half way up the mountain is a house where we had breakfast. The road up & down this mountain has only recently been laid out & constructed. It has been relocated a little to the north of the old road, and is so good that when you are up you hardly realize you are on such a mountain. One approaches it by a long gradual slope, rising steadily, so that when one reaches the mountain proper one is already pretty high. The road up is constructed the same way as on the Blue Mountains, so that if you do not have a load you can ride up and down at a good speed. The mountain is not very broad on top, & the road along the mountain is quite clear of stones. Formerly Sideling Hill was much dreaded by travellers because of the rough steep road and the huge rocks on it. . . . There is something peculiar about the country round here. When you are on top of one mountain you see another and sometimes several more ahead of you. . . . 11 miles from the house on Sideling Hill we came to the Juniata, at a place called the Crossing, on a branch of the Juniata known as the Raystown Branch. The road approaching it goes over and through the mountains. . . . The Juniata flows through [Wills, Tussey, or Great Warriors] mountain, cutting it in two. The road runs along beside the Juniata and is perfectly level. . . .

On the 24th we set off for Bedford, which lies 5 miles beyond Snakespring. A few miles this side of Bedford we crossed Denning's [Dunning] Creek, not far from where it enters the Juaniata. . . . A quarter of a mile before you reach Bedford you cross the Juniata again by another bridge. . . . The Juniata flows past Bedford on the north side of the town, so we had to cross it again farther on. As there is no bridge at that place and the water had risen very high, we had to go back and cross the bridge [at Bedford] and make a detour round [the north-east side of] the Juniata. . . . Our detour took us 4 miles through woods, swamp, and deep water. . . . By noon we reached our friend Bonnet's 4 miles beyond Bedford. . . . Here the great road to Pittsburg divides into two main roads, the one called the Pennsylvania Road [by way of Ligonier], the other the Glades Road [by way of Berlin], which come together again 12 miles this side of Pittsburg.

On the 25th we had a good road for 5 miles farther till we came to Anderson's at the foot of the famous Allegheny Mountain. This is not, of course, the actual mountain. You continue to ascend for several more miles. The mountain is higher than it appears to be, for it rests, as it were, on other mountains on which you are already standing when you really see it. Several miles beyond Anderson's is Ryan's [Lyon's] Inn, which is still some distance from the mountain proper. This innkeeper has a sign, the Black Lion, which is the only inn sign between Bedford & Pittsburg. There was nothing to be had here except a little whiskey, & no oats for the horses. We kept right on climbing till we reached the real mountain. . . . A strong wind was blowing as we climbed, and it was still blowing hard while we were on top. The road up the mountain is rather stony. . . . It is not particularly steep, and you can get up if you climb slowly and don't mind tired legs. . . . It is flat on top of the mountain, and it continues like that with some little variations to Laurel Hill, so that it may be said that Laurel Hill stands on Allegheny Mountain. . . . In many places the road is rather stony; it is like a morass when it rains and pretty bad in spots. At Stadler's, a tolerable inn on the mountain 11 miles from Anderson's, the road used to veer to the right through Edmond's Swamp; but as this swamp is so very bad the road now bears more to the left, to Stony Creek, which is 9 miles from Stadler's. The way there is rather stony. . . .

On the 26th we could not get warm all day. We crossed Laurel Hill today, which is 12 miles from Stony Creek, and has a very good road. . . . The road over Laurel Hill is full of large & small flat stones, but on the east side it is good. On the west side it is much steeper and descends farther, but it is not nearly so bad as it used to be when it ran a little more to the north. . . . The summit of the mountain is fairly level, but not particularly broad. 9 miles beyond the east side of the mountain is Ligonier. There is scarcely a sign to be seen of the fort; there is nothing there now but a good plantation. . . . Now the mountains had come to an end and we were in the western part of the country. There was still Chestnut Ridge ahead, which from a distance looks like a mountain, but when you come up to it, it is so small & insignificant that compared with the mountains it seems no more than a small hill. 2 miles from Ligonier we crossed Two Mile Run, & 2 miles farther on crossed Four Mile Run, both of which are considerable streams. . . . 9 miles from Ligonier, at the 9 Mile Run, we spent the night with a German named Ried, who keeps a good inn. . . .

On the 27th we went on to Greensburg, 11 miles from here. . . . The road was very muddy & bad, the soil a black, sticky loam.

Consequently we were unable to reach Greensburg before 12 o'clock. . . .

On the 28th we rode 12 miles through good country to Turtle Creek. It is another 12 from here to Pittsburg. . . . By 2 o'clock in the afternoon we had the quiet Allegheny on our right hand and Pittsburg ahead of us. . . .

Down the Allegheny River

ON THE Allegheny River immigrants who had crossed Pennsylvania met those who had traversed New York. Before them lay another journey by rude raft or boat down the Allegheny and the Ohio. Conditions for the river passage probably did not vary greatly at any time during the late eighteenth and early nineteenth centuries. Tilly Buttrick, Jr., made such a journey in 1815, which he described in his Voyages, Travels and Discoveries (Boston, Mass., 1831). The following passage is from Reuben Gold Thwaites (ed.), Early Western Travels (32 vols., Cleveland, Ohio, 1904), VIII, 56–58.

I . . . travelled . . . to the head of the Allegheny river; what they call the head of navigation. This place is called Olean Point . . . there were forty or . . . fifty shanties, or temporary log houses, built up, and completely filled with men, women and children, household furniture thrown up in piles; and a great number of horses, waggons, sleighs, &c., &c. These people were emigrants from the eastern States, principally from . . . Maine, and bound to different States down the Ohio river. Two gentlemen undertook to take a number of these people, and found it to be about twelve hundred, of all ages and sexes. They had a large number of flat-bottomed boats built for their conveyance; these were boarded up at the sides, and roofs over them, with chimneys suitable for cooking, and were secure from the weather. There were also many rafts of boards and shingles, timber and saw logs, which would find a ready market at different places on the Ohio river. There are many saw-mills on the streams above this place, where these articles are manufactured from the fine timber which grows in vast quantities in this vicinity. The river at this time had risen full bank, and I should suppose was navigable for vessels of fifty tons burden; but was frozen over to the depth of ten or twelve inches; this was the cause of so many people being assembled here at this time, as many of them had been here two months waiting an opportunity to descend the river. I waited about ten days, which brought it nearly to the close of March. On Saturday night sat up late, heard some cracking of the ice, several of us observing that we should soon be on our way; went to bed. Next morning at daylight found the river nearly clear, and at eight o'clock it was completely so. The place now presented a curious sight; the men conveying their goods on board the boats and rafts, the women scolding, and children crying, some clothed, and some half clothed, all in haste, filled with anxiety, as if a few minutes were lost their passage would be lost also. By ten o'clock the whole river for one mile appeared to be one solid body of boats and rafts. What, but just before, appeared a considerable village, now remained but a few solitary huts with their occupants. Myself with the adventurers now drifted on rapidly with the current, and in six days we were in the Ohio river, and should have been much sooner had it been safe to have run in the night.

A more picturesque description appears in François André Michaux, Travels to the West of the Alleghany Mountains (London, 1805), reprinted in Thwaites (ed.), Early Western Travels, III, 166.

All the boats or barges, whether those in the Kentucky or Mississippi trade, or those which convey the families that go into the eastern or western states, are built in the same manner. They are of a square form, some longer than others; their sides are raised four feet and a half above the water; their length is from fifteen to fifty feet; the two extremities are square, upon one of which is a kind of awning, under which the passengers shelter themselves when it rains. I was alone upon the banks of the Monongahela, when I perceived, at a distance, five or six of these barges, which were going down the river. I could not conceive what these great square boxes were, which, left to the stream, presented alternately their ends, sides, and even their angles. As they advanced, I heard a confused noise, but without distinguishing any thing, on account of their sides being so very high. However, on ascending the banks of the river, I perceived in these barges several families, carrying with them their horses, cows, poultry, waggons, ploughs, harness, beds, instruments of agriculture, in fine, every thing necessary to cultivate the land, and also for domestic use.

Wilderness Road

PIONEERS to the Southwest had to travel the rugged Wilderness Road to Kentucky or to the Cumberland Valley. Abraham Steiner, the acute Moravian observer, left a description of his journey through frontier Tennessee in 1799. The following extract, published in the North Carolina Historical Review, XXI (October, 1944), 334–367, was translated and edited by Adelaide L. Fries. The original journal is in the archives of the Moravian Church, Bethlehem, Pa.

Nov. 2. [1799] . . . we rode . . . down the Carolina, or Great Watauga Road. . . . In the afternoon we reached Sullivan County, in the state of Tennessee. . . .

Toward evening we again crossed the Holston, which there was a stream of some size, and made a great noise as it rushed over the rocks. . . .

The 3rd . . . This morning we passed the Watauga, one of the chief tributaries of the Holston. It runs very rapidly and the ford is deep, so we were thankful that a German, who owns land there and is acquainted with the ford, piloted us through it. Ten miles from the Watauga we reached Jonesboro, in the Nolachuky neighborhood. . . .

Jonesboro consists of one long street, has about thirty houses, and—like all towns of the back country—it is growing. . . .

Ten miles farther on Green County begins, in which we this afternoon passed through Leesburg, or New Washington, which is a quite new town, and not bad looking for the short time it has been in building. . . .

We had been traveling the Great Road leading to Kentucky and Cumberland, and . . . we reached the place where the road forked, going right to Kentucky and left to Cumberland. This is the neighborhood of which we were warned yesterday, as many thieving rascals harbored there. We passed through a region which for lack of water is called Pine Barrens. The soil looked thin and not very good. . . . From Braselton we had eight miles to Macby's ferry, where we were set across to the north side of the Holston; we had come down stream on the south side. Here the river is broad and deep; in a dry season a man can ride through it higher up.

The sixteen-mile ride from the ferry to Knoxville was very unpleasant, on account of the rain and slippery roads across the hills.

Some of the mountains are stony, and the road is covered with limestone. We were glad when we reached Knoxville safely in the afternoon about four o'clock. . . .

The 21st . . . We had our horses re-shod, so that they might not go lame in the wilderness and on the rocky Cumberland Mountains. In the afternoon about four o'clock we left Knoxville, and took the great road to South West Point. A few miles from the town we met a man, who advised us to take a short cut, where we would find good houses and plenty of forage for our horses. We soon found that we were on a road which had been opened recently, and that many stumps were left in it, through which it was very unpleasant to ride in the dark. We were received willingly in a clean house by the road. The owner told us that he had come from Pennsylvania four years before; that the country along the Holston was thickly settled; that an acre of land was sold for four or five dollars.

On the 22, we passed many mills, and ten miles farther again reached the great road. The land was partly level, partly broken and mountainous, but mostly good, resembling the uplands on the Tennessee. We saw many people, with wagons, going to Cumberland. . . .

The [23rd.] We . . . set out on our farther way, and in about a quarter of a mile reached the ferry over Clinch River. A man on horseback, who joined us not far from there, asked leave to ride across the wilderness with us, for which we were glad especially when he said that he had ridden through often and knew the way. . . . By his advice we inquired at the ferry house and got a satisfactory breakfast. Besides the inn there were several other buildings, including a store. . . . This [is] the only road which leads from the east to Mero District on Cumberland River, and also from here to Kentucky and the Ohio. . . .

We were ferried across the Clinch River, which here is wide, and so clear that even where it was deep we could see the stony bottom. The so-called Wilderness begins at this river, which is an entirely unsettled tract belonging to the Indians, which is used by them only for hunting. The Wilderness lies between the Tennessee and Cumberland settlements, and one must travel eighty miles before reaching the first house. Concerning the miles in this Wilderness it should be noted that something more than a quarter of a mile extra is included in each mile, so that the eighty miles make more than a hundred ordinary miles. Through this Wilderness one must take all provision for man and beast, which we purchased yesterday. Corn for the horses cost more and more the nearer we came to the boundary line. First we paid one-third of a dollar for a bushel, then one-half, three-quarters, and yesterday a whole dollar.

Through this Wilderness runs a great road. On it we had first a level and then a mountainous way through pretty chestnut woods, until we reached Little Cane and Big Cane Creek, where it became very marshy. Here we found some thirty persons who were moving to Cumberland with a wagon and five carts, and were slowly working their way through the marsh and mud-holes, in which the carts often sank to the axle. For half a mile we had a road that seemed to have no bottom, then we passed dry hills where only shrubs and grass grew, though we could see a few small trees. The road, however, was good and dry.

Twelve miles from Clinch River we came to the foot of the Cumberland Mountains. . . . The Cumberland Mountains are not high, but are steeper and more difficult than they seem at first glance. Over the first ridge we led our horses. On the second, which is covered with rocks of sandstone, we found a family whose wagon had upset as they drove up, and they were now carrying their belongings up piece by piece.

Soon after we came to Mammy's Creek, a clear mountain stream, with high spruce and white pine on the banks. It did not look deep, but at the first step the water rose to the belly of the horses.

We rode on through the mountains until it grew dark. The road was covered with flat stones, and so bad that we went many miles on foot. We camped in the forest at a tiny brook beside a steep hill. Here in the Wilderness men let their horses run about a little in the evening, then feed them, and tie them securely to a tree near camp when they go to sleep. Travelers must take special care of their horses in the Wilderness, for many are stolen by the Indians, who slip about in the mountains, hunting. Today we have seen sixty-six persons in the Wilderness.

Sunday, the 24th. We had slept well in the starry night by our fire, which burned beside a fallen chestnut tree. Early in the morning we passed the famous Spencer's Hill. The mountain took its name from a certain Spencer, one of the first settlers in Cumberland, who often during the war rode alone through the Wilderness without being stopped by the Indians, until finally they shot him here, on a cliff between rocks. The road is so steep and stony it looks scarcely possible to take a wagon over it. In the beginning the road led directly down the mountain, but was as steep as a house-roof. Then roads went down the mountain to right and to left, all very steep and covered with flat stones, some of them lying above and directly across the road. A man passed us who had been obliged to harness seven horses together to draw an empty wagon up the mountain. Wagons cannot descend the mountain unless all wheels are locked and in addition a great tree is fastened behind the wagon. All the trees on top of the mountain have already been cut.

Now we came into a pretty valley on the so-called Crab Orchard. This piece of land . . . would . . . be a great help for travelers if they could find shelter here in the Wilderness in bad weather. . . .

At noon we reached the Cumberland River in Summer County. It has high, rocky banks, but is not wide. We crossed the ferry to the north side, near Fort Blount. . . .

This place is sixty-six miles from Nashville, and leaving it we traveled westward over a new, marshy road, through narrow valleys, whose hillsides were covered with tall cane. This continued until evening. Because of the bad road we turned early into a large plantation which belonged to a widow Young. Soon a family arrived which was going down the river to Clarksville, one hundred and fifty miles from Nashville. They too spent the night. They told us that the land was settled to where they lived, and still further, but not thickly, for there were many dry hills where no one lived and between them lie the settlements.

The 27th. The night was cold, and in the morning it was so very cold that a pitcher of water that had just been filled was covered with ice in a few minutes. We were thankful for our good night's lodging even though we had to pay dearly for it.

We traveled then on a half-frozen, marshy road for five miles through the cane till we came to a well located plantation called Dickson's Spring, where the Caney Fork road unites with the Fort Blount road. The strong spring flows from under a ledge of rock and makes at once a pretty, wide creek, which not far below turns mills. Now we had a better way which was not so wet. We saw more farms. In the afternoon the road led us through the well known Bledsoes Lick, which lies in an open space and is somewhat depressed in the middle. At various places there are springs of black water, which smells like gunpowder; it is rich in sulphur. The first settlers saw great herds of buffalo here, which licked the water and the sulphur which it deposited on the old stumps. The cattle from the entire neighborhood assemble in summer around the springs. Near by is a large plantation with an inn. Here we saw the first orchard in Cumberland, with apple and peach trees.

Farther on we came to a place . . . called Crag Fort. Here large, stone mills are built on a creek, which was not large when we saw it but at certain seasons of the year is so wide and deep that it cannot be forded. . . .

The 28th. For the first half hour after we left it snowed heavily, then cleared, but the whole day was raw. We saw a number of fine plantations with good houses and level cornfields, some of them excellent camp sites where during the Indian war there were posts for protection against the wild men. The fine growth of trees and the loose, black soil showed that the land was rich. But the people here complain much of sickness, especially of intermittent fever which appears toward the end of summer, and this year was more general than ever before. The cause of the fever seems to be that when the Cumberland River is full to the tops of its banks the water backs into the small streams which flow into it and the land is flooded.

Today we saw a number of persons moving from the more settled parts into the Caney Fork neighborhood, as there the cattle can feed on the cane without work on their part; others were moving back to Georgia; others again to Illinois or to Natches. The wandering spirit is in people, always seeking a paradise and never finding it.

In the afternoon, near Nashville, we crossed the Cumberland River for the second time. From a distance we heard the trumpets and saw the flags flying, for it was general muster here today.

III

Land Speculation

8. Operations of Land Companies

AMONG THE MEN most influential in opening the West were the entrepreneurs and promoters who speculated in land. They operated before and after the federal government took over the jurisdiction and sale of most of the western territory. But their efforts, in some cases bordering on the illegal, were particularly ambitious before 1788 in those regions where jurisdiction was not clear or was disputed between colonies or states. All speculators, whether resident or nonresident in the West, sought a profit, but some made a positive contribution by stimulating migration and settlement.

Among the earliest to engage in large-scale speculation were Virginians, who organized into companies, obtained grants for hundreds of thousands of acres of land, and sought to settle families on them. The earliest into the field were the Loyal and Greenbriar companies. They were shortly followed by the Ohio Company. The following extract from the minutes of an Ohio Company meeting illustrates its promotional activity. It is taken from the George Mercer Papers at the Darlington Memorial Library, University of Pittsburgh, printed in Lois L. Mulkearn (ed.), George Mercer Papers Relating to the Ohio Company of Virginia (Pittsburgh, Pa., 1954), pp. 144–147.

An Ohio Company Meeting

At a Committee of the Ohio Company at M.ʳ Mercers at Marlborough in Stafford County February 6.ᵗʰ 1753.

On the Application of M.ʳ John Pagan Merch[ant] to know what Encouragement the Company would give to [any] German Protestants who would come into this Colony to settle their Lands on the Ohio, he being now on a Voyage to Great Britain and intending to Germany from thence in Expectation of Engaging a great number of families to remove for that purpose in Case the prejudices that have been artfully propagated among those people can be effectually removed and they can be convinced they may on equal if not better terms settle in this Colony than in Pensylvania or the other adjoining provinces. The Committee being satisfied that a large Accession of foreign Protestants will not only be advantageous to this Colony but the most effectual method of promoting a speedy Settlement on the Ohio, and extending and securing the same, before mentioning their own proposals think proper to observe.

That with regard to their religious Liberties, all foreign Protestants may depend on enjoying in this Government the Advantage of the Acts of Toleration in as full and ample manner as in any other of his Majesties plantations whatsoever, as great numbers of them have already experienced.

As to their civil Rights, they will be entitled to Naturalization which will be attended with all the Privileges and Advantages of English natural born Subjects which are too many to be here enumerated. That of electing their Representatives in the Legislature is the greatest can be enjoyed by any Subjects, And the English Laws of Liberty and property are universally allowed to be the best in the World for securing the peoples lives and fortunes against Arbitrary power or any unjust Encroachments whatsoever.

The Levies in this Government which will be better understood by the name of Taxes are of three kinds Public, County, and Parish, The first of which is imposed by Act of Assembly on every person in the Colony liable to pay Levies for defraying the public Charge of this Colony once in two or three years, the second for defraying each County's Charge by the people living therein which is annually imposed, as is the last on the parishioners for maintaining the Minister and other parochial Charges. All these are paid in Tobacco the Staple of the Countrey, but no Male under sixteen years of Age or any white Woman is obliged to contribute thereto. These however are so moderate that We can venture to affirm that taking them all together one Year with the other they don't amount to above the Value of eight shillings Sterling per poll, and no Tax or Imposition is laid on anything necessary for food or raiment or the Subsistence of Life, Officers fees of all kinds and Law charges amount to little more than one half of the Charge of that Sort in the adjoining Colonies, Nor do we know any single place in his Majesties Dominions where the Subject is supported in all his Rights at so easy an Expence, Our Militia renders Soldiers useless and We have no Ecclesiastical Courts.

The Legislature by an Act made last year hath exempted all foreign protestants coming to Settle West of our Great Mountains from paying Levies of all kinds for the term of ten Years from their Settlement As by a Copy of the Act hereto annexed.

As the Committee looks on these Advantages to be sufficient to invite any Strangers not bypassed by some Prejudice to settle in this Colony preferably to any other of his Majesties plantations, which they are very desirous of, so for a further Encouragement they propose and undertake in behalf of the Company.

That as the said Company is intitled to five hundred thousand Acres of Land upon the River Ohio which is exempted from Quit rents for ten years after which term the Quit rent is no more than two Shillings Sterling yearly for every hundred Acres. Every foreign protestant coming in to Settle on the said Land shall have a good title made to him for as much as he desires at the rate of five pounds Sterling for every hundred Acres discharged of Quit rents for the same time allowed to the Company.

That all such as come in on those terms shall be supplied with Warehouses for their Goods convenient carriages for removing them to their Lands and such Quantity of Wheat Flour and Salt as they may want for their present Subsistence at the same Rates the Company pays for them, And such of them as have not ready money to pay for the Lands they desire to purchase shall be allowed two years Credit paying five per cent per Annum Interest[.]

As no Countrey in the world is better or more conveniently watered than Virginia the most convenient Passage will be into Potomack River which is Navigable by the largest Ships within ten Miles of the Falls. The Companys Store house at Rock creek where they may land and have their Goods secured is sixty miles from Connococheege a fine road from whence they may go by Water in the Companys Boat to their Store house at Wills Creek about forty miles and from thence the Company have cleared a Waggon Road about sixty miles to one of the head branches of the Ohio navigable by large flat bottomed boats where they proposed to build Storehouses and begin to lay off their Lands. From this place there is no Obstruction to prevent such Vessels passing into the Mississippi which by the best Calculation is near a thousand miles, and as the Ohio from thence branches all the way down in numberless Branches it not only affords the convenience of making most of the Settlements by Water carriage but will enable the Settlers by the same carriage to carry on their Trade and supply themselves with every produce of those parts. The Rivers are Stocked with fine Fish and wild Fowl and the Woods abound with Buffaloes Elks Deer wild Turkeys and other Game of divers kind. The Land itself is universally allowed to be as good as can be far exceeding any Lands to the East of the great Mountains well Stocked with Timbers of all kinds and Stone for building, Slate Limestone Coal, Salt Springs and various Minerals. In short it is a Countrey that wants nothing but Inhabitants to render it one of the most delightful and valueable Settlements of all his Majesties plantations in America, And as the Value of those back Lands is now discovered and all the nations of Indians in those parts and for some hundred miles round are not only in Strict Amity and friendship with this Government but have faithfully promised to Assist and protect the English Settlements on the Ohio which has tempted many other persons to take up Lands in those parts and people are daily going to Settle them, there can be no doubt but the Settlement in those parts will soon be a very considerable one.

The Committee further Engages in behalf of the said Company for the greater Encouragement of such foreign protestants to lay off two hundred Acres of Land for a Town to be called Saltsburg in the best and most convenient place to their Settlement to be divided into Lotts of one Acre each, Eight of which to be appropriate for a Fort Church and other public buildings and every Tradesman or other person Settling and living three Years in the said Town to have one Lot forever paying the Quit rent of one farthing a Year. . . .

Minutes of a Meeting of the Susquehanna Company

A BROADLY based company for the development of frontier lands was the Susquehanna Company, formed in 1753 by farmers and merchants of eastern Connecticut. Claiming that the upper reaches of the Susquehanna River fell within Connecticut's jurisdiction by the boundaries specified in the colony's charter of 1662, the company made a questionable purchase from the Six Nations in 1754 of what became known as the "Wyoming" District. Due to hostilities with the French and Indians and a dispute with Pennsylvania over jurisdiction of the region, the Yankees did not begin significant settlement until the royal government had negotiated for a revision of the boundary line with the Indians in 1768. The company's plan for establishing settlements is revealed in

the minutes of its meeting on December 28 of that year. These minutes
are among the company papers in the Connecticut Historical Society
and are printed in Julian P. Boyd (ed.), The Susquehanna Company
Papers (4 vols., Wilkes-Barre, Pa., 1930), III, 43–47.[1]

At a Meeting of the Susq[h] Company duly Warned & Convened
at Hartford on ye 28th day of Decembr A D 1768. . . .
. . . Voted that 40 Persons upwards of the Age of Twenty one
years proprietors in s[d] purchase and approved by the Committee
hereafter nominated & appointed proceed to enter upon and take
Possession of s[d] Lands for and in behalf of s[d] Company by the first
Day of February next and that 200 more of s[d] Company of the age
afores[d] and approved as afores[d] proceed and Join s[d] 40 on the lands
afore s[d] as early in the spring as may be for the purpose afores[d] not
later than the first day of may next and that in order to encourage
s[d] 40 Persons to proceed settle and take Possession of the Lands
afores[d] for and in behalf of s[d] Company[.] That there be paid into
the hands of a Committee appointed and hereafter named to and
for the use of s[d] 40 the sum of £200 to be laid out by s[d] Committee in providing proper materials, sustenance and provision for s[d]
40 at the Discretion of s[d] Committee shall be thought proper &
needful[.] and for the further Incouragement of s[d] 40, as also for
the Incouragement of s[d] 200 who may Join them in the spring according to the foregoing Vote it is further considered & Voted to
lay out 5 Townships of Land within the Purchase of said Company
and within the line settled with the Indians afores[d] of five miles
square each three on the one side of the river and two of them on
the opposite side of the river adjoining and opposite to each other
only the river parting at such place on s[d] river as they may think
proper each of s[d] Townships to be 5 miles on the river and to run
and extend in equal width back five miles, to be and belong to
the said 40 and the sd 200 persons over and above their respective
shares and proportion in the remainder of the general Purchase
in manner following Viz, that the s[d] 40 have their first choice of
one of s[d] 5 Townships which they shall chuse to be & belong to
the s[d] 40 and the other four to be and belong to the s[d] 200 to be
divided out to them by 50's in a Township as they shall think

proper reserving and appropriating three whole rights or shares in each Township for the Publick use of a Gospel ministry & Schools in each of s^d Towns and also reserving for the use of s^d Company and for their after disposal all beds of mine, Iron oar & Coal that may be within said Townships the afores^d Townships, to be held by the s^d 40 & and the s^d 200, on Condition of their entering upon and taking Possession according to the above vote and also of their Continuing thereon holding and improving the same by them-selves[,] Heirs or assigns under s^d Company for the space of 5 years after their entry as afores^d and that they shall not so disorderly Conduct and behave themselves as shall by the Company be Judged Inconsistent with the Good & Interest of s^d Company and that they hold not the same or any other part of s^d Purchase under pretence of any other claim but of s^d Company and if the first Number approved by s^d Committee shall fall short of 40 or of those approved to join them in the spring shall fall short of 200, Never-theless, those that do proceed according to the above Vote to be Intituled to their respective parts or shares in the s^d 5 Townships in full as though the whole Numbers were Compleated. And in order that proper Persons & such as may appear to be most sub-servient to the Benefit of said Company may be orderly Intro-duced as first settlers on said Lands, Voted that a Committee be appointed in each County in this Colony as also some meet Person or Persons in the Neighbouring Colonies to admit and approve of such Persons who may offer themselves for the first settlers ac-cording to the foregoing Votes. . . . Isaac Tripp Esqr[,] Mr Ben-jamin Follet, Mr John Jenkins, Mr Wm Buck[,] & Mr Benjn Shoe-maker be and they are hereby appointed a Committee to approve admit, oversee, superintend, manage and order the affairs & proceed-ings of the first 40 settlers to receive and order the monies granted to their use to lay out and prepare a Convenient road to said Susq^h river for which purpose they are to receive £50 to be laid out in preparing a road as afores^d for the Benefit of s^d Company and to account with the standing Committee of s^d Company therefor, and upon any or either of s^d last mentioned Committee failing to at-tend s^d Trust to which they are appointed the Place or Places of such to be supplied by such other Person or Persons as shall be chosen by the major part of s^d 40 first settlers, and upon the ar-rival of the 200 proposed to Join the s^d 40 in the spring, they may if they see cause together with the s^d 40 by their Major Vote add to s^d Committee so as to make the whole to the Number of Nine who shall then be a Committee to oversee order and regulate the affairs of s^d settlers and others of s^d Company who may Join them until further or otherwise ordered by s^d Company which s^d Committee by a major Vote of the settlers there present duly convened may expel from them any Person or Persons among them who shall so disorderly conduct and behave as shall by them be Judged Inconsistent with the Good & Interest of s^d Company and may declare the right of such Person forfeit, which shall so remain unless the s^d Company at any after meeting upon hearing the Cause of Complaint shall otherwise determine.

Voted that some proper well disposed Person or Persons be procured by those Persons who shall undertake to settle on the Susqueh^h Lands according to the above vote, in order to be as a head or Teacher, to carry on religeous In[s]truction and Worship among those settlers, Viz, of such Denomination as by any Particular Number may be agreed upon & to be at the expence of those Persons of such Denomination as such Person so procured shall be until some further Regulation can be had.

9. Promoters and Entrepreneurs

ONE OF the most audacious and unscrupulous of the land speculators was William Blount of North Carolina and Tennessee. Yet his methods varied from those of others only in degree, not in kind; the following correspondence illustrates tactics used by many speculators. Blount and his associates formed the Tennessee Company for the purpose of obtaining title to the land encompassed by the great bend or "bent" of the Tennessee River, an area claimed both by Georgia and North Carolina. Lachlan McIntosh, John Morrell, William Downes, and Stephen Heard were commissioners for Georgia, while John Sevier, John Donelson, and Joseph Martin represented the state of North Carolina. Martin was also North Carolina's Indian agent. The first two letters below are from the Draper Collection, printed in Publications of the Southern History Association, VII (Washington, D.C., 1903), 264–266. The following two are in manuscript in the North Carolina State Department of Archives and History, printed in Alice Barnwell Keith (ed.), The John Gray Blount Papers (2 vols., Raleigh, N.C., 1952), I, 168–169.

William Blount

BLOUNT TO MARTIN

Hillsborough [N.C.], October 26, 1783

I am very glad to find that you have made the Purchase of the Indians of the Bend of Tenesee and I think cheap enough[.] The most of the Goods to make the Payment with were purchased in Philadelphia early in September. . . . I am told that a certain Dispute has arose between the States of Georgia and South Carolina by the latter claiming a Right to back lands as far West as to the Missisippi now if South Carolina has any back lands the Bend of Tenesee must be a Part of it. This dispute between the two States will in my opinion be very favorable to our Designs of obtaining the Georgia Title or the South Carolina Title and either will answer our Purpose equally well for we shall surely settle the Country before the Dispute can be determined and in order to procure a Title from one or both of those States I will certainly attend both their next Assemblies and I have not the least doubt but I shall succeed. . . .

A Number of People have here entered lands which I am sure they know lays without the limits of the State and in the Bent within the limits of our Purchase. And expect to get Grants from this State I hope Care will be taken to have the line of this State well known that the Persons making surveys without the limits may not be able to plead Ignorance. It would seem to me that every Person I have seen here envyed Us the Purchase and wished to own a Part of the Bent of Tenesee. . . .

BLOUNT TO DONELSON

March 9, 1784

. . . The Commissoners of the State of Georgia with whom I had several meetings are very well disposed[.] I could not wish for better then Those of North Carolina were some nominated by myself in the fullest confidence that each of them would act. It is unnecessary to say anything to induce you to act but to beg your attention to the Resolutons especially that Part which impowers the Commissioners to make. The Company such Compensation as may be adequate and satisfactory[.] Nothing will more readily influence the Commissioners of Georgia to grant the Company a large quantity of Land than an appearance of many People being about to remove to the Bent under the Influence of the Company[.] therefore you will necessarily keep up a Report of as many being about to remove as you possibly can whether true or not— I really intend moving out there to live and I have no doubt but I shall bring with me fifty Families at least—I want much to go out with you to explore the Country which I cant do but I hope to be able to meet you in June at the long Island of Hoston tho' before that I expect the Pleasure of seeing you at Hillsboro. . . . You will see I have made use of Bledsoes name altho he had never signed the Articles my Reasons for so doing were he was known to be an able Mountain Man and of much Influence consequently in the Eyes of the State of Georgia gave Weight to the Petitioners. You will please mention this Circumstance to him. . . .

Blount to Donelson, Martin, and Sevier

May 31, 1784

. . . Should the Report of Indians or any other Circumstance prevent the Exploring the Bent I hope you will so manage the Business as not to let them return without executing a Grant to the Company as large as you can obtain—If you can't get a Grant for the whole get it for as much as you possibly can—If you find the Assembly of Georgia will set after the Return of the Commissioners before next Spring some one of you must attend it in Behalf of the Company in Order to assist the Companys Agents viz Majors Call and Long to compleat the Business as advantageously as possible. If you should think proper to open the offur to grant Warrants at ⅛ of a dollar per Acre enter as much as you can and make use of any Names fictious one will do I suppose, If not you may use the Names of Blount, Williams Johnson Allen, Winnan, Ogden and almost any other Name you please ad[d]ing such Christian Names to them as You please and You need not fear but I can find the People to transfer their Rights to the Company.

You must not fail to impress on the Minds of your Brother Commissioners the Value of western lands to individuals and the little Advantage it will be to the State of Georgia, and may offer as a Reason for both the Cessions that have taken place in this State and Virginia and that will certainly and unavoidably take Place in Georgia in a Short Time. May it not be good Policy [to] Set some new Scheme on foot in Partnership with the Gentlemen of Georgia to make further Purchases over the Tenesee or on the Missisippi in down near the Natches for they must if possible be fixed with a thirst for back lands to effect which no Pains must be spared—Western lands since the Session are here estimated at 20/ per Acre—

There is at Nash Ville—Col. Daniel Smith of whom I have heard a very high Character and a great Mathematicien if possible I wish you could get him to assist in running the line[.] the Company will pay him and if he does go with you I would wish him to report to the Assembly of North Carolina his opinion with respect to the precissun with which he thinks it is run—and it ought to be run as exact as possible to prevent future Disputes—Particular [sic] Instrution is unnessary you know the Grand Object is to get as much land as possible and how that is to be accomplished you will be best able to judge who are on the Place of Action but let no trifling Expence disappoint as in the Main Object—If your brother Commissioners should construe the Word *accepting* into an Intention of the Company to give gratis a joint part be it so, or if they purpose to pay a Propeortionable [sic] Part of the Expenses they may [pay] it at their leisure—You will observe to give them Writings if they choose on the part of the Company

BLOUNT TO McINTOSH, MORRELL, DOWNES, AND HEARD

May 31, 1784

. . . The Object of the Tenesee Company in purchasing the Bent and (I suppose) your's in Accepting the appointment as commissioners must have been the same, *I mean private Emolument* and in Order that we may both obtain our *purposes* it is Necessary, We should understand each Other and that our Acts should tend to our mutiose advantage, that is that our Intrust should be joint which can only be by each of you, Accepting an equal Share with the original Petitioners whose Names are known to you and if this is agreeable to you, please signify your Approbation to Misser[es]. Dondeldson, Martin & Severe and it shall bend the company to admit you each as joint Adventurers, and if you think writings Necessary they will on the part of the Company enter into such as may be proper. You have power, *to make the company such, compensation as may be deemed Adequate and satisfactory,* No Bond nor no Oath has been required nor no Instructions, given you from whence as well as the General disposition of the best informed part of your legislature, I think it ardent they intended and wished you to be liberal and if you accede to my Proposition of our Interest being the same you will have a share of your own liberty—It was the Opinion of Gen[l]. M[c].Intosh that the whole of the bent should be granted the company without any other consideration except that of settling a Number of People on it; for these seven Weeks past I have been attending the legislature of this State, now siting at this place that body have passed an act ceeding to the Congress of the United States all the Teretory owned by this State lying West of the Apalachan mountain the leading step to this act was a similar Act passed by the State of Virginia and I suspect Your State will also be under the Necessity of following her Example and should this be the case as I am sure it will had you not at any rate better make a liberal Grant to the Company than leave it for the State to give to Congress—The quantity of Land contained in the Bent is unknown in my Petition, I composed it to contain 300.000. Acres more or less it may contain some more tho Not much so that should you grant the whole of the bent for 300.000 Acres more or less I think it would *be most prudent* but should you think otherwise, I wish whatever quantity you may think best to grant should be bounded by Natural Boundaries except the Northern line & that may be bounded by the Southern line of this State and let it be expressed to contain as much more or less. Your Brother Commissioners will Show you a letter I have just recved from my frend in Congress by which you will see it will be very eaesey to people the Bent, Such Another appertunity may never present itself of Making a Spec and there's an old Proverb which says "make Hay while the sun shines," of which I wish you to be mindfull—the long siting of the Assembly prevents my meeting you at the long Island [of the Holston River] which I much wished but I will either meet you at your Return or I will visit you in Georgia at your spring Session. . . .

John Cleves Symmes

In October, 1787, John Cleves Symmes, a New Jersey promoter and entrepreneur, petitioned the Continental Congress to be allowed to purchase with depreciated Continental certificates a million acres of land between the Great Miami and Little Miami rivers on the right bank of the Ohio. He advertised in the eastern press and had actually begun to lay out his projected colony on the Ohio when he received word that Congress would only allow him a twenty-mile strip east of the Great Miami. Many of his plots lay outside his grant and the ensuing confusion over land titles delayed actual settlement in the region. The text of the first selection is from an advertisement by Symmes in the Brunswick Gazette and Weekly Monitor, January 8 and 22, 1788, reprinted in Beverly W. Bond, Jr. (ed.), The Correspondence of John Cleves Symmes (New York, 1926), pp. 281–284. The letter to Dayton is from a manuscript in the Thomson Collection, College Hall, Cincinnati, and printed in Bond, ibid., pp. 63–65.

Brunswick Gazette, January 8 and 22, 1788

The subscriber having succeeded with Congress in obtaining that most excellent tract of land on the northwest bank of the Ohio, between the great and little Miami rivers, begs leave to state some particulars to those gentlemen who may not meet with a small pamphlet already published on the subject.

In the first place it ought to be observed, that no dispute respecting titles in the first instance, can possibly arise, these will be clear and certain, as the whole purchase will be surveyed into sections of one mile square, and every line well marked, and the sections numbered, and every number which may be sold shall be recorded to the first person applying to the subscriber therefor. The land is allowed (all circumstances considered) to be the best tract in the federal country: It lies in north latitude thirty-eight degrees, and the same with Virginia. Horses, cattle and hogs can live well in the woods, where there is abundance of food through the winters, which are very moderate: Every kind of grain and vegetable raised in the middle states grows here, with the addition of cotton and indigo, which may be raised in sufficient quantities for family use. The land is generally free from stone and a rich, easy soil for tillage. There are no mountains and few hills, so that the country for the most part is level! It is extremely well watered throughout, and surrounded on three sides by rivers navigable in the boating seasons: Vessels may be built here of two hundred tons burden, and being fully freighted may be navigated with safety to New York, or any other sea-port. The finest timber of every kind known in the middle states, with many other sorts of more southerly production, grow in plenty here, but there is very little underwood or brush. Millstones and grindstones are found in some of the hills. Wild game and fish may be taken in abundance. Salt is now made to any quantity, in Kentucke, opposite this tract on the south-east side of the Ohio, where seven counties are already considerably settled and where any number of neat-cattle may be had very cheap.

A plat for a considerable town will be laid out in the spring, on the point of land formed by the Ohio and great Miami; the lots will be 60 feet wide and 120 feet deep, and every other lot, beginning at a corner and numbering the lots around every separate square shall be given freely forever to any person who shall first apply for the same, and build even a log-house thereon within two years after the first payment made to the treasury board, and live, or keep some family therein for the first three years after building; and every such person shall have the privilege of cutting gratis on the subscriber's adjacent lands as much timber for building, as he shall have occasion for in three years from the time when he begins to build. This town will be fortified and garrisoned with continental troops. The farmers profits here must be great, as horses and oxen may be raised free of expense, save a little salt which is cheap; and they may be drove to Philadelphia for less than four dollars a head. The subscriber is of opinion that if the excellence of this country was fully known, thousands would soon emigrate thither, especially young men, and others who have little or no land. The price of the land is five shillings prock or two-thirds of a dollar per acre in certificates, which must be paid to the treasury-board, and which for the better security of the purchasers, if they chuse, may be deposited in the hands of the loan-officer of the states of New York, New Jersey, or Pennsylvania and his receipt for the contents to be credited to the subscriber by the honorable the commissioners of the treasury-board, shall be received in the purchase of a land-warrant, preferable to the original certificate: And one penny farthing per acre in money to defray the surveying and other expences. Certificates to any amount may be had cheap at the brokers in New York and Philadelphia. Any industrious, sober person or family of good characters who will go and settle on the land in the course of the present year, and may not be able to provide themselves with bread-corn, after coming on the ground, until the same may be raised; the subscriber will furnish such persons with indian-corn wherewith to make their bread for six months, at his expence, provided they reimburse him the full of such expence, with interest, either in money, or in grain or labor, at a price to be agreed between the parties; and that within two years after such supplies are furnished; in which time the same may be replaced with great ease from the produce of the sale.

JOHN CLEVES SYMMES

New Brunswick
January 1, 1788

P.S. Land-warrants may be had of the following gentlemen viz. Edward Fox, Esq., Philadelphia. Michael D. Henry, Esq., New York, and in New Jersey of Joseph Bloomfield, Esq. Burlington; Eli Elmer, Esq. Cumberland; Franklin Davenport, Esq. Gloucester; Samuel W. Stockton, Esq. Trenton; Richard Stockton, Esq. Princeton; Johnathan Rhea, Esq. Monmouth; Andrew Kirkpatrick, Esq. New Brunswick; Daniel Hunt, Esq. South Branch, Raritan; Archibald Mercer, Esq. Millstone; Major William Lowrey, Alexandria; George Cotnam, Esq. Oxford, in Sussex; Thomas Anderson, Esq. New-Town, Sussex; Major William Holmes, Hacketts-Town; Joseph Lewis, Esq. Morris-Town; Mr. James Henry, Lamerton; Daniel Marsh, Esq. Rahway; Rev. Rune Runyan, Piscataqua; Doctor Elmer, Westfield; Mr. Elias Dayton, jun. Elizabeth-Town; Mr. John Burner, Newark; Nehemiah Wade, Esq. Hackensack; Mr. Timothy Day, in Chatham; and Capt. Benjamin Stites, Scotch Plains.

SYMMES TO JONATHAN DAYTON

Northbend, Ohio, May 18, 1789

. . . We landed about three of the clock in the afternoon . . . [and] raised what in this country is called a camp, by setting two forks of saplins in the ground, a ridge-pole across, and leaning boat-boards which I had brought from Limestone [Kentucky], one end on the ground and the other against the ridge-pole: encloseing one end of the camp, and leaving the other open to the weather for a door where our fire was made to fence against the cold which was now very intense. In this hut I lived six weeks before I was able to erect myself a log-house & cover it so as to get into the same with my family & property. . . .

I resolved . . . without loss of time to lay out a number of house-lots in order to form a village on the spot where we were; the ground being very proper for a project of that kind on a small scale.

Forty eight lots of one acre each was accordingly laid off, every other one of which I proposed to give away, retaining one for each propriety, upon condition only of the donees building immediately thereon.

These 24 donation lots were soon taken up, and further applications being made, I have extended the village up and down the Ohio, until it forms a front one mile and an half on the river; in which are more than one hundred lots; on forty of which, observing the order of every other lot, there is a comfortable log-cabin built & covered with shingles or clabboards, and other houses are still on hand, so that there remains not three donation lots unappropriated. This village I have called Northbend, from its being situate in the most northerly bend of the Ohio. . . . Northbend being so well improved by the buildings already erected and making; and fresh applications every few days being made to me for house lots; I was induced to lay off another village about seven miles up the Ohio from Northbend, being one mile in front on the river. The ground was very eligible for the purpose, and I would have continued further up and down the river, but was confined between two reserved sections. This village I call Southbend from its being contiguous to the most southerly point of land in the purchase. In this village several houses are almost finished, and others begun; and I make no doubt but the whole of the donation lots will soon be occupied if we remain in safety.

Moses and Stephen Austin

TWO OF the most ambitious land entrepreneurs were Moses Austin and his son, Stephen F. Austin. The elder Austin, born in Connecticut, was for some years a merchant in Philadelphia and Richmond, Virginia, where his son was born. In 1798 the family moved to what was then Spanish Missouri, to mine lead, but after a financial failure the elder Austin traveled to Spanish Texas, where in 1821 he secured a concession to colonize three hundred American families. After returning to Missouri, Moses died, but the settlement scheme was carried out by Stephen, who succeeded his father as empresario in 1822. The following documents from the Austin Papers at the University of Texas, printed in Eugene C. Barker (ed.), The Austin Papers, American Historical Association, Annual Report for 1919, I (Washington, D.C., 1924), i, 521–523, 703–705, illustrate the great interest in Texas lands and the conditions for settlement.

SAMUEL AYERS AND OTHERS TO AUSTIN

Lexington (Ky), June 6ᵗʰ 1822

DEAR SIR.

We the undersigned, being appointed a Committee by the Texas Emigrating Society of this place, for the purpose of writing letters to you and Joseph H. Hawkins Esqʳ of New Orleans, by our agent Mʳ Elijah Noble, who is also one of the members of our Society; Beg leave to state that the object of the Society is to receive and obtain through him, such Information as we can certainly depend on, relative to the Province of Texas, and whether it would be advisable for us to settle there. The Individual members of this Society have been Informed, more than twelve months ago, of the existence of a large Grant of Land made to you by the King of Spain, on the Condition of your settling on the Grant, a Certain Number of American Families; such as Farmers, Mechanics etc; Since, or about that time, we have seen Published in some of our News Papers abstracts of letters said to be from yourself and others, stating that great offers in land were made to settlers who would emigrate to that Country, being However, unwilling to Venture so Important an undertaking, without a Certainty (having heard various and contradictory accounts from there, both as to its local situation and advantages, and its political situation). The Company determines to send a Commissioner, on whom they can depend for all the necessary Information. We would therefore feel ourselves under great obligations to you, for such Information as you may deem necessary as well as satisfactory answers to the following questions. Is it a Rich and Healthy Country possessed of the advantages of Navigation? and to what extent? Is your Grant an Indisputable Title, and how large is Its Boundary? Have you yet made up the Number of settlers which you designed to receive? If so, can other grants be obtained, and upon what terms? If your Number is not made up, what quantity of Good Land do you offer to settlers, and their Families and upon what Terms? What is the present Policy of your Country, and what the future prospects? Will it ever become a republic, so desirable generally to the people of the United States? Will the Liberty of Conscience, and of speech, be Granted to the present settlers, and the Right of worshiping their God according to the dictates of their own consciences? Will the Province of Texas be a separate Government or will it be under the same government and Laws, as that of Mexico? and will free access through the Country be Granted to Travellers and Traders. Your full and unreserv'd answer to the foregoing Interrogatories, together with such other Information as you may think Interesting to the society; in writing, will be Very Desirable, and thankfully received. This society is Composed of Farmers, and Mechanics and Manufacturers, with a few Merchants and Professional Characters. Some of them are wealthy, others have been wealthy, but have fallen Victims to the Changes and difficulties of the time, through the unguarded Policy of our Country, and some are young beginers: all of whom are respectable and industrious, and will carry with them such letters of recommendation as you may require (for we will not receive any but such as we believe are such) and would if encouraged be a great acquisition to any new Country. We formed ourselves into a society with a Constitution and Laws for our Government subject to the laws of the Land to which we may emigrate, which we think will not only Facilitate our Journey and safety in moving; but will very much add to our security and Happiness, when we reach there. Should your answers be satisfactory to Mr Noble, our Friend and agent, and he should be pleased with the country generally we have authorized him to make arrangements for at least from Thirty to Fifty Familys.

SAM^l AYERS
RICH^d SHARPE
DANE HALSTEAD
Wm HANSON
Members of the Com[mit]te[e]

AUSTIN TO ———

San Felipe de Austin, Oct. 20 1823

DR SIR,

I rec^d your letter dated 5 April 1822 only a few days since, and am much pleased to see your inclinations directed towards this quarter.

You have doubtless heard much of, and concerning me and my prospects etc, it is true they have been at times brighter than at others, tho there never has been any just cause to doubt of final success in the completion of my business with the Government. The revolution [in Mexico] coming on at the critical time it did threw some difficulties in the way that were never even dreampt of, but time and perseverance has overcome them all, and I am now engaged surveying the lands to the settlers.

The terms on which emigrants are rec^d [are] as follows— No one will be rec^d as a settler or be permitted to remain in the Province who does not bring the most unequivocal evidence from the highest authority and most respectable men of the state and neighborhood Where he resides, that his character is *perfectly unblemished*, that he is a moral and industrious man, and absolutely free from the vice of intoxication—those who presume so far on the lenity of this Government as to intrude themselves upon its territory without such evidence will be immediately ordered to leave the Province and if the order is not obeyed within the time specified (which will be ten, twenty, or thirty days according to the situation of the family) they will be sent off under guard and their property seized and sold to pay the expenses, and should any resistance be made they will be whipped or condemned to hard labor on public works with a ball and chain attached to them according to the nature of their offence.

Those who are received as settlers have everything to hope—they will get one league of land if they wish for so much and as much less as they please which will cost at the rate of twelve dollars and a half p^r hundred acres—The land will be surveyed and the titles delivered at the houses of the settlers and all the records made complete without any additional charge—a very large family, or a person who brings a valuable capital and erects mills or establishes any useful and extensive branch of business that will be of real benefit to the Colony, can get as much as five leagues of land if he wishes at the same rate—

The Government is yet unsettled tho there is now no doubt of its being a federal republic on the plan of the United States in every particular except toleration, the Roman Catholic is the established religion to the absolute exclusion of all others and will so continue for a few years, but the natural operation of a Republic will soon change that system—private worship will never be enquired into, but no public preaching of exorting will on any account be permitted, and I should feel myself compelled to silence any preacher or exorter who would attempt it within my jurisdiction.

You may think me rather tyranical relative to those who come without proper recommendations, but I have been much imposed upon, no recommendation from justices of the Peace will be noticed unless I personally know them, and all bad or idle and worthless men who come here will have abundant cause to curse the hour they crossed the limits—the welfare of this Colony requires the most rigid police, and my orders from the Gov^t on this subject are imperative and must be obeyed.

No credit will be given for lands and nothing taken in payment but money or negros—this is the general rule, but if you and a few more of my old friends come you may have your own time to pay in. If you see any worthless and idle men on the way here try and turn them back.

TERMS OF SETTLEMENT

The terms on which Settlers are admitted into the Colony forming by Stephen F. Austin in the Province of Texas are as follows—

No one will be received as a Settler, or even be permitted to remain in the country longer than is absolutely necessary to prepare for a removal who does not produce the most unequivocal and satisfactory evidence of unblemished character, good Morals, Sobriety, and industrious habits, and he must also have sufficient property to begin with either as a farmer or mechanic besides paying for his land—No frontiersman who has no other occupation than that of a hunter will be received—no drunkard, nor Gambler, nor profane swearer no idler, nor any man against whom there is even probable grounds of suspicion that he is a bad man, or even has been considered a bad or disorderly man will be received. Those who are rejected on the grounds of bad character will be immediately ordered out of the Count[r]y and if the order is not obeyed they will be sent off under guard and their property seized and sold to pay the expences, and should forcible resistence be made by them, the guard will be ordered to fire on and kill them—

Those who are received as Settlers will get one league of land if so much is wanted, to be chosen by the emigrant, which land will cost at the rate of twelve Dollars and fifty cents p^r hundred acres payable in cash or Spanish Cattle or negros on receipt of title, which will be in full for surveying, title deeds, recording, and all other charges.

The above only applies to men of families—Single men will be examined as to character more particularly than men of families and ten of them must unite to form a family and they will be entitled to one League of land to be divided between them. An exception will be made to this rule in favor of single men who bring a considerable capital into the country all such will be ranked as a family and draw one League—

A person who brings in a large capital and who has a large family will draw more than a league should he wish it. The head of each family will be held personally responsible for the good conduct of every member of his family.

The Roman Catholic is the established religion of the Mexican nation and the law will not allow of any other in this Colony—
October 30 1823—

IV

Land Policy

10. British Land Policy in the
Later Colonial Era

FROM THE middle of the eighteenth century the alienation of western lands was set down in policies determined first by the royal government in London, then by some of the newly independent states, and finally, after the cession of the western lands in the 1780's by the states, by the Congress of the United States.

Two considerations generally prevailed in British land policy for North America: the amount of revenue received through quit rents and the need to build up a human buffer against the French and the hostile Indians who sided with them. Consequently land was almost given away to white Protestant settlers. An individual could receive land for every member of his family, child or adult, black or white, slave or servant—up to 1,000 acres—on condition that he actually cultivate his holdings. Under this generous policy speculators were able to obtain multiple grants merely by listing bogus names for fictitious grantees. During the French and Indian War, royal and provincial officials, in order to bring peace to the frontiers, sought to satisfy the complaints of the Indians over encroachments on their lands by temporarily prohibiting settlement in territory claimed by the tribesmen. This policy was confirmed by a royal proclamation on October 7, 1763—a document which laid down policies for all the territories in Africa, North America, and the West Indies acquired from France and Spain during the late war. The former French colony of Canada was reduced in size and renamed Quebec. The previous Spanish and French territories in the south were divided into two new British provinces, East and West Florida.

The portions of the proclamation which follow are from a copy in the Archives of Canada, printed in Milton W. Hamilton (ed.), The Papers of Sir William Johnson (13 vols. Albany, N.Y., 1951), X, 981–984.

By The King
A Proclamation
George R.

. . . And whereas We are desirous, upon all Occasions, to testify Our Royal Sense and Approbation of the Conduct and Bravery of the Officers and Soldiers of Our Armies, and to reward the same; We do hereby command and impower our Governors of Our Three New Colonies, and all other Our Governors of our several Provinces on the Continent of North-America, to grant without Fee or Reward, to such reduced Officers as have Served in North-America during the late War, and to such private Soldiers as have been or shall be disbanded in America, and are actually residing there, and shall personally apply for the same, the following Quantities of Lands, subject at the Expiration of Ten Years to the same Quit-Rents as other Lands are subject to in the Province within which they are granted, as also subject to the same Conditions of Cultivation and Improvements, viz.

To every Person having the Rank of a Field Officer, Five Thousand Acres.—To every Captain, Three Thousand Acres.—To every Subaltern or Staff Officer, Two Thousand Acres.—To every Non-Commission Officer, Two Hundred Acres.—To every Private Man, Fifty Acres. . . .

And whereas it is just and reasonable, and essential to Our Interest and the Security of Our Colonies, that the several Nations or Tribes of Indians, with whom we are connected, and who live under Our Protection, should not be molested or disturbed in the Possession of such Parts of Our Dominions and Territories as, not having been ceded to, or purchased by Us, are reserved to them, or any of them as their Hunting Grounds; We do therefore, with the Advice of Our Privy Council, declare it to be Our Royal Will and Pleasure . . . that no Governor or Commander in Chief in any of Our other Colonies or Plantations in America, do presume, for the present and until Our further Pleasure be known, to grant Warrants of Survey, or pass Patents for any Lands beyond the Heads or Sources of any of the Rivers which fall into the Atlantick Ocean from the West and North-West, or upon any Lands whatever, which not having been ceded to or purchased by Us as aforesaid, are reserved to the said Indians or any of them.

And We do further declare it to be Our Royal Will and Pleasure, for the present as aforesaid, to reserve under Our Sovereignty, Protection, and Dominion, for the Use of the said *Indians*, all the Lands and Territories not included within the Limits of our said Three New Governments, or within the Limits of the Territory granted to the *Hudson's Bay* Company, as also all the Lands and Territories, lying to the Westward of the Sources of the Rivers which fall into the Sea from the West and North West, as aforesaid; and We to hereby strictly forbid, on Pain of Our Displeasure, all Our loving Subjects from making any Purchases or Settlements whatever, or taking Possession of any of the Lands above reserved, without Our especial Leave and Licence for that Purpose first obtained.

And We do further strictly enjoin and require all Persons whatever, who have either wilfully or inadvertently seated themselves upon any Land within the Countries above described, or upon any other Lands, which not having been ceded to, or purchased by Us, are still reserved to the said *Indians* as aforesaid, forthwith to remove themselves from such Settlements.

And whereas great Frauds and Abuses have been committed in the purchasing Lands of the *Indians*, to the great Prejudice of Our interests, and to the great Dissatisfaction of the said *Indians*; in order therefore to prevent such Irregularities for the future, and to the End that the *Indians* may be convinced of Our Justice, and determined Resolution to remove all reasonable Cause of Discontent; We do with the Advice of Our Privy Council, strictly enjoin and require that no private Person do presume to make any Purchase from the said *Indians* of any Lands reserved to the said *Indians*, within those Parts of Our Colonies where We have thought proper to allow Settlements; but that if, at any Time, any of the said *Indians* should be inclined to dispose of the said Lands, the same shall be purchased only for Us, in Our Name, at some Publick Meeting or Assembly of the said *Indians* to be held for that Purpose by the Governor or Commander in Chief of our Colonies respectively, within which they shall lie; and in Case they shall lie within the Limits of any Proprietary Government, they shall be purchased only for the Use and in the Name of such Proprietaries, conformable to such Directions and Instructions as We or they shall think proper to give for that Purpose: And We do by the Advice of Our Privy Council, declare and enjoin, that the Trade with the said *Indians* shall be free and open to all Our Subjects whatever; provided that every Person, who may incline to trade with the said *Indians*, do take out a Licence for carrying on such Trade from the Governor or Commander in Chief of any of Our Colonies respectively, where such Person shall reside; and also give Security to observe such Regulations as We shall at any Time think fit, by Ourselves, or by Our Commissaries to be appointed for this Purpose, to direct and appoint for the Benefit of the Said Trade; And We do hereby authorize, enjoin, and require the Governors Commanders in Chief of all Our Colonies respectively, as well those under Our immediate Government as Those under the Government and Direction of Proprietaries to grant such Licence, without Fee or Reward, taking especial care to insert therein a Condition, that such Licence shall be void, and the Security forfeited, in case the Person to whom the same is granted, shall refuse or neglect to observe such Regulations as We shall think proper to prescribe as aforesaid.

And we do further expressly enjoin and require all Officers whatever, as well Military as those employed in the Management and Direction of *Indian* Affairs within the Territories reserved as aforesaid for the Use of the said *Indians*, to seize and apprehend all Persons whatever, who, standing charged with Treasons, Misprisions of Treason, Murders, or other Felonies or Misdemeanors, shall fly from Justice; and take Refuge in the said Territory, and to send them under proper Guard to the Colony where the Crime was committed of which they stand accused, in order to take their Tryal for the same.

Given at Our Court at St. Jame[s]'s the Seventh Day of *October*, One Thousand Seven Hundred and Sixty Three. In the Third Year of Our Reign.

Instructions to a Royal Governor

DESPITE *the prohibition on settlement beyond the crest of the Allegheny Mountains contained in the proclamation of 1763, much land was thrown open to settlers in the broad piedmont of the South. Moreover, in 1765 the British Indian superintendents began negotiating with the tribes to clear more land of Indian title. As a result of three treaties negotiated in 1768 and 1770 the Indian boundary line was extended westwards, in some cases as far west as the Ohio River. Nonetheless aggressive squatters and speculators operated with impunity, locating lands indiscriminately and purchasing spurious titles to the soil from*

Indians who had no right to sell. The almost chaotic state of affairs led to an attempt by the royal government to institute some system of regular survey and sale. Additional instructions issued in the name of the king to the royal governors (those to the governor of New York are printed in Edmund B. O'Callaghan [ed.], Documents Relative to the Colonial History of the State of New York [15 vols., Albany, N.Y., 1857], VIII, 410–412) contained the provisions of the new program. In some respects they were paralleled by aspects of the policy adopted in 1785 by the Continental Congress.

We do hereby revoke and annul all and every Part of the said [previous] Instructions, and every Matter and Thing therein contained, in so far forth as they relate to the laying out and passing Grants of Land within our said Province, and to the Terms and Conditions upon which the said Grants are to be made. And it is our further Will and Pleasure, and we do hereby direct and appoint, that the following Rules and Regulations be henceforth strictly and punctually observed in the laying out, allotting and granting such Lands. Tenements and Hereditaments, as now are, or hereafter shall be in our power to dispose of, within our said Province. That is to say.

First. That you our said Governor, or our Governor, or Commander in Chief of our said Province for the Time being, with the Advice and Assistance of our Lieutenant Governor of our said Province, our Surveyor General of Lands for the Northern district of North America, our Secretary, our Surveyor General of our Lands, and our Receiver General of our Quit-Rents for our said Province of New York, or any three of them, do from time to time, and at such times as you shall, with the Advice aforesaid, judge most convenient, cause actual Surveys to be made of such parts of our said Province not already granted or disposed of, the Settlement and improvement whereof You shall think will be most advantageous to the public Interest and welfare; taking care that such districts so to be Surveyed and laid out, as aforesaid, be divided into such a number of Lots (each Lot to contain not less than one hundred, nor more than one thousand Acres) as our said Surveyor General shall judge best adapted to the Nature and Situation of the District so to be Surveyed.

2ᵈ That when the said Survey shall have been made, a Map of the district so Surveyed, with the several Lots marked and Number'd thereon, be hung up in our Secretary's Office within our said

Province, and Duplicates thereof transmitted to Us by one of our Principal Secretary's of State, and to our Commissioners of our Treasury, accompanied with a report in writing signed by our said Surveyor General descriptive of the Nature and Advantages, not only of the whole district in general, but also of each particular Lot.

3ᵈ That so soon as the said Survey shall have been made and returned, as aforesaid, You our said Governor or Commander in Chief of our said Province for the time being, do, with the Advice of our Council of our said Province, and of the Officers herein beforementioned, appoint such time and place for the Sale and disposal of the Lands contained within the said Survey to the best bidder, as you and they shall think most convenient and proper, giving previous Notice thereof at least four Months before such Sale by printed Advertisements, to be published not only within our said Province, but also in the other Neighbouring Provinces, and that You do proceed to such Sales at the Times appointed, unless you shall first receive directions from Us to the Contrary under our Signet and Sign Manual, or by our Order in our Privy Council.

4ᵗʰ That you our said Governor, or our Governor, or Commander in Chief of our said Province for the Time being, do, with the Advice and Assistance aforesaid, fix the price per Acre, at which the several Lots shall be put up to Sale, according to the Quality and Condition thereof, taking care, that no Lot is put up to such Sale at a less Price than six pence per Acre, and all such Lots are to be Sold subject to a Reservation to Us, our Heirs and Successors, of an Annual Quitrent, of one half penny Sterling per Acre.

5ᵗʰ That the printed Advertisement, containing Notice of the Time and place of Sale, so as to be published, as aforesaid, be as full and explicit as may be, as well in respect to the Number and Contents of the Lots to be sold, as the Terms and Conditions, on which they are to be put up to Sale, and the general Situation of the Lands, and the Advantages and conveniency thereof.

6ᵗʰ That the Person, who at such Sale shall bid most for any Lot, shall be the Purchaser, and shall, upon payment of the purchase Money into the hands of our Receiver General, or his Deputy, who is to attend at such Sales, receive from him a Bill of Sale of the Lot or Lots so purchased, upon producing whereof to you our Governor, or to our Governor, or Commander in Chief of our said Province for the time being, he shall be forthwith entitled to a grant in Fee simple of the Land, so purchased, as aforesaid, by Letters Patent under our public Seal of our said Province, subject to no Conditions or Reservations whatever, other than except the Payment to Us, our Heirs, and Successors of the annual Quit Rent of one halfpenny per Acre, as aforesaid, and also of all Mines of Gold, Silver or Precious Stones.

7th That the Fees to be paid by purchasers of Land in manner herein before recited, be such as are allowed by Law and no other, and that neither our Governor, or Commander in Chief of our said Province, or any other Officer or Officers entrusted with the Execution of these our Instructions, do for the present and until some other Arrangement be made for that purpose take any other or greater Fees.[1]

And it is our further Will and Pleasure, that neither you our Governor, nor our Governor, or Commander in Chief of our said Province for the Time being do, upon any pretense whatever, presume to grant any Lands, Tenements or Hereditaments within our said Province, which are in our Power to dispose of, upon any other Terms, or in any other manner than as herein before recited, without our express Authority for that purpose under our Signet, and Sign Manual, or by our order in our Privy Council, except only

1. 7th That the Fees to be paid by purchasers of Land in manner herein before recited be as followeth and that neither Our Governor or Commander in Chief of Our said Province or any other Officer or Officers entrusted with the execution of these Our Instructions do take any other or greater Fees, that is to say

To the Governor

	£	s	d
For every Grant of 100 Acres	0	10	0
For every Grant above 100 Acres and not more than 500 Acres	0	15	0
For Every Grant above 500 Acres	1	—	—

To the Secretary

	£	s	d
For every Grant of 100 Acres	0	5	0
For every Grant above 100 acres and not more than 500 Acres	0	10	0
For every Grant above 500 acres		15	0

To the Receiver General

	£	s	d
For a Bill of Sale of a Lot of 100 Acres	0	5	0
For a Bill of Sale of a Lot above 100 Acres not more than 500 Acres	0	10	0
For a Bill of Sale of a Lot above 500 Acres	0	15	0

in the Case of such Commission Officers and Soldiers, as are entitled to Grants of Lands in Virtue of our Royal Proclamation of the 7th of October 1763, to whom such Grants are to be made and passed in the proportions, and under the Conditions prescribed in the said Proclamation.

And it is our further Will and Pleasure, that in all Districts, which shall hereafter be Surveyed, in order to a sale of the Lands in Manner herein before recited, there be a Reservation of such Parts thereof, as shall appear from the Report of the Surveyor to be necessary for public Uses. . . .

11. Land Policy Under the United States

WITH THE success of the Revolution against Great Britain, the Continental Congress inherited the problems of the West. Several developments made it imperative to devise some policy for selling the western territories the states were then in the process of ceding to the Confederation government. It was apparent that Congress, lacking the power to tax, needed some method of raising money and of liquidating the Revolutionary debt. Moreover, in the West, many pioneers—dissatisfied with the land policy adopted by Virginia, which seemed to ensure the rights of early speculators over latecoming settlers—were actually occupying federal lands. Some were threatening to renounce their allegiance altogether and migrate to Spanish territory. Finally, something had to be done to satisfy the demands of a lobby of Continental Army officers for lands promised them by Congressional resolution on September 16, 1776. Colonels were to receive 500, majors 400, captains 300, lieutenants 200, and noncommissioned officers and private soldiers 100 acres of land.

The immediate pressures in the Northwest are revealed by the following documents, printed in Archer Butler Hulbert (ed.), Ohio in the Time of the Confederation (Marietta, Ohio, 1918), III, 137–140, 103–106, 98–99, 106–109. The original manuscripts are in the Papers of the Continental Congress, Library of Congress.

Petition of Kentuckians
for Lands North of Ohio River

To the Honourable Continental Congress
The Petition of a Number of the true and Loyal Subjects of the United States of America at large most humbly Sheweth

That your Petitioners having heretofore been Inhabiters of the different States of America; Since the Commencement of the Contest with Great Britain for the Common cause of Liberty; Have ventured their lives in a Wild uncultivated part of the Continent on the Western Waters of Ohio called by General Name of Kentuckey—Where they have made Improvements; on what they allowed was Kings Unappropriated Lands before the Commencem[en]t of the said Contest; and that in the face of a savage Enemy with the utmost hardships and in daily Geopardy of being inhumanly murdered—Your Petitioners further allowed that the Honorable Congress would allow them a Reasonable in Lands for the Services your Petitioner[s] did, in defending and Settleing, on their own expence, the Country aforesaid, to the weakening of the Enemy, and the Strengthening of the United States, whenever the common contest with Britain should be desided in favour of America—

In the full Assurance of which your Petitioners Sold all their livings in the Settled parts of the Continent, and have removed with their Wives[,] Families and all their Effects to the Country aforesaid, in order to take possession of their improvements aforesaid—But when they came found almost all their Improvements granted away by a Set of men which Acted or preten[d]ed to Act under the late Act of Virginia [1779]; which Act, also Allows large grants without any reserve of Settling and improving the same. By which means almost the whole of the lands in the Country aforesaid are Engrossed into the hands of a few Interest[ed] men, the greater part of which live at ease in the internal parts of Virginia; while your Petitioners are here with their Wives and Children daily Exposed to the Murders of the Savages to whom Sundry of their Acquaintance have fell a Sacrifice since their Arrival though as yet but a Short time; Again the late Acts of Virginia require your Petitioners to take a New Oath of Allegience to that State; renouncing all other Kings[,] princes and States; and be true to the State of Virginia only; and the prospect of Military Government taking place shortly in this place; give your Petitioners the greatest apprehension of the most Severe usage unless they comply with their mandates

Your Petitioners considering all those grievances would gladly return into the Settled parts of the Continent again; But having come Seven hundred Miles down the River Ohio, with the expence of the greater part of their fortunes find it Impracticable to return back against the Stream with their Wives and Children, were they to suffer the most cruel death—

Your Petitioners being drove to the Extremity aforesaid, have but three things to chooese; One is to Tarry in this place take the Oath of Allegience to Virginia, and be true to that State only, and also become Slaves to those Engrossers of Lands and to the Court of Virginia; The other is to Remove down the River Ohio, and land on some part of Mexico and become Subjects to the King of Spain; And the third to Remove themselves over the River Ohio; with their Wives Children and their small Effects remaining; which is now in possession of the Savage Enemy, to whome they are daily Exposed to murders; The Two former appearing to your Petitioner to have a Tendancy to weaken the United States; and as it were Banish the Common Cause of Liberty; Humbly pray the Honorable Continental Congress to grant them Liberty of Taking the latter Choise; and removing with their Wives Families and Effects to the Indian side of the Ohio, and take possession of the same in the name of the United States of America at large; where your Petitioners suppose to Support themselves in an Enemies Country on their own risque and expence; which they humbly Conceive will have a Tendancy to Weaken the power of the enemy, Strengthen the United States at large, and Advance the Common caus of Liberty—Your Petitioners further pray the Honorable Congress, to grant them liberty of making such Regulations amongst themselves as they shall find necessary to Govern themselves by, being subject to the United States at Large, and no other State or power whatsoever—Your Petitioners Humbly Pray the Honorable Continental Congress to Consider their Case and Grievances in its true light, and grant them such Relief, as You, in your great Wisdom shall see Meet as such meashures which are at this time adopted by Designing men are Likely to Lessen the Exertion of a Great number of people which otherwise are Well attached to the General Cause—And your Petitioners in duty Bound shall ever pray—

Ensign John Armstrong's Report to Colonel Josiah Harmar

Fort McIntosh, 12th April, 1785

Sir:

Agreeable to your orders, I proceeded with my party, on the 31st of March, down the [Ohio] river. On the first instant we crossed Little Beaver [Creek], and dispossessed a family. Four miles from there, we found three families living in sheds, but, they having no rafts to transport their effects, I thought it proper to give them until the 31st inst., at which time they promised to demolish their sheds and remove to the east side of the river.

At Yellow creek, I dispossessed two families and destroyed their building. The 2d inst., being stormy, nothing was done. The 3d, we disposed eight families. The 4th we arrived at Mingo Bottom, or Old Town. I read my instructions to the prisoner, [Joseph] Ross, who declared they never came from Congress, for he had late accounts from that honorable body, who, he was convinced, gave no such instructions to the [Congressional] Commissioners [for Indian Affairs]. Neither did he care from whom they came, for he was determined to hold possession, and if I destroyed his house he would build six more within a week. He also cast many reflections on the honorable the Congress, the Commissioners, and the commanding officer. I conceived him to be a dangerous man, and sent him under guard to Wheeling. Finding that most of the settlers at this place were tenants under the prisoner, I gave them a few days, at which time they promised to move to the east side of the Ohio river, and to demolish their buildings. On the evening of the 4th, Charles Norris, with a party of armed men, came to my quarters in a hostile manner, and demanded my instructions. After conversing with them some time, and showing my instructions, the warmth with which they first expressed themselves began to abate, and for some motive lodged their arms with me till morning. I learned from the conversation of the party that at Norris' Town (by them so called), eleven miles farther down the river, a party of seventy or eighty men were assembled with a determination to oppose me. Finding Norris to be a man of influence in that country, I conceived it to my interest to make use of him as an instrument, which I effected by informing him it was my intention to treat any armed parties I met as enemies of my country, and would fire on them if they did not disperse.

On the 5th, when I arrived within two miles of the town, or place where I expected to meet with opposition, I ordered my men to load their arms in the presence of Norris, and then desired him to go to the party and inform them of my intentions. I then proceeded on with caution, but had not gone far when paper No. 1[1]

1. See the next two documents for papers No. 1 and 2.

was handed me by one of the party, to which I replied, that I would treat with no party, but intended to execute my orders. When I arrived at the town there were about forty men assembled, who had deposited their arms. After I had read to them my instructions, they agreed to move off by the 19th inst. This indulgence I thought proper to grant, the weather being too severe to turn them out of doors. The 6th I proceeded to Hoglin's, or Mercer's Town, where I was presented with paper No. 2, and, from the humble disposition of the people and the impossibility of their moving, I gave them to the 19th, and I believe they generally left the settlement at that time. At that place I was informed that Charles Norris and John Carpenter had been elected Justices of the Peace; that they had, I found, precepts, and had decided thereon. I then proceeded on till opposite Wheeling, where I dispossessed one family and destroyed their buildings. I hope, sir, that the indulgences granted some of the inhabitants will meet your approbation. The paper No. 2 is a copy of an advertisement, which is posted up in almost every settlement on the western side of the Ohio.

Paper No. 1

ADVERTISEMENT

March 12, 1785

Notice is hereby given to the inhabitants of the west side of the Ohio River that there is to be an election for the choosing of members of the convention for the framing of a constitution for the governing of the inhabitants, the election to be held on the 10th day of April next ensuing, viz: one election to be held at the mouth of the Miami River, and one to be held at the mouth of the Scioto River, and one on the Muskingum River, and one at the dwelling-house of Jonas Menzons; the members to be chosen to meet at the mouth of the Scioto on the twentieth day of the same month.

I do certify that all mankind agreeable to every constitution formed in America, have an undoubted right to pass into every vacant country, and there to form their constitution, and that from the confederation of the whole United States, Congress is not empowered to forbid them, neither is Congress empowered from that confederation to make any sale of the uninhabited lands to pay the public debts, which is to be a tax levied and lifted (collected) by authority of the Legislature of each State.

John Emerson [Amberson]

Paper No. 2

[April 11, 1785]

To the Honourable the President of the Honourable Congress of the United States of America

The Petition, of us the subscribers now Residing on the western side of the Ohio; Humbly sheweth our grateful Acknowledgments to those Patriots of our Country who under Divine Providence so wisely Directed and Steered the Helm of Government: in that Great and Unparalel[e]d Conflict for Liberty: Bringing to a happy Period the Troubles of the states Laying the Foundation (by the most Salutary means) of the most Glorious form of government any People on Earth Could ever yet boast of; and that we have nothing more at hart than the Safety and happiness of the Common wealth in all its members from the highest to the Lowest Station in life: unwilling to Act any thing Directly: or Indirectly: that is of a Publick Nature without the Consent and Advice of the Legislature; notwithstanding when the Joyfull sound of Peace had Reached our Ears; we had scarce Enough left us to Support the Crying Distresses of our families Occasioned wholy by being Exposed to the ravages of a Cruel and Savage Enemy; on an Open Frontier where the most of us had the Misfortune to Reside through the whole Continuance of the war; where the only Recourse was to Sit Confin[e]d; in forts for the Preservation of our lives; by which we were Reduced allmost to the Lowest Ebb of Poverty; the Greatest part of us having no property in Lands: our stocks Reduced almost to nothing: our Case seemed Desperate But viewing as it Appeared to us an Advantage Offering of Vacant Lands which with the Alarming Nesesitys we were under Joined with the future Prospect of Bettering our Circumstances: invited us to Enter on those Lands fully Determined to Comply with Every Requisition of the Legislature: which we knew to be our Indispensible Duty Pregnant with hopes of Future Happiness we sat Content in the Enjoyment of our Scanty morsel: thinking ourselves Safe under the protection of Government: when on the fifth of this Instant we were Visited by a Command of men Sent by the Commandant at fort McIntosh; with orders from Government on purpose to Dispossess us and to Destroy our Dwellings: which the Executed in part when the first set out but our principles and our Duty to Government Obligded us to make an offer of Performing the Task ourselves which was agreed to on Conditions it were Executed Against the Nineteenth of this Instant; by which order it now Appears our Conduct in Settling here is Considered by the Legislature to be prejudicial to the Common good; of which we had not the Least Conception till now; we are greatly Distressed in our present Circumstances; and humbly pray if you in your Wisdom think proper to grant us Liberty: to Rest where we are and to grant us the preference to our Actual Settlements when the Land is to be settled by order of Government: where we shall Count it our Interest to be Subject to such Law and Regulations as the Legislature in their wisdom may think proper to prescribe Consistent with the Rights and privileges of the good people of these states. . . .

Land Ordinance of 1785

THE FIRST, and it became the basic, ordinance passed by Congress for selling land in the national domain was passed on May 20, 1785. The initial proposal brought in by a committee reflected the New England system of regular survey and settlement by groups in townships as opposed to the southern practice of individual, indiscriminate occupancy of the land. The ordinance as finally passed provided for some measure of direct, individual purchase. The law printed here is from John C. Fitzpatrick, et al. (eds.), Journals of the Continental Congress (34 vols., Washington, D.C., 1904–1937), XXVIII, 375–381.

May 20, 1785

An ordinance for ascertaining the mode of disposing of lands in the Western Territory.

Be it ordained by the United States in Congress assembled, that the territory ceded by individual states to the United States, which has been purchased of the Indian inhabitants, shall be disposed of in the following manner: . . .

The surveyors . . . shall proceed to divide the said territory into townships of 6 miles square, by lines running due north and south, and others crossing these at right angles, as near as may be. . . .

The first line, running north and south as aforesaid, shall begin on the river Ohio, at a point that shall be found to be due north and south from the western termination of a line, which has been run as the southern boundary of the state of Pennsylvania;[1] and the first line, running east and west, shall begin at the same point, and shall extend throughout the whole territory. . . . The geographer shall designate the townships, or fractional parts of townships, by numbers progressively from south to north; always beginning each range with No. 1; and the ranges shall be distinguished by their progressive numbers to the westward. The first range, extending from the Ohio to lake Erie, being marked No. 1. . . .

The plats of the townships respectively, shall be marked by subdivisions into lots of one mile square, or 640 acres, in the same direction as the external lines, and numbered from 1 to 36; always beginning the succeeding range of the lots with the number next to that with which the preceding one concluded. . . . And the surveyors, in running the external lines of the townships, shall, at the interval of every mile, mark corners for the lots which are adjacent, always designating the same in a different manner from those of the townships. . . .

As soon as 7 ranges of townships, and fractional parts of townships, in the direction from south to north, shall have been surveyed, the geographer shall transmit plats thereof to the board of treasury, who shall record the same, with the report, in well bound books to be kept for that purpose. And the geographer shall make similar returns, from time to time, of every 7 ranges as they may be surveyed. The secretary at war shall have recourse thereto, and shall take by lot therefrom, a number of townships . . . as well from those to be sold entire, as from those to be sold in lots, as will be equal to one-seventh part of the whole of such 7 ranges, as nearly as may be, for the use of the late continental army; and he shall make a similar draught, from time to time, until a sufficient quantity is drawn to satisfy the same, to be applied in manner hereinafter directed. The board of treasury shall, from time to time, cause the remaining numbers, as well those to be sold entire, as those to be sold in lots, to be drawn for, in the name of the thirteen states respectively, according to the quotas in the last preceding requisition on all the states; provided, that in case more land than its proportion

1. This still had not been run.

is allotted to sale, in any state, at any distribution, a deduction be made therefor at the next.

The board of treasury shall transmit a copy of the original plats, previously noting thereon, the township, and fractional parts of townships, which shall have fallen to the several states, by the distribution aforesaid, to the commissioners of the loan-office of the several states, who, after giving notice of not less than two nor more than six months, by causing advertisements to be posted up at the court-houses, or other noted places in every county, and to be inserted in one newspaper, published in the states of their residence respectively, shall proceed to sell the townships . . . at public vendue; in the following manner, viz: The township . . . No. 1, in the first range, shall be sold entire; and No. 2, in the same range, by lots; and thus in alternate order through the whole of the first range. The township . . . No. 1 in the second range, shall be sold by lots; and No. 2, in the same range, entire; and so in alternate order through the whole of the second range; and the third range shall be sold in the same manner as the first, and the fourth in the same manner as the second, and thus alternately throughout all the ranges; provided, that none of the lands, within the said territory, be sold under the price of one dollar the acre, to be paid in specie, or loan-office certificates, reduced to specie value, by the scale of depreciation, or certificates of liquidated debts of the United States, including interest, besides the expense of the survey and other charges thereon, which are hereby rated at 36 dollars the township, in specie, or certificates as aforesaid . . . to be paid at the time of sales; on failure of which payment, the said lands shall again be offered for sale.

There shall be reserved for the United States out of every township, the four lots, being numbered 8, 11, 26, 29 . . . for future sale. There shall be reserved the lot No. 16, of every township, for the maintenance of public schools, within the said township; also one third part of all gold, silver, lead and copper mines, to be sold, or otherwise disposed of as Congress shall hereafter direct. . . .

If any township . . . or lot, remains unsold for 18 months after the plat shall have been received, by the commissioners of the loan-office, the same shall be returned to the board of treasury, and shall be sold in such manner as Congress may hereafter direct.

And whereas Congress, by their resolutions of September 16th and 18th, in the year 1776, and the 12th of August, 1780, stipulated grants of lands to certain officers and soldiers of the late continental army, and by the resolution of the 22d September, 1780, stipulated grants of land to certain officers in the hospital department of the late continental army; for complying therefore with such engagements, Be it ordained, That the secretary at war, from the returns in his office, or such other sufficient evidence as the nature of the case may admit, determine who are the objects of the above resolutions and engagements, and the quantity of land to which such persons or their representatives are respectively entitled, and cause the townships, or fractional parts of townships, hereinbefore reserved for the use of the late continental army, to be drawn for in such manner as he shall deem expedient, to answer the purpose of an impartial distribution. He shall, from time to time, transmit certificates to the commissioners of the loan offices of the different states, to the lines of which the military claimants have respectively belonged, specifying the name and rank of the party, the terms of his engagement and time of his service, and the division, brigade regiment or company to which he belonged, the quantity of land he is entitled to, and the township, or fractional part of a township, and range out of which his portion is to be taken. . . .

Saving and reserving always, to all officers and soldiers entitled to lands on the northwest side of the Ohio, by donation or bounty from the commonwealth of Virginia, and to all persons claiming under them, all rights to which they are so entitled, under the deed of cession executed by the delegates for the state of Virginia, on the first day of March, 1784, and the act of Congress accepting the same: and to the end, that the said rights may be fully and effectually secured, according to the true intent and meaning of the said deed of cession and act aforesaid, Be it ordained, that no part of the land included between the rivers called Little Miami and Sciota, on the northwest of the river Ohio, be sold, or in any manner alienated, until there shall first have been laid off and appropriated for the said officers and soldiers, and persons claiming under them, the lands they are entitled to, agreeably to the said deed of cession and act of Congress accepting the same.

Land Act of 1796

IN 1796 Congress amended the basic act for sale of land in the national domain by raising the minimum price but varying the method of dis-

posing of townships. The text is reprinted from the original statue in the National Archives in Clarence E. Carter (ed.), The Territorial Papers of the United States (25 vols., Washington D.C., 1934), II, 552–557.

An Act providing for the Sale of the lands of the United States, in the territory north-west of the river Ohio, and above the mouth of Kentucky river. . . .

Be it further enacted, That the part of the said lands, which has not been already conveyed by letters patent, or divided, in pursuance of an ordinance in Congress, passed on the twentieth of May, one thousand seven hundred and eighty five, or which has not been heretofore, and, during the present session of Congress, may not be, appropriated for satisfying military land bounties, and for other purposes, shall be divided by north and south lines . . . and by others crossing them at right angles, so as to form townships of six miles square. . . . One half of the said townships, taking them alternately, shall be subdivided into sections, containing, as nearly as may be, six hundred and forty acres each . . . the sections shall be numbered respectively, beginning with the number one, in the north east section, and proceeding west and east alternately, through the township, with progressive numbers, 'till the thirty sixth be completed. . . .

Be it further enacted, That whenever seven ranges of townships shall have been surveyed . . . the said sections of six hundred and forty acres (excluding those hereby reserved) shall be offered for sale, at public vendue, under the direction of the Governor or Secretary of the western territory, and the Surveyor-General. . . . And the townships remaining undivided shall be offered for sale . . . in tracts of one quarter of a township, lying at the corners thereof, excluding the four central sections, and the other reservations before mentioned: Provided always, that no part of the lands directed by this Act to be offered for sale, shall be sold for less than two dollars per acre.

Be it further enacted, That the Secretary of the Treasury, after receiving the aforesaid plats, shall forthwith give notice, in one newspaper in each of the United States, and of the territories north west and south of the river Ohio, of the times of sale; which shall, in no case, be less than two months from the date of the notice; and the sales at the different places shall not commence, within less than one month of each other: And when the governor of the western territory, or Secretary of the Treasury, shall find it necessary to adjourn, or suspend the sales under their direction, respectively, for more than three days, at any one time, notice shall be given, in the public newspapers, of such suspension, and at what time, the sales will recommence. . . .

Be it further enacted, That the highest bidder for any tract of land, sold by virtue of this Act, shall deposit, at the time of sale, one twentieth part of the amount of the purchase money; to be forfeited, if a moiety of the sum bid, including the said twentieth part, is not paid within thirty days . . . and upon payment of a moiety of the purchase-money, within thirty days, the purchaser shall have one year's credit for the residue. . . .

. . . But if there should be a failure in any payment, the sale shall be void, all the money theretofore paid on account of the purchase shall be forfeited to the United States, and the lands thus sold shall be again disposed of, in the same manner as if a sale had never been made: Provided nevertheless, that should any purchaser make payment of the whole purchase money, at the time when the payment of the first moity is directed to be made, he shall be entitled to a deduction of ten per centum on the part, for which, a credit is hereby directed to be given and his patent shall be immediately issued.

The Harrison Land Act

IN THE Harrison Land Act of 1800, Congress retained the minimum price of two dollars an acre but introduced a credit system and allowed a minimum of 320 acres. The text is reprinted from the original statute in the National Archives, in Carter (ed.), The Territorial Papers of the United States, III, 88–91.

[May 10, 1800]

An Act to amend an Act . . . "providing for the sale of the lands of the United States in the Territory North-West of the Ohio. . . ."

Sec. 3. *And be it further enacted,* That the Surveyor General shall cause the townships west of the Muskingum, which by the above mentioned act, are directed to be sold in quarter townships, to be subdivided into half sections of three hundred and twenty Acres each. . . .

Sec. 5. *And be it further enacted,* That no lands shall be sold by virtue of this act, at either public or private sale; for less than two dollars per acre . . . and shall be made in the following manner, and under the following conditions to wit,

1. At the time of purchase, every purchaser shall, exclusively of the fees hereafter mentioned pay six dollars for every section, and three dollars for every half section he may have purchased, for surveying expenses, and deposit one twentieth part of the amount of purchase Money to be forfeited if within forty days, one fourth part of the purchase money including the said twentieth part, is not paid.

2. One fourth part of the purchase money shall be paid within forty days after the day of sale as aforesaid: another fourth part shall be paid within two Years; another fourth part within three Years; and another fourth part within four Years, after the day of sale.

3. Interest at the rate of six per cent a year from the day of sale, shall be charged upon each of the three last payments payable as they respectively become due.

4. A discount, at the rate of eight per cent a Year, shall be allowed on any of the three last payments, which shall be paid before the same shall become due reckoning this discount always upon the sum which would have been demandable by the United States on the day appointed for such payment.

Settlers' Petitions

ALTHOUGH Congress, by an act passed on March 26, 1804, reduced the minimum price to $1.64 an acre and the minimum sale to 160 acres, westerners still complained, particularly since their ability to pay for land depended on the sale of their produce. Due to British interference with American shipping to Europe, the price of western foodstuffs was low from 1805 to 1815. And the boom following the War of 1812 was shortly followed by the Panic of 1819. Many settlers were unable to meet their credit payments. Moreover, since the federal government sold land at public auction there was no guarantee that settlers who had squatted on the land and made improvements could outbid speculators and latecomers when the tract was put up for sale at auction. These grievances, common in both the Southwest and Northwest, are shown *in the following petitions, printed in Carter (ed.), Territorial Papers of the United States, III, 123-124; VII, 314-315; VI, 407-409.*

[Library of Congress, House File]

[1800]

The Senate, and House of Representatives of the United States of America, in Congress Met.

The Petition of the Subscribers, Set[t]lers on the Publick land Be-tween the Waters of Muskingum, and Sciota River, in the Northwestern Territory;—Humbly Sheweth,

That your Petitioners Return their Humble thanks to your Honorable Body for your attention to their Petition at your last Session, in making an Act suplementary to the former Act, for setling the Publick Lands in this Territory, in which among other Advantages to Settlers, is, dividing the Townships, (before di-rected to be sold in Quarter Townships) into half sections, and giving time for the payment of a part of the Money; &ᶜ Yet there is one Circumstance in that Law, which Militates forcibly against your Petitioners, especially the poor Industrious Setlers, an[d] what we wish particularly to represent to your Honorable Body; and that is, that their small improvements, made at a great ex-pence, and labour, emigrating so far thro' a Wilderness without inhabitants, and having their Provisions as well as families to Trans-port, and oftentimes hazarding their lives from the danger of the Savages, and have now formed considerable settlements, should still be exposed to a Publick Vendue to be outbid by an unfeeling Land-Jobber or Speculator, who perhaps has been preying on the Vitals of his Country, untill he has fill'd his pockets, by such we say, the poor honest and Industrious Citizen must submit to have his improvement bought over his head, and him eith[er] submit to become his Tenant, or quit his Country; Great num[bers] have al-ready gone to accept the offers of the British over the Lakes, a[nd of] the Spaniards over the Mississipi, and great numbers more are contemplating to go also, should their own Government which has such a vast Quantity of uncultivated Lands, dispose of it in such a manner, and at such a rate, as puts it out of their power to procure any. Which in fact compels them to renounce their own Govern-ment[,] the Government of their choice that very Government which many of them fought and Bled to procure, and establish, to go to people the Uncultivated wilds of despotic Governments, and add strength and population to them.—We have imigrated from the different states of the Union, some of us with small property, and large families, with a [hope] to make better provision for them. others of us Renters, una[ble] to purchase in the older states on account of the high price [of Land] and came here at a great expence, and labour, and trusting that Congress would grant us some indulgence, as by our settling down in the Wilderness, a way was opened for others to emigrate and tends much to the encouragment of the Sale of the Publick lands. We would Just suggest to your Honorable Body, an Idea that it is our Opinion should you see cause to grant a preemption right, at Two dollars pr Acre, to the oldest improvement made on Sections and half Sections prior to the first of May one thousand Eight hundred and Sell the Rest, at publick Auction, (there being but a small part improved and that along the Publick road) for the most pa[rt] the Unimproved land, selling so much better on account of the settlement, that the money arising from them Sales, together with the preemption, would amount to more money than the whole sold at Publick Auction, had there been no improvements made. These things we would submit to the serious consideration of your Honorable Body, And if you see meet in your Wisdom to grant unto your Petitioners, a Preemption right, to the Sections and half Sections we have improved, at Two Dollars pr Acre, with all the indulgence as to time for payment, your Honorable Body shall see meet, Clear of Interest untill the several payments shall become due; as we conceive the Interest to operate powerfully against us as Settlers, as every means of making money here is yet in its infant State. . . . And whereas numbers of Persons have settled on land reserved by Congress, and not knowing thereof untill after making considerable improvements, We pray that if Congress sees meet to grant that such as are able to purchase their improvements, may have granted to them a like preemption at two dollars, and such as are not may have a right to preempt to lease, least others should take advantage and lease it over their heads by an earlier Application,—These Petitions we prefer to Congress, and trusting to the Justness, and Reasonable ness of them; and a Just, enlightened, and indulgent Legislature, We humbly hope they will grant us; And Your Petitioners as in Duty bound, shall ever pray.—

[House of Representatives Files, 9th Cong.]

[November 19, 1805]

To the Honourable the Senate and House of Representatives of the United States in Congress assembled

The Petition of the Subscribers, purchasers of lands of the United States in the now State of Ohio and in the Indiana Territory . . . and Inhabitants of the same

Most Respectfully sheweth

That at the times when their Contracts for the said lands were made money was not scarce as now, and flowed into the Country from some sources that have been since dried up particularly from the pay of a part of the army then stationed there but since removed, and that New Orleans was the only place to which the produce of the County could be exported, it afforded a tollerable market and the expectations of drawing from thence in return the sums necessary to meet their engagements with the United States was not only reasonable but flattering

That the market at all times easily overstocked became unfavourable, so as that the articles sent there, in many Instances with all the care diligence and economy that could be used, did not return more than the original value at the place of embarcation, and consequently involved the adventurers in great losses and some of them in ruin, and at length, from the deficulties thrown in the way by the Spanish Government the intercourse for a time was totally suspended—that the payments in part already made to the United States, have so much reduced the quantity of circulating money that no kind of produce will scarcely command it at any price, while the expenditures your Petitioners have of necessity been obldiged to make in order to subdue and render productive these very lands have entirely exhausted the money provided and intended for succeeding payments

That the Province of Louisiana and the City of New Orleans having come into the hands of United States a prospect opens to your Petitioners that could they obtain a respite in the payments becomeing due, the market there will become more favourable and from the establishment of commercial Houses with sufficient capitals, the produce of this Country will be bought there for foreign markets and a return made in coin or Bills of Exchange that

would enable your Petitioners to fulfill their engagements with the
Public at no very distant period—

That your Petitioners were compel[l]ed to purchase more lands
than they wished for in many cases a section with its adjoining
Fraction and in no instance less than an entire Section of land
and the whole tract was respectively included in one Certificate—
thus your Petitioners are prevented from disposing of a part because they are unable to assign over the Certificate, for a less quantity than the whole

That under all these Circumstances should the terms on which
your Petitioners contracted be rigorously insisted upon they must
be turned adrift in the World with their families, and others reap
the benefit of their labour, who perhaps have not experienced the
dangers attendant on a long Indian War, nor been subjected to the
extreme hardships and expences of Cultivating a Wilderness nor
had any Share in bringing this country to its present promising
state—But the hopes of your Petitioners are on the magnanimity
and Generosity of Congress, neither they trust will it be forgotten,
mentioned as it is with the utmost diffidence and delicacy that
the high price the wild lands of this country have borne, so greatly
beyond any ever sold by any of the states and the great sums of
money that has been drawn from thence into the public Treasury
have been consequences of their labour

Your Petitioners do therefore most humbly and earnestly request that their case may be taken into consideration and that an
extention of the times for their future payments may be granted
and a remission of Interest on the several instalments. But if this
should be refused (which they with submission hope will not be
the case) that then Congress will be pleased to grant to those who
have purchased under the aforesaid law the preference of re-entering the same on their forfeiting the fourth part already paid.

[Library of Congress, Madison Papers]

[January 11, 1814]

*To the Honorable the Senate and House of Representatives of the
United States of America in Congress Assembled: The Memorial of the Legislative Council and House of Representatives
of the Mississippi Territory in general Assembly convened, respectfully Sheweth. . . .*

. . . The Public Lands which will shortly be forfeited unless
the payments are completed, were purchased at a period of [MS.
torn] prosperity. The purchasers had every rational ground to believe that as the day of payment approached they would be enabled to meet it. They have been disappointed. Property has depreciated. Their funds have vanished. They have no means of
complying with their obligations to the Public. The Public Lands
were purchased in a time of peace. Peace might have permitted
the purchasers to complete their payments. The National Interest,
the National Character called for war. War just and righteous as it
was, has stripped them of the means of fulfilling their engagements[.] They will not say that the Declaration of War was the Act
of the Creditor, and has deprived the Debtor, against his will of the
means of discharging his Debts. No! though your memorialists had
no voice in Declaring war they approved the measure; and are
[proud to be] regarded as parties in it. But if their Lands their
Houses and their Homes, be swept from them in consequence of
the War, they will be more than equal sharers in its disasters. But
it is not the war alone that has involved them in Difficulties. Visi-
tations of providence against which no human foresight could
have guarded, have lasted their crops. The Cotton in the fertile
bottoms of the Mississippi has for two Years been destroyed by
the unusual inundations of that River; and in more interior Situations, the rot has exposed the same article to a nearly equal injury.
If the attentions of Your Honorable body be turned to the Eastern
Section of our Territory what will you See, but a Scene of Savage
devastation? Can the people who have been driven from their
Homes, who have been plundered of their property [and have]
been deprived of the power even of gathering their Crops for the
subsistance of their families; be supposed to be capable of paying
any instalments which may be due from them for the Lands which
they have purchased of the Government? Madison County on the
Tennessee River has also in some measure been visited by a Similar
Calamity. That county moreover was settled under every dis-
couragement and privation. Their country was not only new, but
detached from all other places, affording Shelter to civilised man!
and notwithstanding the disadvantages of the Situation, Yet such
was the expectation of a rapid increase in the value of property in
consequence of the projected Settlement that higher prices were
given for the Lands of Madison County than ever went into the

public coffers [for similar lands], and the period of purchase precluded the people of that county from receiving benefit from former acts of indulgence. And what would be the advantage of insisting upon a Compliance with the Stipulations of the Contract? Would it bring into the Treasury of the United States any sums of money worthy the attention of a great Nation? It surely would not. Past experience will justify this conclusion. When forfeitures have already taken place few indeed are the cases in which the Lands forfeited have sold at an advanced price at public Sale

A change of owners indeed has sometimes taken place. They have been purchased at private Sale at two dollars per acre on account of their improvements: and the monied man with his capital, in the place of the labouring man with his [fluctuating] income a Debtor to the Nation, without enriching it by his industry or giving strength to it by adding any thing valuable to its population. Two Slaves indeed may have occupied the place of one Freeman; but the source of National greatness has been lessened, and the Sinews of National Strength have been relaxed. Alas! the population of our territory is already on its decline Should the Land Laws be enforced at the present inauspicious moment it will still further recede from our borders; And where shall we then look for the Youthful warriors who shall defend the firesides of their Fathers and become the champions of the liberties and honor of their country; Your memorialists therefore pray your Honorable body to secure them still in the occupancy of the fields which they have cultivated [and] the Houses they have built, and to withdraw, till peace shall Smile upon them again, any demand for the instalments due upon their Land, or Interest accruing on payments required, but not discharged in time. But could the purchasers and Actual Settlers on the public Lands be merely Secured in the occupancy of the tracts they hold, and have the privilege of re-entering them within the space of two or three years, they would in many cases probably prefer it, to any postponement of the payment of their present Debt, and Cheerfully submit to the forfeitures of the money already paid into the public Treasury. But previously to the reception of this memorial by your Honorable body, many cases of forfeiture will have occurred; We therefore trust that you will make such provision for those unfortunate sufferers as your wisdom may suggest. Where there has been no change of owners this can be easily effected by extending to the Original purchaser a right of Preemp [MS. torn] thereby giving him an opportunity of saving his improvement from the rude grasp of the Merciless Speculator. Another subject to which the general Assembly of the Mississippi Territory would Solicit the attention of your Honorable body, is the existing regulation with regard to the Sales of fractional parts of Sections. Those fractions frequently extend to the amount of five or six hundred acres. Under the present laws they cannot be divided. Many Settlers would be able and desirous to purchase One hundred and Sixty acres, but are totally unable to purchase a whole fraction. It does not occur to your memorialists, that there is any Solid reason why the same Privilege of subdivision which is enjoyed with [MS. torn] whole sections should not be extended to fractional parts of sections. It would accommodate private purchasers and it would advance the public Interest by encouraging the Sales of Lands.

A Realistic Land Law
and Squatters' Rights

FOLLOWING *the Panic of 1819 Congress passed a realistic land act on April 24, 1820, abolishing the credit system, reducing the minimum price to $1.25 an acre and the minimum sale to 80 acres. And in 1830 Congress passed a pre-emption law for squatters then on the land. The laws printed below are from Richard Peters (ed.), The Public Statutes at Large of the United States . . . (8 vols., Boston, Mass., 1858–1862), III, 566–567; IV, 420–421.*

AN ACT MAKING FURTHER PROVISION FOR THE
SALE OF THE PUBLIC LANDS

[April 24, 1820]

Be it enacted by the Senate and House of Representatives of the United States of America, in Congress assembled, That from and after the first day of July next, all the public lands of the United States . . . when offered at public sale, to the highest bidder, be offered in half quarter sections; and when offered at private sale, may be purchased, at the option of the purchaser, either in entire sections, half sections, quarter sections, or half quarter sections. . . .

SEC. 2. *And be it further enacted,* That credit shall not be allowed for the purchase money on the sale of any of the public lands which shall be sold after the day of July next, but every purchaser of land sold at public sale thereafter, shall, on the day of purchase, make complete payment therefor . . . and if any person, being the highest bidder, at public sale, for a tract of land, shall fail to make payment therefor, on the day on which the same was purchased, the tract shall be again offered at public sale, on the next day of sale, and such person shall not be capable of becoming the purchaser of that or any other tract offered at such public sales.

SEC. 3. *And be it further enacted,* That from and after the first day of July next, the price at which the public lands shall be offered for sale, shall be one dollar and twenty-five cents an acre; and at every public sale, the highest bidder, who shall make payment as aforesaid, shall be the purchaser; but no land shall be sold, either at public or private sale, for a less price than one dollar and twenty-five cents an acre. . . .

AN ACT TO GRANT PRE-EMPTION RIGHTS TO SETTLERS ON THE PUBLIC LANDS

[May 29, 1830]

Be it enacted by the Senate and House of Representatives of the United States of America, in Congress assembled, That every settler or occupant of the public lands, prior to the passage of this act, who is now in possession, and cultivated any part thereof in the year one thousand eight hundred and twenty-nine, shall be, and he is hereby, authorized to enter, with the register of the land office, for the district in which such lands may lie, by legal subdivisions, any number of acres, not more than one hundred and sixty or a quarter section, to include his improvement, upon paying to the United States the then minimum price of said land. . . .

SEC. 5. *And be it further enacted,* That this act shall be and remain in force, for one year from and after its passage.

A Remonstrance from Michigan Settlers

ATTEMPTS *in Congress to enact a permanent pre-emption bill and to institute a policy of graduated prices became enmeshed in sectional politics, but graduated prices for western lands were opposed not only by eastern politicians, who feared the drain on the population of their sections, but also by westerners who looked with distaste on the "lower" elements. The following remonstrance is printed in Carter (ed.),* Territorial Papers of the United States, *XI, 1175–1176.*

[National Archives, State Department]

[March 10, 1828]

To the Honorable the Senate and House of Representatives in Congress assembled,

The Subscribers inhabitants of the Ter[ritory] of Michigan respectfully remonstrate to your Honorable Body, against the passage of a Bill, reported by the Committee upon Public Lands, entitled "a Bill to graduate the price of public lands &ᶜ". We think the Bill is essentially unjust to those who have already purchased of the United States, and have undergone all the labor expense & deprivation of settling a new country—the lands have then become more valuable; but the first settler finds his property falling upon his hands from the fact that new comers can buy for one fifth of what he has paid when the country was a wilderness. Our Territory will be settled by squatters who are a pest to society. By the provisions of this Bill any one may obtain one eighty acre lot by residing upon it and may purchase a thousand acres in its vicinity. Speculation will be the order of the day, immense quantities of land will be purchased at twenty five cents per acre by companies and individuals, a credit system will be established, and the price raised to two or three dollars. The cash system for the disposal of the public lands has produced the happiest results in establishing a moral population for Michigan. The present price secures to the United States a fair compensation for the expenses attendant upon the acquisition and survey of new lands, and secures to the settler a respectable neighbourhood. Your Honorable Body cannot for a moment imagine, that our society would be benefitted by giving away the Public Lands and thus enticing the dregs of community from the old States. We appeal to your Hon[ora]ᵇˡᵉ Body for protection against a system which we think must drive every respectable man out of this country. If your Honorable Body were disposed to establish a place of refuge for the refuse of society, if you were inclined to draw off from the old States, that portion of the people who are a nuisance to any country, we think it might not be amiss to fix upon some place in the interior of the North Western Territory, and to offer lands within a given district to the settler free of expense; but we beg that Michigan may not be selected for that object. We are far from objecting to a grant of land from the United States to the several states and Territories within whose boundaries these lands may lie; but let that grant be made now; now we have roads and bridges and canals to make; let the first settlers be benefitted by these lands; let them have some compensation for the expense of making roads for those who are to come after them. It must be obvious to your Honorable Body, that this Bill if it pass into a law, must procrastinate the settlement of new countries, as emigrants will wait until land falls to its lowest price. We think that this Bill should be entitled, A Bill for the encouragement of squatters and speculators for the destruction of the moral character of new countries, for a tax upon first settlers and a premium to those who come last, and for the establishment of the old credit system.

V

Government and Law

12. Frontier Compacts

THE EARLIEST governments in the West were either county courts extended under the jurisdiction of colonies or states claiming the region, or, where jurisdiction was disputed or undetermined, compacts or agreements arrived at by common consent of the settlers. The latter type did not survive being replaced within a short time by county governments, once state authority was determined.

The following documents from Boyd, Susquehanna Company Papers, IV, 146, 264, 271–272, 276, 377–378,[1] illustrate "blockhouse" government as employed by Connecticut settlers in the Wyoming District when engaged in a conflict with Pennsylvania for control of the Susquehanna lands.

Minutes of a Meeting of the Susquehanna Company
Windham, Connecticut, January 9, 1771

Voted That Col Dyer Nath Wales J^r. Saml Gray & Maj^r Elderkin be a Com^{te} To draw up a schem In Writing agreeable To the minds of the Settlers on s^d Land to be signd by all who now are or shall go on to settle the Susqueh^h Lands so as To Legally bind & oblige all who sign the Same faithfully To perform Each one his Trust and undertakeing according To the True Intent and meaning of such Schem & That none butt such as Voluntarily Sign s^d agreement shall be admitted To hold any right or priviledge There as a Setler untill further orders of s^d Company

Voted That Capt Zeb^n Butler Capt Laz^s Stewart Maj^r John Durke & John Smith Esqr be & they are hereby appointed a Com^{te} To repair To Our setlement att Wyoming with our Setlers & they

1. Reprinted from Julian P. Boyd (ed.), *The Susquehanna Company Papers*, (4 vols., Ithaca, N.Y., 1930), IV. Copyright 1930 ©, by the Wyoming Historical and Geological Society. Used by permission of the Cornell University Press.

or the major part of Them To order and direct In all affairs relating To the Well Governing and ordering s^d setlers and setlement and That the Proprieters of Each of the five Townships laid out att Wyoming shall have full Liberty To Choose one person for Each Town To be a Com^{te} Man To Joyn The above Gen^t the whole To be butt one Intire Com^{te} for the purposes affores^d

Minutes of a Meeting of the Inhabitants of Wyoming

At a meeting of ye Inhabitants of ye 6th township at and Near Wyoming Legally warned August ye 22nd 1771 Capt. Butler was chosen Moderator. This meeting is adjorned to ye 23rd Day at 6 a Clock in ye morning.

This meeting is opened & Held by an adjornt august ye 26th 1771.

Voted, Capt Hopkins, Parshall Terry and Bartholamew Weeks are appointed to take care of ye cows in ye Day time and to see that ye cows are Brought up in season.

Voted, That Captain Marvin is appointed to Deal out ye milk to Each mess.

Voted, Abel Peirce & Abel Smith is appointed Bacors to Bake Bread for ye Company.

This meeting is adjorned to ye 29th Day of this Instant to 6 a Clock in ye morning.

August 29th, 1771, this meeting is adjorned until ye 2nd Day of September, 6 a Clock in ye forenoon at this place.

September ye 2nd 1771 this meeting is opened & Held by an adjornment &c.

Voted, that any man that will go and secure ye Grain that is now standing and secure ye same Between Now and Next Saturday Night shall be intitled to ye same as his own property Not neglecting his other duty.

Voted, that Capt. William Warner is appointed to live in ye Block House built by ye mills, in order to Gard ye mills, and has ye Liberty to pick out Nine men to assist him in keeping ye same.

Voted, That Capt. Stephen Fuller is appointed to go, with such a Number of men as he shall chuse, this Day to Lackawana & remove all ye Pennemites [adherents to the government of Pennsylvania] that Reside their, and Bring them Down ye River.

Voted, that 20 men to prosede and go forward and clear ye upper Rode Leading to Dellaware River of ye Pennemites &c.

Minutes of a Meeting of the Inhabitants in Wilkes-Barré

Wilksbury, Septr 30th 1771. This meeting is opened & Held by an adjornment, &c.

Voted Mr William Park undertakes to thrash out all ye English grain Now in ye fields—Rye and Wheat—and to take every seventh Bushel for his Thrashing, &c.

Voted that Capt Butler, Capt Stewart & Capt Gore Is appointed as a Comtee to Lott out all ye corn Now standing at Wyoming to the persons now on ye Ground that will undertake to gather & stack ye same and Bring it in to ye fort and crib up ye same, &c.

Voted, That what grain each man shall soe shall be his own to Reap ye Next year for his own private Property Lett it be on his own Land or on any other mans Lott, &c.

Voted, that Docr Joseph Sprague shall Have a settling Right In one of ye five towns.

Voted, that No person that is admitted in as a settler shall go Home or absent himself without Liberty of ye Comtee—if they Do they shall forfitt their settling Right.

This meeting is adjorned untill Fryday ye 4th Day of october next at six a Clock in ye morning at this place.

Minutes of a Meeting of the Inhabitants in Wilkes-Barré

Att a meeting Legally warned and Held in Wilksbury october 12th 1771 Capt Butler was chosen moderator for ye work of ye Day.

Voted, that John Dougherty, Peter mathews, John White, William young, David young, Thomas Robinson, John McDaniel, William Vallentine, Asa Lyon, William Buck, John Depew, Levi Green are to be stationed on ye west side of ye River in ye Block House with Capt Stewart.

Voted that Atherton's Family, Adsel's Family & Anguish & his family is to Have ye Liberty to Live on ye west side of ye River provided they move to ye Block House with Capt Stewart.

Voted that all ye Persons that are Not stationed in ye Block-house on ye west side of ye River & in ye Blockhouse at ye mills is to move into ye fort at this Place.

Voted that David Sanford & William Vallentine is to Have a settling Rite In one of ye towns Now laid out &c.

Voted that ye Com^{tee} shall Dispose of ye Pennemites cows to such Persons as they think Proper.

Minutes of the Proprietors and Settlers in Kingston

Voted that Capt Zebulon Butlar, Mr Stephen Jenkins Capt Benjamin Follet be a Committee for leaying out the 3 Division in this town.

Voted that they proceed to lay out the 3 Division in the town of Kings[ton]

Voted that the Committee above written be empowered to lay out such highways and Roads as they in their Judgements may Judge will best accomodate the Town and public.

Voted that Each settler now in this town shall have an equal share in the grain now growing on the intervals.

Voted That Thomas Bennet Simon Draper & Israel Jones be appoint to divide the grass to the several settlers in this town.

Voted that this meeting be adjourned to the center of the Town viz, at the houses building on the bank of the River near the great Springs on the first Tuesday in July next at 2 oClock in the afternoon.

Tuesday July 3rd A D 1770. At a meeting held in Kingstown this day by adjournment.

Voted that this meeting be adjourned until Saterday the 7th day of Instant July at 2 O Clock afternoon at this place.

Voted that the Rales which are on the land and which were split and cut either in fence and otherwise before the 1st of May shall belong to the public youse and shall be moved into a fence on the East side of a two Rods road which runneth thro' the intervale in this town.

July 7th A D 1770

At a meeting held at Kingston this 7th of July A D 1770 by adjournment

Voted that Reuben Davis and Jonathan Dean are appointed to draw the Third Division of land in this town.

The Watauga Compact

JUST AS the Yankees used their familiar New England town governments on the Pennsylvania, and later the Ohio, frontier, so Virginians and North Carolinians used the institution of the county court in the

Tennessee wilderness. The following petition, printed in Samuel Cole Williams, Tennessee During the Revolutionary War *(Nashville, Tenn., 1944), pp. 19–21, shows the origin of the "Watauga Compact" and its relation to Virginia county government and laws.*

[July 5, 1776]

To the Hon. the Provincial Council of North Carolina:

The humble petition of the inhabitants of Washington District, including the River Wataugah, Nonachuckie, &c., in committee assembled, Humbly Sheweth, that about six years ago, Col. [John] Donelson, [actually John Stuart] (in behalf of the Colony of Virginia), held a Treaty with the Cherokee Indians, in order to purchase the lands of the Western Frontiers; in consequence of which Treaty, many of your petitioners settled on the lands of the Wataugah, &c., expecting to be within the Virginia line, and consequently hold their lands by their improvements as first settlers; but to their great disappointment, when the line was run they were (contrary to their expectation) left out; finding themselves thus disappointed, and being too inconveniently situated to move back, and feeling an unwillingness to loose the labour bestowed on their plantations, they applied to the Cherokee Indians, and leased the land for a term of ten years, before the expiration of which term, it appeared that many persons of distinction were actually making purchases forever; thus yielding a precedent, (supposing many of them, who were gentlemen of the law, to be better judges of the constitution than we were,) and considering the bad consequences it must be attended with, should the reversion be purchased out of our hands, we next proceeded to make a purchase of the lands. . . .

Finding ourselves on the Frontiers, and being apprehensive that, for the want of a proper legislature, we might become a shelter for such as endeavored to defraud their creditors; considering also the necessity for recording Deeds, Wills, and doing other public business; we, by consent of the people, formed a court for the purposes above mentioned, taking (by desire of our constituents) the Virginia laws for our guide, so near as the situation of affairs would admit; this was intended for ourselves, and was done by the consent of every individual; but wherever we had to deal with people out of our district, we have ruled them to bail, to abide by our determinations, (which was, in fact, leaving the matter to reference,) otherways we dismissed their suit, lest we should in any way intrude on the legislature of the colonies. . . .

We shall now submit the whole to your candid and impartial judgment. We pray your mature and deliberate consideration in our behalf, that you may annex us to your Province, (whether as County, district, or other division,) in such manner as may enable us to share in the glorious cause of Liberty; enforce our laws under authority, and in every respect become the best members of society; and for ourselves and constituents we hope, we may venture to assure you, that we shall adhere strictly to your determinations. . . .

The Transylvania Convention

IN THE spring of 1775, after making a dubious purchase of land from some Cherokee Indians, Judge Richard Henderson and other North Carolina associates attempted to set up an independent colony in the Kentucky Basin. Since many of the settlers were from Virginia and threatened to ignore his claims, Henderson decided on a convention to draft a compact to bind all the settlers to the new colony, Transylvania. The venture failed the following year when Virginia extended its jurisdiction over the infant stations and created the county of Kentucky. In 1780 the region was subdivided into three Virginia counties. The following extracts from Henderson's journal of the Transylvania Convention are printed in George W. Ranck, Boonesborough Its Founding . . . and Revolutionary Annals, Filson Club Publications No. 16 (Louisville, Ky., 1901), pp. 196–212. A manuscript copy is in the Draper Collection, The State Historical Society of Wisconsin.

JOURNAL OF THE PROCEEDINGS OF THE HOUSE OF DELEGATES OR REPRESENTATIVES OF THE COLONY OF TRANSYLVANIA

BEGUN ON TUESDAY THE 23D OF MAY, IN THE YEAR OF OUR LORD CHRIST 1775, AND IN THE FIFTEENTH YEAR OF THE REIGN OF HIS MAJESTY, KING OF GREAT BRITAIN

The proprietors of said colony having called and required an election of Delegates or Representatives to be made for the purpose of legislation, or making and ordaining laws and regulations for the future conduct of the inhabitants thereof, that is to say, for the town of Boonesborough six members, for Harrodsburg three, for the Boiling Spring settlement four, for the town of St.

Asaph four, and appointed their meeting for the purpose aforesaid, on the aforesaid 23d of May, *Anno Domini* 1775:—

It being certified to us here this day, by the secretary, that the following persons were returned as duly elected for the several towns and settlements, to-wit:

For Boonesborough,	*For Harrodsburg,*
Squire Boone,	Thomas Slaughter,
Daniel Boone,	John Lythe,
William Cocke,	Valentine Harmon,
Samuel Henderson,	James Douglass;
William Moore, and	
Richard Callaway;	
For Boiling Spring,	*For St. Asaph,*
James Harrod,	John Todd,
Nathan Hammond,	Alexander Spotswood Dandridge
Isaac Hite, and	John Floyd, and
Azariah Davis;	Samuel Wood.

Present—Squire Boone, Daniel Boone, Samuel Henderson, William Moore, Richard Callaway, Thomas Slaughter, John Lythe, Valentine Harmon, James Douglass, James Harrod, Nathan Hammond, Isaac Hite, Azariah Davis, John Todd, Alexander Spotswood Dandridge, John Floyd, and Samuel Wood, who took their seats at convention.

The House unanimously chose Colonel Thomas Slaughter Chairman, and Matthew Jouett Clerk, and after divine service was performed by the Rev. John Lythe, the House waited on the proprietors and acquainted them that they had chosen Mr. Thomas Slaughter Chairman, and Matthew Jouett Clerk, of which they approved; and Colonel Richard Henderson, in behalf of himself and the rest of the proprietors, opened the convention with a speech, a copy of which, to prevent mistakes, the Chairman procured.

Ordered, that said speech be read—read the same which follows:

Mr. Chairman, and Gentlemen of the Convention:

You are called and assembled at this time for a noble and an honorable purpose—a purpose, however ridiculous or idle it may appear at first view, to superficial minds, yet is of the most solid consequence; and if prudence, firmness, and wisdom are suffered to influence your councils and direct your conduct, the peace and harmony of thousands may be expected to result from your deliberations; in short, you are about a work of the utmost importance to the well-being of this country in general. . . .

We, gentlemen, look with infinite satisfaction on this happy presage of the future felicity of our infant country, and hope to merit a continuation of that confidence you are pleased to express in our veracity and good intentions.

While our transactions have credit for the integrity of our desires, we can not fail uniting with the delegates of the good people of this country, fully persuaded that the proprietors are zealously inclined to contribute every thing in their power which may tend to render it easy, prosperous, and flourishing.

May 25th, 1775   RICHARD HENDERSON,
                            For himself and the company

26th May. Met according to adjournment. . . .

On motion made by Mr. Todd, ordered, that Mr. Todd, Mr. Lythe, Mr. Douglass, and Mr. Hite, be a committee to draw up a compact between the proprietors and the people of this colony. . . .

Transylvania, 27th May, 1775. . . . Ordered, that Mr. Calloway and Mr. Cocke wait on the proprietors with the laws that have passed, for their perusal and approbation.

The committee, appointed to draw up the compact between the proprietors and the people, brought in and read it, as follows, viz:

Whereas, it is highly necessary, for the peace of the proprietors and the security of the people of this colony, that the powers of the one and the liberties of the other be ascertained; We, Richard Henderson, Nathaniel Hart, and J. Luttrel, on behalf of ourselves, as well as the other proprietors of the colony of Transylvania, of the one part and the representatives of the people of said colony, in convention assembled, of the other part—do most solemnly enter into the following contract or agreement, to wit:

1. That the election of delegates in this colony be annual.

2. That the convention may adjourn, and meet again on their own adjournment; Provided, that in cases of great emergency, the proprietors may call together the delegates before the time ad-

journed to; and, if a majority do not attend, they may dissolve them and call a new one.

3. That, to prevent dissension and delay of business, one proprietor shall act for the whole, or some one delegated by them for that purpose, who shall always reside in the colony.

4. That there be perfect religious freedom and general toleration; Provided, that the propagators of any doctrine or tenets, evidently tending to the subversion of our laws, shall, for such conduct, be amenable to, and punished by, the civil courts.

5. That the judges of the superior or supreme courts be appointed by the proprietors, but be supported by the people, and to them be answerable for their malconduct.

6. That the quit-rents never exceed two shillings sterling per hundred acres.

7. That the proprietors appoint a sheriff, who shall be one of three persons recommended by the court.

8. That the judges of the superior courts have, without fee or reward, the appointment of the clerks of this colony.

9. That the judges of the inferior courts be recommended by the people, and approved by the proprietors, and by them commissioned.

10. That all other civil and military officers be within the appointment of the proprietors.

11. That the office of surveyor-general belong to no person interested or a partner in this purchase.

12. That the legislative authority, after the strength and maturity of the colony will permit, consist of three branches, to wit: the delegates or representatives chosen by the people; a council, not exceeding twelve men, possessed of landed estate, who reside in the colony, and the proprietors.

13. That nothing with respect to the number of delegates from any town or settlement shall hereafter be drawn into precedent, but that the number of representatives shall be ascertained by law, when the state of the colony will admit of amendment.

14. That the land office be always open.

15. That commissions, without profit, be granted without fee.

16. That the fees and salaries of all officers appointed by the proprietors, be settled and regulated by the laws of the country.

17. That the convention have the sole power of raising and appropriating all public moneys, and electing their treasurer.

18. That, for a short time, till the state of the colony will permit to fix some place of holding the convention which shall be permanent, the place of meeting shall be agreed upon between the proprietors and the convention.

To the faithful and religious and perpetual observance of all and every of the above articles, the said proprietors, on behalf of themselves as well as those absent, and the chairman of the convention on behalf of them and their constituents, have hereunto interchangeably set their hands and affixed their seals, the twenty-seventh day of May, one thousand seven hundred and seventy-five. . . .

Ordered, that the delegates of Boonesboro be a committee to see that all the bills that are passed be transcribed, in a fair hand, into a book for that purpose.

Ordered, that the proprietors be waited on by the chairman, acquainting them that all the bills are ready for signing.

The following bills this day passed and signed by the proprietors, on behalf of themselves and their partners, and the chairman of the convention, on behalf of himself and the other delegates:

1. An act for establishing courts of jurisdiction and regulating the practice therein.
2. An act for regulating a militia.
3. An act for the punishment of criminals.
4. An act to prevent profane swearing, and Sabbath breaking.
5. An act for writs of attachment.
6. An act for ascertaining clerks' and sheriffs' fees.
7. An act to preserve the range.
8. An act for improving the breed of horses.
9. An act for preserving game.

All of the above mentioned acts were signed by the chairman and proprietors, except the act for ascertaining clerks' and sheriffs' fees, which was omitted by the clerks not giving it in with the rest.

Ordered, that at the next meeting of delegates, if any member be absent and doth not attend, that the people choose one to serve in the room of such absent member.

Ordered, that the convention be adjourned until the first Thursday in September next, then to meet at Boonesboro.

MATTHEW JEWITT,
Clerk

13. Government, Law, and Politics

UNIFORM government for the West came with federal control. After some of the states—particularly Virginia, which had the most extensive claims—had ceded their western lands to the Confederation, Congress in 1787 passed an ordinance establishing procedures for government. An early ordinance drafted in 1784 by Thomas Jefferson never went into effect, and Congress did not take action in 1787 until pressure developed from officers and speculators interested in developing the Northwest. The later ordinance provided for three stages of government with limited representation, some home rule, and—when sufficient population justified it—admission into the Union as a state. With little alteration this statute remained the basis for territorial government for more than a century. The qualifications for voting and officeholding in the 1787 ordinance reflected comparable requirements in the original states at the time. The extracts printed below are from Fitzpatrick et al. (eds.), Journals of the Continental Congress, XXXII, 334–343.

An Ordinance for the Government of the Territory of the United States Northwest of the River Ohio

[July 13, 1787]

Be it ordained by the United States in Congress Assembled that the said territory for the purposes of temporary government be one district, subject however to be divided into two districts as future circumstances may in the Opinion of Congress make it expedient.

Be it ordained by the authority aforesaid, that the estates both of resident and non resident proprietors in the said territory dying intestate shall descend to and be distributed among their children and the descendants of a deceased child in equal parts. . . .

Be it ordained by the authority aforesaid that there shall be appointed from time to time by Congress a governor, whose commission shall continue in force for the term of three years, unless sooner revoked by Congress; he shall reside in the district and have a freehold estate therein, in one thousand acres of land while in the exercise of his office. There shall be appointed from time to time by Congress a secretary, whose commission shall continue in force for four years, unless sooner revoked; he shall reside in the district and have a freehold estate therein in five hundred acres of land while in the exercise of his office; It shall be his duty to keep and preserve the acts and laws passed by the legislature and the public records of the district and the proceedings of the governor in his executive department and transmit authentic copies of such acts and proceedings every six months to the Secretary of Congress. There shall also be appointed a court to consist of three judges any two of whom to form a court, who shall have a common law jurisdiction and reside in the district and have each therein a freehold estate in five hundred acres of land while in the exercise of their offices, and their commissions shall continue in force during good behaviour.

The governor, and judges or a majority of them shall adopt and publish in the district such laws of the original states criminal and civil as may be necessary and best suited to the circumstances of the district and report them to Congress from time to time, which laws shall be in force in the district until the organization of the general assembly therein, unless disapproved of by Congress; but afterwards the legislature shall have authority to alter them as they shall think fit.

The governor for the time being shall be Commander in chief of the militia, appoint and commission all officers in the same below the rank of general Officers; All general Officers shall be appointed and commissioned by Congress.

Previous to the Organization of the general Assembly the governor shall appoint such magistrates and other civil officers in each county or township, as he shall find necessary for the preservation of the peace and good order in the same. After the general Assembly shall be organized, the powers and duties of magistrates and other civil officers shall be regulated and defined by the said Assembly; but all magistrates and other civil officers, not herein otherwise directed shall during the continuance of this temporary government be appointed by the governor.

For the prevention of crimes and injuries the laws to be adopted or made shall have force in all parts of the district and for the execution of process criminal and civil, the governor shall make proper divisions thereof, and he shall proceed from time to time as circumstances may require to lay out the parts of the district in which the indian titles shall have been extinguished into counties and townships subject however to such alterations as may thereafter be made by the legislature.

So soon as there shall be five thousand free male inhabitants of full age in the district upon giving proof thereof to the governor, they shall receive authority with time and place to elect representatives from their counties or townships to represent them in the general assembly, provided that for every five hundred free male inhabitants there shall be one representative and so on progressively with the number of free male inhabitants shall the right of representation encrease until the number of representatives shall amount to twenty five after which the number and proportion of representatives shall be regulated by the legislature; provided that no person be eligible or qualified to act as a representative unless he shall have been a citizen of one of the United States three years and be a resident in the district or unless he shall have resided in the district three years and in either case shall likewise hold in his own right in fee simple two hundred acres of land within the same; provided also that a freehold in fifty acres of land in the district having been a citizen of one of the states and being resident in the district; or the like freehold and two years residence in the district shall be necessary to qualify a man as an elector of a representative.

The representatives thus elected shall serve for the term of two years and in case of the death of a representative or removal from office, the governor shall issue a writ to the county or township for which he was a member, to elect another in his stead to serve for the residue of the term.

The general assembly or legislature shall consist of the governor, legislative council and a house of representatives. The legislative council shall consist of five members to continue in Office five years unless sooner removed by Congress any three of whom to be a quorum and the members of the council shall be nominated and appointed in the following manner, to wit; As soon as representatives shall be elected, the governor shall appoint a time and place for them to meet together, and when met they shall nominate ten persons residents in the district and each possessed of a freehold in five hundred acres of Land and return their names to Congress; five of whom Congress shall appoint and commission to serve as aforesaid; and whenever a vacancy shall happen in the council by death or removal from office, the house of representatives shall nominate two persons qualified as aforesaid, for each vacancy, and return their names to Congress, one of whom Congress shall appoint and commission for the residue of the term, and every five years, four months at least before the expiration of the time of service of the Members of Council, the said house shall nominate ten persons qualified as aforesaid, and return their names to Congress, five of whom Congress shall appoint and commission to serve as Members of the council five years, unless sooner removed. And the Governor, legislative council, and house of representatives, shall have authority to make laws in all cases for the good government of the district, not repugnant to the principles and Articles in this Ordinance established and declared. And all bills having passed by a majority in the house, and by a majority in the council, shall be referred to the Governor for his assent; but no bill or legislative Act whatever, shall be of any force without his assent. The Governor shall have power to convene, prorogue and dissolve the General Assembly, when in his opinion it shall be expedient.

The Governor, Judges, legislative Council, Secretary, and such other Officers as Congress shall appoint in the district shall take an Oath or Affirmation of fidelity, and of Office, the Governor before the president of Congress, and all other Officers before the Governor. As soon as a legislature shall be formed in the district, the Council and house assembled in one room, shall have authority by joint ballot to elect a Delegate to Congress, who shall have a seat in Congress, with a right of debating, but not of voting, during this temporary Government.

And for extending the fundamental principles of civil and religious liberty, which form the basis whereon these republics, their laws and constitutions are erected; to fix and establish those principles as the basis of all laws, constitutions and governments, which forever hereafter shall be formed in the said territory; to provide also for the establishment of States and permanent government therein, and for their admission to a share in the federal Councils on an equal footing with the original States, at as early periods as may be consistent with the general interest,

It is hereby Ordained and declared by the authority aforesaid, That the following Articles shall be considered as Articles of compact between the Original States and the people and States in the said territory, and forever remain unalterable, unless by common consent, *to wit*,

Article the First. No person demeaning himself in a peaceable and orderly manner shall ever be molested on account of his mode of worship or religious sentiments in the said territory.

Article the Second. The Inhabitants of the said territory shall always be entitled to the benefits of the writ of habeas corpus, and of the trial by Jury; of a proportionate representation of the people in the legislature, and of judicial proceedings according to the course of the common law; all persons shall be bailable unless for capital offences, where the proof shall be evident, or the presumption great; all fines shall be moderate, and no cruel or unusual punishments shall be inflicted; no man shall be deprived of his liberty or property but by the judgment of his peers, or the law of the land; and should the public exigencies make it necessary for the common preservation to take any person[']s property, or to demand his particular services, full compensation shall be made for the same; and in the just preservation of rights and property it is understood and declared; that no law ought ever to be made, or have force in the said territory, that shall in any manner whatever interfere with, or affect private contracts or engagements, bona fide and without fraud previously formed.

Article the Third. *Religion, Morality and knowledge being necessary to good government and the happiness of mankind,* Schools and the means of education shall forever be encouraged. . . .

Article the Fourth. The said territory, and the States which may be formed therein shall forever remain a part of this Confederacy of the United States of America, subject to the Articles of Confederation, and to such alterations therein as shall be constitutionally made; and to all the Acts and Ordinances of the United States in Congress Assembled, conformable thereto. . . .

Article the Fifth. There shall be formed in the said territory, not less than three nor more than five States . . . and whenever any of the said States shall have sixty thousand free Inhabitants therein, such State shall be admitted by its Delegates into the Congress of the United States, on an equal footing with the original States, in all respects whatever; and shall be at liberty to form a permanent constitution and State government, provided the constitution and government so to be formed, shall be republican, and in conformity to the principles contained in these

Articles; and so far as it can be consistent with the general interest of the Confederacy, such admission shall be allowed at an earlier period, and when there may be a less number of free Inhabitants in the State than sixty thousand.

Article the Sixth. There shall be neither Slavery nor involuntary Servitude in the said territory otherwise than in the punishment of crimes, whereof the party shall have been duly convicted; provided always that any person escaping into the same, from whom labor or service is lawfully claimed in any one of the original States, such fugitive may be lawfully reclaimed and conveyed to the person claiming his or her labor or service as aforesaid. . . .

Settlers' Complaints About Territorial Government

COMPLAINTS against many of the provisions for territorial government were numerous, ranging from a host of petty grievances on the county level to basic issues such as the lawmaking powers of appointive officials, limitations on the franchise, and—north of the Ohio River—the restriction on slavery. The following extracts are printed in Carter (ed.), *Territorial Papers of the United States,* V, 63–66; XI, 324–325; and VI, 411–413. The original of the presentment is in the Pickering Papers, Massachusetts Historical Society, Boston, Mass.; the report is from the manuscript in the Library of Congress, House File, 17th Cong.; and the memorial from the manuscript in the House of Representatives Files, 13th Cong.

PRESENTMENT OF THE GRAND JURY OF ADAMS COUNTY, MISSISSIPPI TERRITORY

[June 6, 1799]

At a Court of general quarter Sessions held for the County of Adams on the sixth day of June in the year 1799—

We the grand Jury for the County aforesaid present that whereas a law directing the manner in which money shall be raised and levied to defray the charges which may arise within the several Counties is in several instances oppressive and may be attended with the most baleful consequences—We consider it as an imposition upon the good Citizens of this Territory and protest against the same in the manner following—

1st We the grand Jury aforesaid consider it as a great grievance to the good people of this Territory that a law should be passed to assess and levy a tax on the County of Adams previous to the census of the people being taken

2^d We present as a great grievance that the amount of the sum proposed to be levied should be vested in the Governor and one Judge alone—We present as a very great grievance the present ruinous State of the roads and bridges throughout the whole of this Territory to the great injury of an industrious and civilized people and furthermore that money should be levied for the purpose of repairing said roads and bridges which can be much more easily effected and less burthensome by the manuel labor of the male inhabitants and negroes as was the custom heretofore practised—

3^d We present as a very great grievance the want of a white man for an indian Interpreter which has hitherto been effected by a negro slave to the great shame of a free and independent people—

4th We present as a grievance that Commissioners should be appointed and vested with a power of valuing the property of the Citizens of this Territory and adding an unlimited per Cent thereon—

5th We present as a grievance that lands which may be sold that are the property of none residents may be attended with baleful consequences to the purchasers by it being afterward proved they belong to the united States when they are only allowed a reimbursement of the purchase money with interest—a compensation by no means adequate to having put buildings thereon to the amount perhaps of some thousand dollars exclusive of other improvements—

6th We present as a grievance that the Inhabitants of this Territory may be subject to great impositions by being liable for the appearance of hireling lodgers and sojourners residing in their house at the time the Commissioners are taking a list of the names of such people who may elope or absent themselves without their previty or knowledge

7th We present as a grievance that any Sheriff in this Territory should be vested with power according to the eight[h] section of a law passed to levy a tax for defraying the expences of the same in each County to comit any Citizen of said Territory to the common gaol without sufficient proof of his or their default and without complaint warrant or commitment

8th We present as a grievance that an unlimited time is allowed to the Assessors to make out their assessments which may swell their accounts to an enormous sum and thereby become burthensome to the good people of this Territory—

9th We present as a grievance that qualified persons are not appointed to visit and examine the several public and private cotton gins throughout this Territory as the success and prosperity of this Country chiefly depend upon our particular care and attention to that valuable branch of agriculture and to prevent any frauds and neglects in preparing it for exportation—

10th We present as a grievance that any person should be vested with the sole power of contracting on their own terms for the erecting of the public buildings in this Territory and proper persons be not appointed as Commissioners to examine their accounts and inspect the said buildings during the time of their erection on failure of which great frauds may be commited to the manifest injury of the good citizens of this Territory.

11th We present as a manifest grievance and a nuisance the great number of idle and disorderly people who assemble and meet at the different public houses in the town of Natchez on sabath day particularly during divine service to the interruption of well disposed christians and to the great encouragement of vice profaness and immorality—

12th We also present as a grievance the want of attention in the Inhabitants of the town of Natchez in suffering negro slaves & playing about the fences of the out lotts at cards dice and chuck penny upon the above day—

13th We present as a grievance that the Citizens of this Territory should be ameanable to any law of the same previous to the publication thereof as thereby many good people may be injured thro ignorance who have been guilty of a breach of the same—

14th We present as a very great grievance the impositions daily practised upon the good Citizens of this Territory particularly the poor & ignorant part thereof by not having the weights & measures properly regulated and established by law—

15th We present as a great grievance the number of hogs which are suffered to run at large thro the town of Natchez to the great injury & annoyance of the Inhabitants thereof—

16th We present as a grievance the taxing of batteaux and boats carrying above twenty barrels as it will thereby prevent the freighting our produce & necessaries to and from New Orleans in our own boats to the manifest injury of our own people employed in that line—

17th We present as a grievance the want of a proper place for a market within the town of Natchez and the necessary buildings which are requisite for the same—

18th We present as a great grievance the gaol having been erected upon the spot where it now stands as it will manifestly be attended with great expence & inconvenience to the public in furnishing the same with wood & water and other necessaries for the maintenance of prisoners when a place more centrical healthy & less expensive can be had

19th We present as a grievance that the Citizens of this Territory should be taxed according to limits and not according to number or property which may tend to the great injury of the poor and other good and faithful Citizens of the same

20th We present as a great & enormous grievance that a code of laws said now to exist in this Territory have been framed by people not well acquainted with or who did not pay that attention to the local circumstances and interest of the good people of this Territory that they required—particularly the section wherein no term was allowed for removing their negroes out of the spanish Territory into this of the united States—to the great injury and ruin of a number of many of it's Inhabitants—whereas had a number of men of abilities and experience been consulted an exception in that case would have been provided And we the grand Jury as the guardians of the good people of this Territory humbly conceive & assert that the situation and circumstances of this Territory at the commencement was intirely different from any other ever yet formed within the united States and ought therefore to enjoy every indulgence as a free people It was not a matter of choice our coming into this Territory as belonging to the united States—We were found here by them a useful industrious and we flatter ourselves not an unenlightened set of people much prejudiced in favor & wishing to become subjects of the U States a people descended from the same stock possessed of the same principles and animated with the same desire of freedom and expecting to enjoy in the fullest extent the same previledges and immunities in common with the rest of our fellow Citizens—We remark that in the formation of new Territories heretofore made the Inhabitants may be said to have had a vote in the government of them as they consisted of Individuals immigrating from the several different states of the union all of which are represented in Congress—they knew that laws of such a nature were to exist they had the choice as before observed of going into or staying out of said new Territory—Whereas we the good people of this Territory have no alternative not even the opportunity of being advised with a previlege always enjoy[ed] by us heretofore when subject to a despotic government and to the honor & benevolence of that gov[t] it can be proven that the voice of the Inhabitants generally regulated the operations of government in what respected their own immediate concerns 21st We totally disapprove of the unexampled oppression and enormous fees demanded by law for licences in particular—which supasses any thing ever yet heard of 22[d] We know from woeful experience that imperfections & impositions with their attendant concomitants apathy cruelty & oppression in time prevail in the wisest & best of governments and we are sorry to find that ours even in its present infancy is fetching large strides to attain that disgraceful & fatal period which it is our duty as guardians of the people of this Territory to prevent with that dignity energy and spirit becoming a free people—at the same time we think it incumbent on us to acknowledge our loyalty & attachment to government with zeal & firmness & determined resolution to support and defend it with our lives & fortunes—In testimony of which we have hereunto subscribed o[u]r names—Sutton Banks foreman & others

REPORT OF A COMMITTEE OF INHABITANTS OF WAYNE COUNTY, MICHIGAN TERRITORY

[November, 1822?]

We the undersigned committee of the Inhabitants of Wayne county who were appointed to take into consideration and pursue such measures as may be best calculated to give effect to the Memorial of the inhabitants of Michigan, transmitted to congress at their present Session submit the following as among the prominent reasons which have prompted the people of this Territory to apply to Congress for a change in the form of their present Government.

They ask for a repeal of so much of the ordinance of [17]87 as makes the Governor and Judges Legislators and that the Legislative power may be entrusted to a Legislature elected by themselves

That the ordinance of 87 which forms the fundamental Law of this Territory, has been in our opinion continually violated by the Governor and Judges in the *making* Laws instead of Adopting them from the Statute Book of the original states

That many statutes are passed without reference to the Laws of the States whence they purport to be adopted, and where in fact many of their provisions do not exist.

That many important Laws involving the rights and interests of the whole Territory, are passed without sufficient deliberation or discussion by the Legislative Board assembled for that purpose, but are carried for signature to the different Lodgings of the members.—

That the Legislative Board do not meet to do business at the time fixed by their own Statute for that purpose and they have no known place of Meeting. and when they do meet no public notice of the time or place is given—And when that can be ascertained by enquiry, they are found sometimes at a Tavern—sometimes at private Rooms or offices where none have a right, and few except those immediately interested in the passage of Laws have the *assurance* to intrude themselves or can find room or seats if they should.—

That Laws are frequently passed and others repealed, which take effect from the date and vitally affect the rights of the citizens and are not promulgated or made known to the community for many months—

That no expose of the receipts or disbursements of the Treasury of the Territory has ever yet been published by them; that no statement is published of the amount of Taxes or of the manner in which they are expended—and except in one or two recent instances the appropriation Laws have not been published.—

That even when a statute happens to be really *adopted* from the Laws of one of the states, the Judges (3 out of 4 who adopted the Law) have declared from the Bench that they will not be bound by the known and established constructions and decissions of the state whence it was taken; thus entirely altering the intent of the ordinance of 87, the paramount Law.—

That it is believed that the Judges make decissions without statutory provisions to warrant them, directly in violation of the rights of the citizens by the Common Law, the benefits of which are guaranteed by the ordinance

That the decissions of the Supreme Court are in Similar cases so discordant that they furnish no guide to conjecture what will be their decissions on the same points in future; it having even been declared by them that their own decissions shall not be obligatory as precedents.—

That a Single Judge has been known to open and immediately adjourn the Supreme Court without the attendance of either Clerk, Sheriff, Constable, or crier. And even without the records or even pen, ink, or paper, and that when cases were before the court for argument, leaving the Suitors and officers of the court and the other Judges to find out if they can when and where it will please the court to open itself again.—

That the Supreme Court during a great part of a four months session held its sessions during the night instead of the day time. and with out the knowledge of the people. at, private offices, where not only the suitors but the officers of the court, at such hours, had no right to intrude and could not be accommodated with seats if they should.—

That at these night sittings. among other important business, a multitude of rules of the court were entered of record, vitally affecting the rights of the Suitors, some of which annulled rights at Com[mon] Law. others were palpable Legislative enactments, and one at least going to alter an act of Congress.—

That Judicial proceedings are often embarrassed, and their validity rendered even more dubious by the absence of one of the Judges from the Territory or from the Bench when within it.—

Memorial from the Mississippi Territorial House of Representatives

[January 11, 1814]

To the Honorable the Senate and House of Representatives of the United States of America in Congress assembled;

The memorial of the House of Representatives of the Mississippi Territory respectfully Sheweth; That your Memorialists in behalf of their constituents inhabitants of the Mississippi Territory respectfully pray that while it may be deemed expedient by your honorable body to withhold from us the Privileges of Self Government, an alteration, mitigating the burthens of a Territorial Government may be made in that part of the Act of Congress Which requires the possession of a Freehold, or of a Town Lot of the value of One hundred dollars as a qualification entitling a citizen to Vote;[1] And that hereafter all free white males of Twenty One years of Age and upwards and who shall have resided in the Territory twelve months; or who may have been assessed at least three months previous to the Election, and who shall reside in the county at the time, shall be permitted to vote at Elections for members of the House of Representatives, and a Delegate to Congress.—

They solicit this important amendment of the existing constitutional Laws for the following reasons

1. The disqualification of all but Landholders does not seem strictly compatible with Republican principles. The Laws are made for the common good. They operate alike upon all. The life the liberty and the property of every man is affected by them, Every man therefore ought to have an agency in their formation. The principle of the union of taxation and Representation was one of the leading points on which the revolutionary contest was founded; and it surely ought not to be lost sight of wherever it can apply.—

2. The situation of this country does not admit of the application of the principle that Land holders Only, have that interest which will secure a judicious choice of representation In old countries landed property is more permanent and secures a stronger interest than in new countries. Those associations of ideas which are formed in early life attach the owner to his farm, and to every thing connected with it—A new settlement does not admit of attachments equally strong. Landed property is also more a subject of traffic than in Old countries. It is transfered as frequently as personal property. That peculiar and settled interest which is presumed when the right of Election is confined to Landholders does not really exist. The man who has a large Stock of cattle, or a considerable Property in Slaves, has surely more interest in the country in which they are located than the man who ownes fifty acres of Land which may not be worth as many cents, and are verry probably, not worth more than One hundred Dollars.—

1. Act approved Jan. 9, 1808 (2 Stat. 455).

3. Men who are able to purchase Lands, who came to the Territory with that view; and continue here with the same view, have not in many cases had an Oppertunity. In some of our counties no Land has yet been sold Many who are able to purchase have fixed their mind on particular spots which have not yet been exposed to public Sale Their object is an establishment for life: and they feel in fact the same interest in the country and its Laws, as those who have been more fortunate.—

4. The existing system has produced a most preposterous inequality of Representation.—The Ordinance provides that for every 500 free male inhabitants, there shall be one Representative in the general Assembly. This has been so construed as to give a distinct representation to every county that has that number. In some counties the Qualified Voters are extremely few. In one case their number did not exceed thirteen. In another case it does not exceed fifteen. Seven men therefore in one part of the Territory have as much weight in enacting the Laws for its Government as five hundred in Another.—

5. The present system is a source of intrigue and corruption, subversive of the rites of the people and of the principles of morality It opens a wide door to fraud. Where man as man has an agency in makeing the Laws there will be no disputes about qualifications. Where his right to vote depends on landed property; titles framed for that Occasion will be brought forward: And as much must necessarily be left to the discretion of the Judges of an Election, there is too great a field not only for honest misconception, but for base partiality The provision authoriseing voters on Town Lots though liberally intended has magnified the evil. If a Town in the woods be laid off and established, the owner of a Lot worth Nominally One hundred Dollars obtains a Vote, whilst his neighbour though possessing Stock and Slaves of the value of ten thousand is deprived of the right of Suffrage.—

6. In an Election of a Delegate to the Congress of the United States, no certain conclusion can be drawn of the real will even of the qualified electors, from the result of the polls.—In some counties in consequence of the Misconception of the Judges of Election of their own Powers, all citizens are suffered to vote. In others they are rigid in enforcing the qualifications required by Law. In a country so extensive as the Mississippi Territory it would be almost impossible to rectify the errors which must be produced by this dis-

cordant mode of proceeding Your memorialists therefore respectfully solicit your honorable body to take the subject into your
serious consideration and to extend to the people of the Mississippi Territory that right of general suffrage which is so dear to freemen, and so truly correspondent with the principles of republicanism.—

Efforts to Alter the Franchise

SEVERAL efforts were made to alter the franchise qualifications. In the
following circular letter to his constituents, George Poindexter, delegate
to Congress from the Mississippi Territory, discusses the franchise question. The text of the letter is reprinted from John F. H. Claiborne,
Mississippi as a Province, Territory and State (Jackson, Miss., 1880),
pp. 364–365. The following extracts are printed from Carter (ed.),
Territorial Papers of the United States, VII, 687; VIII, 111–113; XVI,
199–202; XIV, 456–458.

GEORGE POINDEXTER TO HIS CONSTITUENTS

Washington City, February 13th, 1808

DEAR SIR

In compliance with the obligations of my duty, I now communi-
cate to you, the several acts which have passed during the present
session of Congress, in relation to the local police, and internal
welfare of our territory.

The act extending the right of suffrage, in the Mississippi Territory, and for other purposes, passed the House of Representatives,
in its most desirable shape, requiring that the elector should be a
citizen of the United States, resident in the Territory one year,
and have paid a tax assessed, at least six months previous to an election. This qualification would have extended the elective franchise
to the great body of the community, liable to perform militia duty,
and subject to bear a portion of the public burdens; which in my
judgment is a right inseparable from freemen, and cannot be
abridged, without an infraction of the principles on which our republican institutions are founded. Another consideration also,
rendered me particularly solicitous that this just and liberal system
should have been adopted. The payment of a tax is a matter of fact,
capable of direct and immediate proof, by a reference to the roll of
the tax collector, who is an officer of public responsibility, and
therefore, no fraudulent voter could have imposed himself upon

the inspectors appointed to preserve the chastity of Elections. Experience has shown us that the free-hold qualification is liable to the abuse of fraudulent conveyances made for the express purpose of enabling a dishonest candidate to obtain a factitious majority over the virtuous and worthy citizen who will not stoop to the violation of the plain dictates of morality, and the known laws of the land, to acquire either surreptitious fame or illegitimate power; but the Senate, for wise reasons, no doubt, thought proper to restrict the right of suffrage to the holders of real estate. I assented to this modification because its provisions are more expansive than those comprised in the ordinance for the government of the Mississippi Territory. There were numerous citizens of wealth and respectability, residing in the city of Natchez and other small towns in various parts of the territory, owning town lots of considerable value, who were not heretofore enabled to vote for representatives to the general assembly; to this class of citizens, and to purchasers under the United States, and also to those possessed of equitable estates in fifty acres of land, the right of suffrage is extended. I therefore trust, that although the law may not meet our wishes in their fullest extent, it will put the subject at rest until the arrival of that auspicious period, in which we shall be entitled to the enviable privileges of self-government. In the formation of a constitution suited to the genius of a free people, the elective franchise will be fixed on the basis of equality as the best means of securing the liberty and independence of the citizens.

PETITION OF THE INHABITANTS OF CLARK COUNTY, INDIANA TERRITORY

[1809]

To the Honorable Senate & House of Representatives of the United States of America in Congress Assembled—

We your Petitioners of Clark County & Indiana Territory Beg leave to represent to your Honorable Body that agreeably to the Ordinance of Congress for the government of this Territory a great part of the Inhabitants are excluded from the right of suffrage though at the same time compelled to do milita duty & contribute to the suport of the Territorial Government—

Having lately experienced the fostering care of Government for this portion of the union by an extension of the right of suffrage

We hope with the greater confidence that Congress will extend that right to all free Males who have attaind the age of 21 years done milita duty & paid taxes

And as we hope and belive that Congress are disposed to make any concession of priviledges to us that may be conducive to our Interest and not compatible with that of the Union Beliving that it would have the most happy effect in restoring to the people of this Territory that confidence in their Goverment, to which they have long been strangers; If the choice of the Officers thereof, were granted to the People; We therefore pray your Honorable Body that All Officers of the Militia, except General Officers, Magistrates Sherriffes & Coroners may be elected by the People and that All other Officers hitherto appointed by the Governor may hereafter be appointed by the Legislature. We are well convinced that Officers who owe their appointments to the People will be more faithful in the discharge of the duties of their Offices than when they hold them independent of Public Oppinon

And whereas by the Laws of this Territory almost all Officers civil & military being eligible to a seat in the Legislature by appointing them as heretofore, the Executive may have an undue influence and prevent the wishes of the Majority from being known

We feel no doubt that your Honorable Body will give these representations that attention which they shall merit And your Petitioners as in duty bound &ᶜ. . . .

AN ACT TO EXTEND THE RIGHT OF SUFFRAGE IN THE INDIANA TERRITORY

[March 3, 1811]

Be it enacted by the Senate and House of Representatives of the United States of America, in Congress assembled, That each and every free white male person, who shall have attained the age of twenty one years, and who shall have paid a county or territorial tax, and who shall have resided one year in said territory, previous to any general election, and be at the time of any such election, a resident of said territory shall be entitled to vote for members of the legislative council and House of Representatives of the territorial legislature and for a delegate to the Congress of the United States for said territory.

Sec. 2. *And be it further enacted,* That the citizens of the Indiana territory entitled to vote for representatives to the general assembly thereof, may on the third Monday of April next, and on the third Monday of April biennially thereafter (unless the general assembly of said territory shall appoint a different day) elect one delegate for said territory to the Congress of the United States, who shall possess the same powers heretofore granted by law to the same.

Sec. 3. *And be it further enacted,* That each and every sheriff that now is, or hereafter may be appointed in said territory who shall either neglect or refuse to perform the duties required by an act, entitled "An act extending the right of Suffrage in the Indiana territory, and for other purposes," passed in February, one thousand eight hundred and nine, shall be liable to a penalty of one thousand dollars recoverable by action of debt in any court of record within the said territory, one half for the use of the informer, and the other for the use of the territory.

Sec. 4. *And be it further enacted,* That any person holding, or who may hereafter hold any office of profit from the governor of the Indiana Territory (justices of the peace and militia officers excepted) shall be ineligible to, and disqualified to act as a member of the legislative council or House of Representatives, for said territory.

Sec. 5. *And be it further enacted,* That each and every sheriff in each and every county that now is or hereafter may be, established in said territory, shall cause to be held, the election prescribed by this act, according to the time and manner prescribed by the laws of said territory and this act under the penalty of one thousand dollars, to be recovered, in the manner, and for the use pointed out by the third section of this act.

GOVERNOR NINIAN EDWARDS TO RICHARD M. JOHNSON

Elvirade, Randolph County, Illinois Territory, March 14. 1812
DEAR SIR

I hope the sincere desire which I feel to serve the people of this territory & their having no delegate in congress will be accepted as an apology for the trouble which this letter will give you.

At no time since the first organization of this gov[t] have the people as far as I can learn been better satisfied with their territorial officers than at the present juncture. But a variety of different wishes and motives have combined to induce them to wish to enter the second grade of territorial gov^t merely for the purpose of obtaining a delegate to congress—which I always supposed might with as much propriety have been allowed them without their being obliged to incur for that purpose alone the expences of the second grade—more especially since if the same rights should be extended to them that are enjoyed by the Indiana territory the delegate will be wholly independent of the legislature—

The population of this territory as appears by the late census amounts to 12,282 in the whole of which there does not exceed between two & three hundred freeholders (two hundred and twenty I am convinced is the extent of the number) this is owing to the sale of public lands having been postponed much beyond any period that was anticipated from the appointment of a register & receiver to this district—

This very small portion of freeholders have the exclusive right, of determining upon the contemplated change of gov^t after which they alone will have the right to vote for the members of the legislature who will be elected for two years with the right to nominate the Council who will be appointed for five years by which a small minority will have the power to fix upon a very large and respectable majority of their fellow citizens a course of measures which may not be changed however disagreeable to the majority for five years—Even if the danger to be apprehended should be considered problematical still such are the jealous and independent dispositions of freemen that they never will be satisfied to depend for the security of their rights upon the mere courtesy of others—

A number of petitions have been presented to me by the freeholders in favor of organizing a general assembly—and not one against the measure has been rec^d so that I have no doubt that the change will very soon take place and I have this day issued a proclamation for taking in a formal manner the sense of the freeholders on the subject—

Under these circumstances I am sure I do not miscalculate when I suppose your attachment to republican principles will lead you to wish to extend their salutary influence to the people of this territory by extending endorsing the right of suffrage—It is the more just and necessary because it is not the fault of the people that they are not freeholders for many of them are able and anxiously waiting to buy land as soon as the public sales are open

—Those sales will certainly commence shortly and the number of freeholders will thereby be greatly augmented yet unless immediate provision be made for them, they may for the reasons before given be excluded from the benefits of representation for five years—

These considerations also demonstrate the propriety of giving the people of the territory the right to elect their delegate to congress, as was done for Indiana. whilst this territory was an integral part of that—A delegate was designed to represent the whole people of the territory & not any particular description of citizens only —except as to the right of voting in congress—he stands precisely in the same relation to the people of a territory that any representative in congress does to the people of his district. Why then should the election of the one be made by the legislature and the other by the people themselves—It is more necessary that the people here should have this right secured to them, than any where else, for owing to the peculiar situation of this territory, in consequence of the sale of public lands being so long delayed. one hundred and thirty freeholders having an interest distinct from that of the great body of the people have by uniting would constitute the majority of the freeholders and could elect the delegate in opposition to the interest and wishes of all the rest of a population consisting of 12282 persons—It surely is enough that such an inconsiderable . . . minority should possess the power of . . . legislating for the whole territory—But to secure also the additional advantage of a delegate to congress is a reason strongly urged to press into the second grade of gov^t before the public sales shall open and thereby increase the number of persons who could have a right to participate in the equal rights of free government—

Independent of the . . . reasons growing out of the peculiarity of our situation in favor of the measure. It is strongly recommended by considerations of justice & policy upon general principles—Our house of representatives will consist of seven members the legislative council of five making in the aggregate, twelve—Whilever these men have the sole right to elect the delegate, scenes of intrigue or to use a Kentucky term loggrolling will constantly present themselves—which . . . while they may gratify the ambition of individuals will . . . greatly disturb the repose and tranquility of any territorial gov^t and hazard much of the best interest of the best citizens thereof—

The situation of the setlers between Kaskaskia and the Ohio most cogently demands consideration—The appointment of a register & receiver to this district several years ago induced those people to believe (as the obvious and common duty of such officers is to sell land & receive the money) that the sales would very shortly thereafter commence. by which means . . . they were induced to settle on the land they proposed to buy—they now constitute at least one third of the whole population of the territory —and a great portion of them will become freeholders as soon as the sales shall be open—Yet unless Congress interpose to extend to them the right of suffrage &c they must be deprived of the benefits of representation—The ordinance & laws amendatory thereof require that so soon as the Governor shall receive satisfactory evidence that the organization of a general assembly in the territory is the wish of a majority of the freeholders—he shall order an election for representatives whose number shall not be less than seven nor more than nine and these he shall apportion to the several counties in the territory according to the number of free males above the age of 21 years—at present there are but two counties in the territory. so that I must give at least four representatives to one and three to the other—This power is given to the Governor for the purpose of getting the second grade of gov^t in operation after which he has no power to apportion the representation by taking a member from one or both the counties to which he had previously given him. this must depend on the legislature of which consists of the representatives of two counties only and it is not a safe calculation that they will have magnanimity enough to relinquish all that justice would require—the people of whom I have spoken as residing between Kaskaskia and the Ohio are in Randolph County—will be counted for it in the apportionment of representatives and yet will have no vote—If I seperate those people from Randolph by laying off a new county (which I have only been prevented from doing in consequence of their being in legal estimation intruders on public land) and should apportion to them their share of representatives still I do not know that there is one man among them that is qualified to be a representative by having a freehold of 200 acres of land. and not more than three or four qualified to vote by having a freehold in fifty acres . . . which are the qualifications fixed by the ordinance—Convinced as I am that nothing more than a fair representation of the situa-

tion of the people of this territory at the present time to congress
can be necessary to procure them the justice which their situation
imperiously calls for. I beg leave in their behalf most earnestly
to intreat your aid in procuring the passage of law to extend the
right of suffrage, in all cases . . . and for the election of the delegate to Congress by the people at large instead of by the legislature. An early passage of the law alone can secure . . . the advantages
which it may propose, as otherwise the second grade will be forced
ov [MS. torn] so as to defeat its beneficial purposes. . . .

I would thank you to inform me what may be the prospect of
having the right of suffrage extended, because should I be assured
that that event w^d certainly take place I would certainly postpone
the elections a little beyond the period I should otherwise appoint
for them. . . .

AN INHABITANT OF ARKANSAS DISTRICT, LOUISIANA TERRITORY,
WRITES TO JOSEPH CHARLESS, IN THE *Louisiana Gazette*,
AUGUST 8, 1811

[July 1, 1811]

MR. CHARLESS,

My neighbours have again commenced the discussion of the second grade of government. One opposes it because he alledges the
taxes will be higher, that the people have not virtue enough to be
trusted with the government of themselves, and that we shall soon
be a *State* by remaining as we are; and says he will not sign the
petition for a change. Another advocates it because he says we have
virtue and information enough, at least some fifteen or twenty
in the Territory, to assist in making laws for ourselves. That in the
first grade a bad law may be imposed on us, whereas in the other,
no law can be made but by the consent of those chosen by the
people. That local matters and local laws, are best known by those
upon whom they operate. That the legislative and judicial powers
ought never to be combined in one man or set of men, that taxes
ought not to be imposed on us without our Consent. That we have
no direct communication with the general government, except
through agents (many of whom are worthy men) appointed and
paid by the government, representing it, and not the people, and
not dependent upon the people for the tenor of their offices. That
oppression is often suffered rather than to encounter the perplexi-

ties of complaining in a circuitous and uncertain manner. That we have no one chosen by us to defend our rights, nor protect our interests at the seat of government. That most of the titles to land are in a precarious and dangerous situation; rejected either for not coming within the strict letter of the law, with many equitable circumstances in their favor, or because, fluctuating decisions in them have not enabled a common man to know what it was necessary to prove.

That the commissioners will soon make their report to Congress and individual claimants are either obliged to abandon their claims to what constitutes the best support of their families, or expend money, hard to earn, and difficult to attain, in paying an agent, and that agent vested with no power, authority or privilege to speak, except when the *committee* shall deign to permit him. That for want of a delegate, to which they would be entitled under the second grade of government; the contracts for carrying the mail and for furnishing the troops are taken by persons not resident in the Territory, who carry away all the profits and specie out of the country: a mere bargain of speculation, and the shameful irregularities and failures of the mail, are not corrected. That the labour of the husbandman, whose industry clears a field, is now taxed under the name of lands in actual cultivation; while unimproved lands which are rising in value and belong chiefly to the affluent are not taxed, by which the industrious pay, and the idle are exempt. That one of our legislators and Judges reside out of the territory and therefore cannot be made acquainted with the wants and necessities of the people, and that economy and prudence in our fiscal concerns would enable us to support the second grade of government with very little or no additional taxes.

The Slavery Question

ONE OF the most controversial political issues in the Old Northwest was the question of slavery in the territories. In Ohio, Indiana, and Illinois, where there had been heavy migration from the slaveholding areas of the south, the issue was particularly discussed. Strongly opposed to the institution was the writer of the following letter, John (Jean) Louis Badollet. Born in Geneva in 1758, he arrived in the United States sometime in the mid-1780's. After living in western Pennsylvania for eighteen years, he spent the rest of his life in and about Vincennes, Indiana. Through the influence of his friend Albert Gallatin, he was appointed by President Jefferson as register for the newly created land office at Vincennes. *The following extracts from his letters to Gallatin in the New-York Historical Society collection are printed in Gayle Thornbrough (ed.), The Correspondence of John Badollet and Albert Gallatin, Vol. XXII, Indiana Historical Society Publications (Indianapolis, Ind., 1963), 91–93, 97.*

Slavery continued to be a hot political issue even after statehood. In Illinois attempts were made to amend the state constitution to provide for slave labor. The following extracts of letters from Governor Edward Coles to Nicholas Biddle are printed in The William and Mary College Quarterly, 2nd series, VII (April, 1927), 100–103.

JOHN LOUIS BADOLLET TO ALBERT GALLATIN

[December 21, 1807]

. . . The Legislature of the Territory have been every year pestering Congress with petitions for the admission of slavery into it. Apprehending little danger, the opponents of that scheme have hitherto remained, but will not always remain silent. They place too much reliance upon the enlightened views of the national Legislature, they firmly believe, that the spirit of justice, philanthropy & sound policy which animates them, will not permitt them to introduce into this part of the union such a nefarious system, against which the faith & honour of Congress stand solemnly pledged, and they rather indulge the hope that the efforts of all good men, will be united in endeavours, to remove by every practicable means that national disgrace. . . .

. . . Besides, my office of Register has put me in possession of a fact of which few here have any knowledge, namely that almost all the emigrants from the Southern states to a man, who have purchased or do purchase land in this office are flying from the evils of slavery, to this only part of the United States, the climate of which will permit them to cultivate the products, to the raising of which they are accustomed, without meeting the evils they so much wish to avoid. I am informed by them that a considerable population from both North & South Carolina, of whom wealthy Quakers form a great proportion, are preparing to remove here (some have already arrived), that, could the apprehensions created by the petitions above alluded to, be quieted & the belief be solidly impressed, that Congress will not yield to those clamours, but perform their solemn promise of not permitting the introduction of slavery in this Territory, then the emigration from the aforesaid States would be very great and as it were unceasing. The emigration from the neighboring State of Kentucky is chiefly composed either of men who detest slavery from principles, or of such, as being in modest circumstances, & owing their bread to their own labour cannot well brook the haughty manners of their opulent neighbours the slave-holders. The members of our Legislature & their co-adjutors, whatever may be the source of their actions, prejudice or interest, have argued from wrong premises, namely that crouds of slave holders would flock here, raise the price of land and rapidly increase our population. (What sort of population, of poor black slaves, stopping the ingress of free & industrious men) What I have stated above sufficiently demonstrates the fallacy of those reasonings. I'll add but one more observation the former unanimity of the Legislature exists no more, two members of the lower house, in compliance with instructions from the Counties of Dearborn & Clarke, have seceded & opposed the measure. . . .

[January 23, 1808]
. . . I have often admired the ingenuity of Stupidity, as you will choose to call it, with which our first Legislature (with many lawyers too) have trampled on the Ordinance of Congress, in that part of it which relates to Slavery. They have passed an Act permitting owners of negroes emigrating into this Territory to bring them hither and to keep them for a number of days, during which time the poor slave is at *liberty* forsooth to bind himself for a term of years (the favourite term is 99 years) or to be remanded to the state he was brought from & there to be sold. True if the Slave accept of the proferred boon, by signing the indenture (a slave signing a contract!) the master gives bond with security, conditioned for the slave never becoming a charge on the County. A sardonic grin invades my face at writing this. Could humanity, the principles of wise policy which shine in that part of the ordinance, and common-sense be insulted in a more outrageous manner? The executive gave his sanction to the laudable Act! ! ! ! So much for the first exploit performed under the second grade of Government. So much for the Solons, who give us laws.

GOVERNOR EDWARD COLES TO NICHOLAS BIDDLE

Vandalia, Illinois, April 22, 1823
. . . There has long existed in this State a strong party in favor

of altering the Constitution, and making it a Slave-holding-State; while there is another party in favor of a convention to alter the Constitution, but deny that Slavery is their object. These two parties have finally, by the most unprecedented and unwarrantable proceedings (an account of which you have no doubt seen in the newspapers) succeeded in passing a Resolution requiring the sense of the people to be taken at the next general election (Augt: 1824) on the propriety of calling a Convention for the purpose of altering the Constitution. Knowing that this measure would be strenuously urged during the late Session of the Legislature, and that many who professed to be hostile to the further introduction of Slavery would advocate it, and believing that it would have a salutary effect to furnish them an opportunity of evincing the sincerity of their professions; and being also urged by a strong sense of the obligations imposed on me by my principles and feelings, to take notice of the subject, I called the attention of the Legislature, in a speech I delivered on being sworn into office (a printed copy of which I sent you by mail) to the existence of Slavery in the State, in violation of the great fundamental principles of the Ordinance, and recommended that just and equitable provision be made for its abrogation. As I anticipated this part of my speech created a considerable excitement, with those who were openly or secretly in favor of making Illinois a slave holding, rather than making it really as well as nominally, a free State—who wished to fill it, rather than empty it of Slaves. Never did I see or hear, in America, of party spirit going to such length, as well officially as privately, as it did here on this question. Indeed it seems to me that Slavery is so poisonous as to produce a kind of delirium in those minds who are excited by it. This question, and the manner of carrying it, is exciting great interest throughout the State, and has already kindled an extraordinary degree of excitement and warmth of feeling, which will no doubt continue to increase until the question is decided. I assure you I never before felt so deep an interest in any political question. It presses upon me to such a degree, that I shall not be happy or feel at ease until it is settled. It is impossible to foresee the injurious effects resulting to this State, or the unhappy consequences which may arise to the Union, from the success of the Slave party in this State. Many of us who migrated to this State under the solemn assurance that there should exist here "neither Slavery nor involuntary Servitude," will, if the

Slave faction succeeds, be compelled to sacrifice or abandon our property and seek new homes we know not where, or remain in a Community whose principles we shall disapprove of, and whose practice will be abhorrent to our feelings. And already we hear disputed the binding effect of the ordinance—the power of Congress to restrict a State &c &c &c—from which I fear, if the introduction of Slavery should be tolerated here, the discussions on the expediency and unconstitutionality of the measure will not in all probability be confined to the Citizens of this State. But this is a part of the question too painful for me to dwell on. I trust the good sense and virtue of the Citizens of Illinois will never sanction a measure so well calculated to disturb the harmony of the Union, and so injurious to its own prosperity and happiness, as well as so directly opposite to the progress of those enlightened and liberal principles which do honor to the age. But to ensure this it is necessary that the public mind should be enlightened on the moral and political effects of Slavery. You will confer a particular favor on me, and promote the virtuous cause in which I am inlisted, by giving me information, or refering me to the sources from whence I can draw it, calculated to elucidate the general character and effects of Slavery—Its moral, political, & social effects—facts showing its effects on the price of Lands, and general improvement and appearance of a Country—of labour, both as it respects agriculture and manufactures &c &c.

[Edwardsville, Illinois], September 18, 1823

. . . The propriety of calling a convention, or more properly speaking, of making this a slave-holding State, is still discussed with considerable warmth, and continues to engage the undivided attention of the people, being the constant theme of conversation in every circle, and every newspaper teems with no other subject. Unfortunately for the friends of freedom, four out of five of the newspapers printed in this State are opposed to them; and the only press whose Editor is in favor of freedom, altho' a pretty smart Editor, has rendered himself unpopular with many by his foolish and passionate attacks upon many of the prominent men on his side of the question. If however the advocates of slavery have the advantage of us in printing presses, we have greatly the advantage of them in possessing men of the most talents, and most able to wield the pen, and use the press, with effect; and as three out of four of their presses have professed a willingness to admit well written original essays on both sides of the question, we shall have not only the best of the argument but be able, I trust, to present it in the best dress to the public. I am happy in telling you that the advocates of a convention have been losing ground ever since the adjournment of the Legislature; and there is no doubt with me if the question were now to be decided that a majority of the people would be opposed to it. But what will be the state of parties next August is another question. Many of the people in this State are very fickle and credulous, and much can be done by designing and unprincipled partizans: and that every thing which can possibly be done will be done, we cannot but infer from the extraordinary and unwarranted measures resorted to last winter in the Legislature in getting up the question, and the great anxiety evinced, and exertions which have been made, and are still making to prevail on the people to sanction it. But as the friends of freedom are aware of this they will watch the movements of their opponents, and be on the alert to counteract their intrigues and machinations. The object for which a convention is wanted is so justly odious, and the conduct of the friends of the measure so disgraceful, that I cannot bring myself to believe they will succeed. But I regret to state that the advocates of Slavery in this State are gaining strength, from the indiscretion of the advocates of freedom out of the State. Certain leading newspapers in the Atlantic Cities have taken a stand, and held language which is used here in a way calculated to do much mischief. Whether we have the Constitutional right to make this a Slave holding State or not, or whether the opponents of the extension of Slavery, here or elsewhere may think proper hereafter to call for the interposition of the Federal Govt: to restrain the people of this State, it is certainly bad policy at this time very strongly to urge it, and especially in what may be considered dictatorial language; as it is of all other questions the best calculated to arouse the feelings of State pride, and State rights, and that natural love of unrestrained liberty and independence, which is common to our Countrymen, and especially to our frontier settlers, who of all men in the world have the strongest jealousy of authority and aversion to restraint. I wish my friend you would use your influence to prevail on these newspaper writers to let this question alone for the present. If they are sincere in their opposition to the further extension of Slavery, they will not prematurely urge it, when they are assured by so doing they can do no good but much harm.

Western Politics

WESTERN politicians, more violent perhaps than their counterparts in the East, were nevertheless as partisan. Indeed there was often a close connection between political leaders in the sections, especially with the rise of parties. At an early date, westerners were integrated into the national political scene. Edward Turner was appointed register of the land office for the Mississippi Territory by President Jefferson. His letter to John C. Breckinridge, United States Senator from Kentucky, is printed in Carter (ed.), Territorial Papers of the United States, V, 265–266, from the Breckinridge Papers, Library of Congress.

Jefferson County (Mississippi Territory), November 2nd 1803
As an introduction to the subject of this letter, I will make a few remarks on the political affairs of this Territory, and on my Situation with respect to them.

We have here, as you have in the States, federalists, and democratic-republicans. The first of these, or what is properly called the *political party*, is composed of federal emigrants from the States, disbanded officers, persons attached to a Spanish Collonial Government, others friendly to monarchy and aristocracy in general, and of some who were probably at one time inclined to republicanism, but who, from the attention, and support of federalists in power, have become federalists, first, from interest, lastly, from a vainglorious kind of gratitude. The democratic republicans are men, who have at all times, both under the American and Spanish government, under Adams' & Jefferson's administration, been uniform in their principles—here I allude to those republicans who lived here under & since the Spanish Government: there are others who have emigrated here since the american government came into operation, of which number I am one. Under the first grade of our Territorial Government, the Governor and all the officers of the Judiciary, were federal. The opposition among parties ran very high, but the republicans were finally successful in obtaining the second grade of Government, and in obtaining a discontinuance of Colo[nel Winthrop] Sargent in the office of Governor; who was succeeded by Governor [William] Claiborne. The first Territorial Legislature was Republican. It was now that the feds were exerting all their talents in the opposition, and in this situation I found the politics of the Territory when I landed at Natchez in January 1802. I found every gentleman of the Bar except two, in the opposition. I was received as a Republican, and received with cordiality by Governor C. & the old republicans of the Country. My letters of introduction were principally to the leading federalists of the Country, and my brother Henry, a merchant in Natchez, from whom I was to receive a support until I could make the means of supporting myself, was in the opposition likewise—various and powerful were the arguments & persuasions used by him to keep me from going with the Republicans; and I plainly saw that it was my interest *as a lawyer* to be a federalist, and I had no other way of making my bread, but by my profession. I, however, as I had been taught, made enquiries & formed my own opinions, felt superior to the influence of interest over principle, and continued a republican. I took no active part in support of either the one or the other *party*, I avoided news-paper scribling as a trifling business, but advanced and supported my principles when & where ever I found it proper to do so: and my object has ever been to support principles,—not *men*, except so far as they act from principle. I have frequently differed even with republicans. The only remarkable instances in which I have been active as a politician, are, my writing two pieces for the press, pointing out the corruption of the federal party at an election in July 1802; in assisting in drafting a petition to Congress last fall, praying for sundry alterations in our Ordinance, which was founded entirely on principle; in forming a society called "The Mississippi Republican Society," formed for the purpose of promoting Republican principles, of disseminating political information among the people by means of discussion, & circulating political pamphlets & news papers; to prepare the people for the great change which is some day to take place among them, that from a Territorial to a State Government; in delivering an oration for the Society on the anniversary of Mr Jefferson's election to the Presidency; in assisting in drawing up a Bill of rights for this Society, to which all the members Subscribe. In all this time I have been treated by the federalists, as a decided republican. I have been an officer under Governor C. almost ever since I have been here—I was first honored in the military line by being nominated one of His *Aids de camp*; and my civil commission was that of Clerk of a court. My great object has ever been to promote *republican principles*; in doing which I have sometimes differed with *republican men*; for instance, I have generally been upon the *best* terms with Governor C., (and my being a confidential officer under him is a proof of it) who from his official situation has it much in his power to serve me, and who *has* served me in many instances, but yet, when I have found Governor C. acting against principle, for personal popularity, or other objects, where some sacrifice of principle was the consequence, I have withdrawn, in such cases, my support; and would from any man, who, in pretending to serve the Republican cause, would attempt to aggrandize himself, at the expense of such cause.

The County Seat

THE BASIC *unit of government for administering the law was the county court, an institution transferred from England to the eastern colonies and then on to the West. Frontier communities often competed to be chosen as locales for the seat of government, once western counties were established in newly settled areas. In February, 1773, the Pennsylvania legislature created Westmoreland County out of the old jurisdiction of Bedford County. The new county lay west of Laurel Hill and included the whole of southwest Pennsylvania. The county seat was located at "Hanna's Town," founded by William Hanna, thirty miles east of Pittsburgh. Aeneas Mackay, the author of the following letter, was one of the sixteen justices of the peace appointed for the new county. His letter to Arthur St. Clair is printed in William Henry Smith, The Life and Public Services of Arthur St. Clair . . . with His Correspondence . . . (2 vols., Cincinnati, Ohio, 1882), I, 269–270. The following letter from St. Clair to Joseph Shippen is printed in Smith, ibid., 274–275.*

AENEAS MACKAY TO ARTHUR ST. CLAIR

PITTSBURGH, 3rd March, 1773

DEAR SIR:

—Your esteemed favor dated Philada., the 12th ulto., I have had the pleasure of receiving. Every body up this way are well satisfied there is a county granted on this side of the hills, altho' I find every body else as well as myself, observes with infinite concern, that the point in question is not attended with so favorable circumstances as we at this place had reason to expect, from the nature of things. I can not but express my surprise at the point determined in favor of the courts of law first sitting at Hanna's.

Pray may I ask you the question, Where is the conveniency for transacting business on these occasions, as there is neither houses, tables, nor chairs? Certainly the people must sit at the roots of trees and stumps and in case of rain the lawyers' books and papers must be exposed to the weather, yet to no purpose, as they can not presume to write. Consequently, nothing can be done but that of revising fees, by which means every body (the lawyers, only, excepted) going to or attending court, must be sufferers. No doubt but Mr. [Joseph] Irwin and a few more of his party, may find their interest in this glaring stretch of partiality, yet we, at this place, in particular, are too much interested to look over such proceeding in silence. The whole inhabitants exclaim against the steps already taken to the injury of the county yet in its infancy, and that too, before it got its eyes or tongue to speak for itself.

My dear friend, if I had as much to say among the great as you, I would declare it as my opinion that it would be absolutely necessary that the commissioners should be nominated in Philada., by which means I think we could not fail to have the point in question carried in our favor; whereas, should they be appointed up this way, it is ten to one, if Joe Irwin and his associates will not prevail.

I am sorry for our disappointment in our hopes of being indulged with a small garrison at this place, but in failure of that, nothing could afford me greater satisfaction than the prospect of having you, my friend, my neighbor at this place. This I will look for now every day, and if you will send me word when you will set of from Ligonier I will meet you half way and perhaps a Divine and another friend to show you the way up here. As to Ross, he seldom speaks as he thinks—for my part I therefore pay but little regard to his declarations.

The people of this place take great umbrage at the very thoughts of being disappointed of the country town's not taking place here at once, and are, to a man, willing to come to any measure or charges, in order, if possible to frustrate the intrigues carried on by a certain party. I think we can not exert ourselves too much on this occasion, and therefore would be very glad to receive your opinion of the affair and your advice in regard to the most intelligible steps to be pursued in the first setting off.

I would be exceeding glad how soon other affairs could admit of your coming up here, by which means a plan might be concerted, that in my opinion could scarcely fail of succeeding to our wish.

I daily inquire after the welfare of your family, and have the pleasure of informing you that Mrs. St. Clair and the children are well and in good health. . . .

ARTHUR ST. CLAIR TO JOSEPH SHIPPEN, JR.

Ligonier, January 15, 1774

SIR:

—This will be delivered by Mr. Hanna, one of the trustees for Westmoreland county. To some management of his I believe, the opposition to fixing the county town at Pittsburgh is chiefly owing—it is his interest it should continue where the law has fixed the courts, pro tempore; he lives there; used to keep public house there; and has now, on that expectation, rented his house at an extravagant price. Erwin, another trustee, adjoins, and is also public housekeeper. A third trustee lives in the neighborhood, which always make a majority for continuing the courts at the present place. A passage in the law for erecting the county is, that the courts shall be held in the foregoing place (the house of Robert Hanna) till a court house and jail are built; this puts it in their power to continue there as long as they please—for a little management might prevent a court house and jail being built this twenty years. . . .

An Act for the Prevention of Vice and Immorality

DURING the early stage of government in the Northwest Territory, statutes were required to be adopted from those governing the existing states. In the second stage, however, the territorial legislature could enact its own code. The following extract from the reprint of the 1800 edition of Theodore C. Pease (ed.), The Laws of the Northwest Territory, Vol. XVII of The Collections of the Illinois State Historical Library (Springfield, Ill., 1925), 377–380, reflects an attempt to impose morality in an area thought free from such restraints.

Whereas the increase of vice and immorality in a nation, eventually tends, by corrupting the human mind, to wound individual happiness, as well as to destroy national prosperity, it becomes the indispensable duty of the legislature to adopt such measures as may appear most effectual for the suppressing its growth, and preventing its effects: therefore,

Sec. 1. *BE it enacted by the Legislative Council and House of Representatives in General Assembly, and it is hereby enacted by the authority of the same,* That if any person shall be found reveling, fighting, or qu[a]rreling, doing or performing any worldly employment or business, whatsoever, on the first day of the week, commonly called Sunday, (works of necessity and charity only excepted) or shall use or practice any unlawful game, sport or diversion, whatsoever, or shall be found hunting or shooting, on the said day, and be convicted thereof, every such person, so offending, shall, for every such offence, forfeit and pay a sum not exceeding two dollars, nor less than fifty cents, to be levied by distress; or in case such person, being a male, shall refuse or neglect to pay the said sum, or goods and chattels cannot be found, whereof to levy the same by distress, he shall be committed to the charge of one of the supervisors of the highways, in the township wherein the offence was committed, to be kept at hard labor for the space of two days. *Provided always,* That nothing herein contained shall be construed to hinder watermen from landing their passengers, or ferrymen from carrying over the water travellers, or persons removing with their families, on the first day of the week, commonly called Sunday.

Sec. 2. *And be it further enacted,* That if any person of the age of sixteen years and upwards, shall profanely curse, damn, or swear, by the name of God, Christ Jesus, or the Holy Ghost, every person so offending, being thereof convicted, shall forfeit and pay, for every such profane curse, damn, or oath, a sum not exceeding two dollars, nor less than fifty cents, at the discretion of the justice who may take cognizance thereof; and in case he shall refuse or neglect to pay the said forfeiture, or goods and chattels cannot be found, whereof to levy the same by distress, he shall be committed to the charge of one of the supervisors of the highways in the township wherein the offence was committed, to be kept at hard labor, for the space of two days, for every such offence, of which such person shall be convicted.

Sec. 3. *And it further enacted,* That if any person of the age of sixteen years or upwards, shall be found in the public highway, or in any public house of entertainment, intoxicated by excessive drinking of spiritous, vinous, or other strong liquors, and making, or exciting any noise, contention or disturbance, it shall be lawful for any justice of the peace, on complaint or view, to cause such person or persons to be committed to the common jail of the county, there to remain for a term of time not exceeding forty eight hours; and every person, so committed, shall pay the fees arising on such commitment. And if any person shall be found offending, as aforesaid, at any greater distance than five miles from the county jail, it shall be lawful for any justice of the peace to commit such person or persons to the custody of any constable within the township, for the like term of time, to be by such constable confined in any proper and convenient place, for the like term of time; and the said constable shall be entitled to the same fees as are allowed to the keeper of the jail in the like cases.

Sec. 4. *And be it further enacted,* That the judges of the supreme court, every justice of the court of common pleas, and every justice of the peace, within the limits of their several jurisdictions, are hereby empowered, authorized and required to proceed against and punish all persons offending against the preceding sections of this act; and, for that purpose, each of the said judges or justices, severally, may convict such offenders upon his own view and hearing, or shall issue, if need be, a warrant, summons or capias, according to the circumstances of the case, to bring the body of the person accused, as aforesaid, before him; and the same judges or justices shall, respectively, in a summary way, enquire into the truth of the accusation, and upon the testimony of one or more credible witnesses, or the confession of the party, shall convict the person who shall be guilty, as aforesaid, and thereupon shall proceed to pronounce the forfeiture incurred by the person so convicted, as herein before directed; and if the person, so convicted, refuse or neglect to satisfy such forfeiture immediately, with costs, or to produce goods and chattels whereon to levy the said forfeiture, together with costs, then the said judge or justice shall commit the offender to one of the supervisors of the highways, as aforesaid, during such time as is herein before directed. . . .

Sec. 5. *And be it further enacted,* That if any person or persons shall cause to fight any cock or cocks, for money or any other valuable thing, or shall promote or encourage any match or matches of cock fighting, by betting thereon, or shall play at any match of bullets, in any place, for money or other valuable thing, or on any highway or public road with or without a bet, or shall play at cards, dice, billiards, bowls, shovel-board or any game of hazard or address, for money or other valuable thing, every such person, so offending, shall, upon conviction thereof, before any justice or magistrate . . . forfeit and pay three dollars, for every such offence. . . .

Thomas Rodney Comments on Lawyers and Judges in the Southwest Territory

THOMAS RODNEY of Delaware was appointed a judge for the Mississippi Territory. In the following letter to his son, Caesar A. Rodney (printed in the Pennsylvania Magazine of History and Biography, XLV [1921], 182–183), he comments on lawyers in the Southwest and the difficulties facing the judges.

Town Washington M. T., Septr. 30th 1809

MY DEAR SON

I flattered myself some time ago with the hope of having it in my power to visit my friends in Delaware next Winter but Judge Leak went off for his family last June and is not expected back Untill next Spring; and Judge Martin of N. C. our new Judge has not yet arrived nor is it known here when he will come—I received a Letter from him in July in which he proposed being here in that month but July, August & September have passed away and we have heard nothing further from him, so that the whole duties of the Superior Judiciary have remained on my Hands since May, and I have three or four Counties yet to hold the fall Circuit Courts in two others I have already passed through. It is not only Expensive but laborious to be on the Circuit and sit alone for better than two months, Especially in such Uncomfortable Court Houses as we have yet in this new Country—I sincerely hope that when there is occasion to appoint another judge for this Territory that some gentleman of the Law in the Territory will be preferred —Our gentlemen at the bar here are numerous and many of them not inferior to any that Can be had in the States who would come to this Country.

Special Pleading is adhered to in our Courts perhaps with as much Strictness Elegance and propriety as in any of the States, so that Even the Young Lawyers are obliged to read their books and be very attentive to their business or want bread—beside there are

several gentlemen in the territory who have read the Law but
have declined the practice—I have said this much because for 4
years past I have felt the burthen and inconvenience both to myself, by being left so often alone, and to the people by the delay
of their business as it requires two Judges to hold the Supreme
Court and there are so many Counties that one judge unless he
had an Iron Constitution Cannot attend them all the full time
required to git through the business of each—But the unfortunate
situation of the Country for want of a market makes delay at present no very great inconvenience—Indeed there is so little money,
and the Country so much in debt that if the Courts were to go
through their business, the Country would be in a great measure
ruined; for the most wealthy people in it cannot pay their debts
at this time—Yet when this is the Case Suits are always multiplied.

Cases from the Jefferson County Circuit Court

THE NATURE of law as practiced in the courts in the West is demonstrated by the following cases from the Jefferson County Circuit Court,
Mississippi Territory, printed in William B. Hamilton, Anglo-American
Law on the Frontier: Thomas Rodney and His Territorial Cases (Durham, N.C., 1953), pp. 360–362, 381–382.

Munday 2 week March 27th, 1808
The Territory v Bartho Wallace. Horse Stealing—J. Brazeale
P[laintiff]

In Criminal Capital Cases, The Prisoner after being Indicted
is Called To the Bar and Charged—and if he Pleads Not Guilty
—Then a Venire is ordered To Summon a Jury of 36, Including
the original Pannel—The Prisoner is furnished with a Copy of the
Indictment, and a list of the Jurors & witnesses on the Part of
Governmt. 3 days before the day of Trial (Unless the Prisoner
Consents To a Shorter Time) Then the Prisoner is brought To
the bar & ready for Trial. The Sher[iff] and Clerk proceed To
draw the Jury one by One, when the first Jury Man Comes To the
book The Clerk Then addresses The Prisoner Informing him That
as Those good Men Come To the book who are Called on to pass
on his Trial if he Challenges any he Must do as they Come To
The book—Then the Clerk Says, Juror look on the Prisoner—
Prisoner look on the Juror; Do you Challinge him? If the Prisoner

no. then Juror is Sworn—if he Says yes, Then Juror is rejected—but
The usual way is, To ask the Prisoner do you like him?

The Atty. General opened the Case and then proced[e]d to Ex-
am[in]e Evidence.

Brazeale Says he bot. a Horse of Hutchinson and then came up
to Fairbank's where Wallace was and where he was Talking of
Selling Said Horse When Prisoner Said the Horse was his, and
forceably Took the Horse from him—Kentucky Man had been rid-
ing the Horse for Trial—when he returned and light Then he and
Prisoner—Seized The bridle nearly Together but Prisoner Choaked
him and Took the Horse away and beged him for the rope that
had been on the Horse and he gave Wallace the rope there was
agreat number of people Present—He said he bot. him and paid
for him and he owned him he must git him Legally—Wallace
Threw of[f] the Saddle & Bridle—heard nothing of Wallaces offering to return the Horse on his giving Security—after Saddle and
bridle was thrown off Horse run off—Wallace went and brot. him
back by the rope, then Took Rope off The Horse, and gave To
Witness—after this he lent Wallace The Rope—

J. Coulter, Says, he was at Hutchinsons when Brazeale purchased
the Horse and Saw him Delivered—Hutchinson had had the Horse
5 or 6 weeks before—he came up Just as they were Scufling for
the Horse—The Horse got off and Wallace brot. him back—Wallace offered the Horse for Sale next day—Wallace Staid among the
boats all night and kept the Horse there—(27th. of October last)
was Ten or 15 yds from Prisoner & Brazeal when Scuffg. about the
Horse—Brazeale pickt up a bar of Iron To Strike Wallace,—Wallace Claimed the Horse, as his Own. He was present when Wallace
delivered the Horse to Hutchinson and Said he had Sold him and
asked this Witness his Value—He answered 40. dols. Heard
Brazeale Tell Wallace he would prosecute him—

J. Neely, Says, Hutchinson bot. the Horse to his House To Keep
& Said he bot. him of Wallace and heard Wallace say he had Sold
him—afterwards saw Hutchinson Sell him To Brazeale—afterwards
Saw Wallace, Soon after Wallace he had Taken the Horse from
Brazeale the saddle and bridle was then off and Neelly Said he
Should not Take him away and a Scuffle Ensued between them,
and the Horse got away, and Wallace got the better of him—
Brazeale Said he would prosecute Wallace—he Lent Brazeale a

Team [?] and went with him—Witness and Generally the Company were gay—Saw Wallace offer the Rope to Brazeale, but Brazeal would not Take the Rope Without the Horse—Then Said Wallace let me have it—and Brazeale Said if you keep the Horse you Keep the rope—W. offered if Witness would be B. security— he would let him have to ride home—&c.

J. Malone, Says, That He Saw Brazeale Talking of Selling his Horse To a Kentuky Man, who rode him a little way, and he came back and light he Saw Wallace put his arm through the bridle Then he pushed Brazeale off and Choaked him at this Time the Saddle fell off and then the bridle was pulled off and Wallace was leading The Horse off by the Rope, when Brazeale attempted To Take Horse again & Wallace choked him again Then Neely came up and Struck Wallace, and Wallace To defend himself let the Horse go—They Scuffled Some Time, and after This Brazeale Took up a bar of Iron but put it down again—Wallace went then and got the Horse—this Witness left them. but Saw Wallace there at Supper, and Next day—

Fairbanks, Says, he Saw none of the Transaction Saw Wallace with the Horse—he Knew the Horse he had seen Wallace with him the ev[en] i[n]g before

Hutchinson, He got the Horse from Wallace Neilly Owed Wallace $400—which Witness advised him To pay it—paid it in Cotton & Delivered up Neilly Bond—He Saw to the weighing the Cotton —He is overseer for H. Hunt—wallace Sold the Horse to him—for $25. & his Trouble afsd. about weigh[in]g. the Cotton—The 23d. of October The Horse was delivered to him—

Staybraker Says Wallace Owned the Hors[e] and he heard Wallace Say Several Times he had Sold The Horse to Hutchinson— and Said he had been paid for him—End

Sharrow, Says, Hutchinson aided in acting for Neilly & Wallace —and W. Said he would Satisfy Hutchinson for his Trouble—had Two Horses—And afterwards Hutchinson offered one for Sale (The One in question) Bright Eyes he does not know How Hutchinson got possession.

Testimony Closed

Mr. Atty. Genl. opened The argument by Citing 1. Hale 538—1. Haw. 149. Defining Robbery 1. Haw. 147.—Stub. C. C. 636—if purse is Taken and returned Immediately—It is never the less

Robbery—and Said That The Evidence—Supported Point of Robbery—

Mr. Sturgus, acceeded That Horse was Taken but not *animo
Furandi*—1. Hale 534.—"a Man May Take his own property wherever he find it" on this ground The Prisoner acted—as if the Horse
was his Own—

Mr. Shields followed Cited 4. Blac. 332.242. and argued the Case
Very handsomely and Enforced his arguments with Impressive
language and with Method

The Atty. Genl. Concluded. and argued more Strongly
ag[ains]t. the Prisoner Than The Evidence or [one or two words
illegible] would well Justify—

In This Case you are To give the Testimony what wheight you
Please—But you Must believe That The Prisoner Robbed the
owner of his Horse with a Felonious Intent, by Violence, or by
putting The Person Robbed in fear—If you have the least doubt
of This, you Must acquit the Prisoner.

Verdict Not guilty—

[From "Judge Rodneys Doquet Of business Done out of Court
At his Chambers" in the Historical Society of Delaware]

May 13th. 1808

Gilbert Chavers Negro v Joseph Carnes. Habeas Corpus for The
body of a Mullato Girl Named Sally about Ten or Eleven years
Old, which Said Gilbert Claims To be his Daughter by a white
woman he the Said Gilbert being a blackman.

The Said girl being Examined Says She is The daughter of a
white woman, but has not Seen her Mother for 4 years past—That
She has lived Two years past with Joseph Carnes That She is
Well Satisfied with her place of Residence—That She does
not know That Gilbert Chavers is her Father but he used To live
with her Mother, and beat and abused her Cruilly and Took her
Children all but The Youngest away from her. This was in The
Tuckapa over the River.

Chavers Says he was born in Georgia where he Took the Mother
of Said girl to wife and produced a Certificate to Shew that he is a
Free man—And an Order from the Mother of the girl requiring
Carnes To deliver The Child To Gilbert or She will proscut
him &c.

Carnes Says it is True That Gilbert used To live with the Mother of the girl, who is a white woman, And that he Gilbert beat and abused her and most killed her and Then Took all her Children from her but the youngest, and had put this girl Sally at Several places among Negros & Others Till he Gilbert was Imprisoned for Stealing and was whiped—That 2 years ago he brought the girl Sally and put with him and She had remained with him Ever since—That Chavers Tried To git her away in Tuckapa and they were before Jud[g]e White about it and The Judge Would not permit Gilbert To have The Girl, he being a Very bad man and guilty of many attrocious offences &c. That he lately moved from Tuckapa To this Town and brought the girl with him, by Permission of Judge White.

Gilbert having no Other Evidence of his being the father of Sally, or the husband of her Mother—I adjourned The further consideration of this Case Till Tomorrow To give the parties an Opertunity of Obtaining further Testimony[.]

May 14th. 1808

The Parties appeared at My Chambers With Their Witnesses and Counsel.

John Campbell Examined as a Witness on the part of Gilbert claiming To be the father of Sally Said That Gilbert and the Mother of Sally who was a white woman came into the Tuckapas about 4 years ago & passed for man & wife & the woman had four mullato Children—That She & Gilbert lived together about 6 months and Then parted—That one of the Children Died and Gilbert Took the Two Eldest away Sally being one and put them with a Mullato Man of the Name of Chavers,—That Gilbert then worked about and Traded to Mexico &c.

Mrs. Campbell wife of the above Witness being Sworn Said That Gilbert and the mother of Sally lived Together in Tuckapa a few months as man & wife and then parted That the Mother of Sally is a white woman and Gilbert a black man, Sally a mullato That they lived only a few hundred yards from her but She had No Intimacy wth. them and knew but Little about them.

after which and hereing the Counsel on both Sides I Delivered My Opinion That Gilbert being a Blackman and The Mother of Sally a white woman—altho Sally was a Mullato yet there was not Sufficient Evidence To Verify a marriage or That Gilbert was The father of Sally Esspecially as it was not Legal in any of the U. S. for black and white To marry, Therefore where Children are of the mixed breed They follow the Mother Therefore Sally must remain in the possession of Carnes who is ordered To Take due Care of her Until Claimed by her mother or She be Otherwise Legally Disposed Of as an Orphan Child—and

Ordered That Chavers pay the Cost Incurred by this applycation Towit $8.50.

Governor Winthop Sargent Addresses the Militia

THE FOLLOWING address to the militia officers by Governor Winthrop Sargent, printed in Dunbar Rowland (ed.), The Mississippi Territorial Archives 1798–1803 (Nashville, Tenn., 1905), pp. 324–325, illustrates the concern over racial relations and the force used in the Southwest frontier. The Sargent journal is in the Mississippi Department of Archives and History.

To the Commandants, Field Officers, Captains, and Subalterns of Militia, Mississippi Territory, January 12th—1801—Natchez.

The Governors strong anxieties for the safety of the good People of the Territory, impel him again to urge the well ordering and Arming of the Militia.

To the Discretion and firmness of the officers, he may adventure to express himself in Confidence, and without apprehension of Creating unnecessary alarm.

Of the Continuance of Indian Friendship we cannot be assured, and the Crisis of Hostility would be found *fatally* tardy for the essential preparation of Defence.

Almost every day adds to the number of our Slaves, and (Reasoning from the fine feelings of Man) to the number of our most inveterate Enemies *also*.

'Tis more than probable, that in the Lapse of another year, there will be more Blacks than Whites within the Mississippi Territory.—That we deprive them of the sacred Boon of Liberty is a Crime they can never forgive—Mild and humane Treatment may for a Time Continue them quiet, but can never fully Reconcile them to their situation—and Calculating from the Experience of some amongst us, in a War with any European, or even Indian Power *they* might be irresistably stimulated to Vengence.

From those important serious Considerations, the Governour is induced to reiterate Recommendation to the Officers, of most energetic Measures—that Company Districts be fully ascertained without a Moments delay, and every Man Enrolled in the Militia according to Law.—that all deficiencies in Arms and accoutrements be immediately supplied:—to enforce which the penalties should be inflicted, *provided* in every case of Delinquency, for no man of Reason will Deny that the Consequence of Continuing a *mistaken Clemency* and unlawfull Indulgence may be most fatal to ourselves, our Wives and our Children.

Military Officers must Consider it a Point of honour, to Carry into full effect, the Laws for the Regulation of Slaves—Legionary Commandants have been permitted to order out Patrols whenever they shall deem it necessary, and it seems advisable that such should Occasionally be used altho' no suspicions might occur—not unnecessarily to harass the Men, but *more* Strongly to impress the Negroes that we are never off our Guard.

Noncommissioned Officers or others having the order of Patrols, should be specially instructed as Circumstances may Require—and Cautiously to avoid all Violence other than may be absolutely necessary for the apprehending and safe Keeping of Delinquents, and security of the peace.

Some Complaints have been made to the Governour of cruel and Barbarous usage practiced towards Slaves, under a pretended Authority, and which he highly disapproves:

The Military Authority only can Constitute the Legal Patrols, and the evil Consequences of Suffering this Power to be usurped are so obvious that officers will Consider it their Special Duty to guard against and Report Offenders.

Company and Legionary alarm Posts should be assigned to which the Men are to be directed to Repair, in Case of Domestic disturbance and Receive their Instructions from the senior officer present according to the Rules of War—And Communications must be made as early as Possible, to the proper Legionary Commandants, and the Commander in Chief.

The firing of three Guns with an interval of half a Minute between each Discharge is to be Considered as the Legionary Alarm by night or by Day. . . .

VI

The Economy of the West

14. Road and River Transportation

UNTIL the development of railroads and canals, the movement of people and goods in the West depended on roads and particularly rivers. The early Indian trails and traces gradually gave way to improved roads, built often at the expense of the federal government. In the 1750's British troops under Generals Braddock and Forbes opened the earliest roads from Maryland and Pennsylvania west across the Alleghanies to the upper reaches of the Ohio. As shown by the following letter from the Quartermaster General to Lieutenant Frederick L. Griffith, in the Natural Archives, War Department (printed in Carter (ed.), Territorial Papers of the United States, XX, 187–189), the American army continued such work.

Quartermaster General to Lieutenant Griffith, January 27th, 1826

SIR,

You have been selected to superintend the making of a road from a point on the West Bank of the river Mississippi, opposite the town of Memphis in the state of Tennessee, to Little Rock in the Territory of Arkansas, authorized by an act of Congress approved the 31st of January 1824.—Enclosed is a copy of the report of the Commissioners who surveyed the route, with a copy of the plot of the survey.

The road is to be opened in reaches staked out as straight as practicable, keeping in view the general direction of the survey, in the ascent and declivities of hills, and other localities, which cause a necessary deviation from a straight line. It is to be at least twenty four feet wide throughout, and all timber, brushwood, and other rubbish or impediments, are to be removed from it, and all holes within its limits are to be filled with earth. The stumps must be cut as low to the ground as practicable, their height in no instance to exceed two thirds of their diameter, they should be hollowed

towards the centre in cutting them to retain the rain and mois-
ture. Marshy or swampy ground must be causewayed with poles
or split timber, from five to eight inches in diameter at the smallest
end, laid down compactly, side by side across the direction of the
road the causeways to be eighteen feet wide, secured at each side
with heavy timbers or riders firmly and securely staked down.
Ditches four feet wide and three feet deep are to be dug on each
side of the causeways, and the earth and sand taken therefrom to
be thrown upon the causeway so as to render it convex or highest
in the centre—and if the swamps or other grounds be of such a
nature as not to afford earth sufficient to cover the causeways at
least eighteen inches in the centre and six inches at the sides, a
sufficiency is to be brought from other places—At proper distances
in long causeways, or through very wet ground, open log bridges
are to be constructed to let the water pass freely through Where
any separate causeway shall exceed seventy yards in length, it must
be open in the centre or at each distance of seventy yards, to the
width of twenty feet.

The hills on the route are to be dug down and wound round in
such a manner as to make them practicable for carriages or loaded
waggons.

All streams, branches, Creeks, lagoons and rivers, except [blank]
are to be bridged in the most substantial manner—if not more than
ten feet wide with strong and permanent log abutments for the
floor beams to rest upon—if more than ten feet wide with staunch
frame bridges built upon trestles or arches none of which are to be
more than fourteen feet apart—the main timbers of the bridges are
not to be less than twelve by twelve inches, squared & hewed, &
where the uprights are twenty feet in heighth, measuring from the
mudsill to the cap sill, they are to be fourteen by sixteen inches
squared and hewed—The mud sills are to be logs not less than two
feet in diameter hewed on the upper and lower sides, the bark to be
taken off the other two sides, and to extend at least four feet at each
end beyond the exterior sides of the uprights—the uprights are to be
firmly secured into the mud sills and cap sills by mortices and
tenons with two pins in each, and to be firmly braced with timbers
of five inches squared and hewed with mortices and tennons
pinned in like manner. The floor beams of the bridges are to be
four in number, one on each side of the bridge resting at each
end of the cap sill, and immediately over the uprights and the

others between them equidistant from them and from each other —The flooring of the frame bridges is to be of sawed plank three inches thick or of hewed puncheons from three to five inches thick the other bridges may be covered with split or hewed puncheons of the same thickness—the bridges are to be twelve feet wide in the clear—that is twelve feet measuring from the exterior sides of the cap sill—the planks or puncheons are to be securely pinned to the beams at each end—no timber is to be used in the bridges, either under the water, or exposed to the air, but that which is known to be durable.

The bridges are to be built so high above the water that no part thereof from bank to bank shall ever be exposed to danger from the highest freshets—Good and staunch hand rails are to be affixed to the bridges. Such small streams as are never deep enough in freshets to obstruct carriages in passing, and have firm sandy bottoms, with firm banks, may be dug down and left as fords.

You will proceed without delay to Memphis, or some other convenient point near the route of the proposed road to make contracts for opening it. Of the appropriation made by Congress for that purpose there remains unexpended $11.674 $^{18}/_{100}$ if that sum be sufficient to complete the work, contracts will be made for the whole distance—if not, then for so much as the balance of the appropriation will complete.

Public notice must be given for proposals and in order to increase competition, and to enable persons of limited means to become bidders, it is advisable that the road be let out in small sections—no single contract, therefore, shall be made for more than ten miles, and in all cases the lowest responsible bid will be accepted for any distance exceeding three miles. Should the bids in your judgment all be too high they should all be rejected.

Each contract must stipulate that the contractor is to be under your direction or that of some other authorized agent of this Department, in everything relating to the road; & reserve the right to examine it as it progresses, and of annulling it, should the contractor not proceed according to his contract, or should he disregard instructions relative to it.

Advances being prohibited by law, no money can be paid on any contract until the work stipulated be performed; but should any individual contract to make more than one section of the road, he may be paid for them as they be completed and received. . . .

The Mississippi and Ohio Rivers

THE MAJOR arteries for the lifeblood of the western economy were the Mississippi and Ohio rivers, on whose waters were found a variety of craft. The following account from Estwick Evans, A Pedestrious Tour . . . Through the Western States and Territories During . . . 1818 . . . (Concord, N.H., 1819) was reprinted in Thwaites (ed.), Early Western Travels, VIII, 256–257. Evans traveled by boat thirty-five days from Pittsburgh to New Orleans.

The boats which float upon the river Ohio are various:—from the ship of several hundred tons burthen, to the mere skiff. Very few if any very large vessels, however, are now built at Pittsburgh, or indeed at any other place on the Ohio. They were formerly built on this river, particularly at Pittsburgh and Marietta; but the difficulties incident to getting them to the ocean, have rendered such undertakings unfrequent.

An almost innumerable number of steam boats, barks, keels, and arks, are yearly set afloat upon this river, and upon its tributary streams. The barks are generally about one hundred tons burthen, have two masts, and are rigged as schooners, and hermaphrodite brigs. The keels have, frequently, covered decks, and sometimes carry one mast. These and also the barks are sometimes rowed and sometimes moved up the river by poling, and by drawing them along shore with ropes. The flat boat or ark is of a clumsy construction; but very burthensome. Its foundation consists of sills like those of a house, and to these is tunneled a floor of plank. The sides are of boards loosely put together, and the top is covered in the same way. The bottom of the boat, and so much of the sides as come in contact with the water, are caulked. Some of this kind of boat will carry four or five hundred barrels of flour, besides considerable quantities of bacon, cheese, and other produce. On the deck of the ark are two large oars, moving on pivots, and at the stern there is a large stearing oar. The progress of the ark is principally in floating with the current; and the oars are seldom used excepting for the purpose of rowing ashore.

The business carried on by boats, on the Ohio and Mississippi, is immense. The freight of goods up and down these rivers is high; and the freighting business here is exceedingly profitable. No property pays so great an interest as that of steam boats on these rivers. A trip of a few weeks yields one hundred per cent upon the capital employed.

The arks, and, generally speaking, the keels, when they reach New-Orleans, seldom return up the river again. The former are sold for lumber.

The current of the Ohio is about four miles an hour. That of the Mississippi is rather quicker.

James Hall

A MORE picturesque account of the river traffic was given by the Englishman James Hall in his Letters from the West, originally published in London 1828. The following extracts are from pp. 47–49, 87–88, 229–231, 323–324.

I left Pittsburgh in a keel boat of about forty-five tons burthen, laden with merchandise, and navigated by eight or ten of those "half-horse and half-alligator" gentry, commonly called *Ohio boatmen*, whose coarse drollery, I foresee already, will afford us some amusement. There is a small cabin in the stern of the boat, which is occupied by two females—not high born damsels, nor yet young nor lovely; one is the wife of a decent shoemaker, the other is Crispin's maiden sister, and both are verging into the "sear and yellow leaf." I could wish them more attractive, for I already begin to feel romantic, and could find it in my heart to be very gallant; but I fear that after descanting on the silent beauties of nature, or the noisy revels of my male companions, I shall have to confess, that "all the rest is *leather*." My state room is in the bow of the boat, and is formed by leaving a vacancy, large enough for a bed and chair, among the boxes and barrels which encompass me. I have an excellent bedstead, composed of packages and parcels, so disposed as to receive a comfortable mattress, and here I snore among British goods and domestic manufactures, as composedly as if neither of those articles had ever caused us one moment's angry discussion. The ample surface of a huge box is devoted to the functions of a table, and my fare is drawn from a small store provided by myself, and consisting of such articles as are easy of preparation. Of the culinary department, I cannot speak in high praise. The cook is an Irish lad, who says he is "a cobbler by trade, and a republican by profession," as careless and as frisky as any of his countrymen, and withal as dirty a wight as you shall meet with in a summer day. But the captain declares that "Richards is as willing a soul as ever lived," which I suppose must make amends for all deficiencies. The deck or roof of the boat affords ample room for a promenade. . . .

To-day we passed two large rafts lashed together, by which simple conveyance several families from New England were transporting themselves and their property to the land of promise in the western woods. Each raft was eighty or ninety feet long, with a small house erected on it; and on each was a stack of hay, round which several horses and cows were feeding, while the paraphernalia of a farm-yard, the ploughs, waggons, pigs, children, and poultry, carelessly distributed, gave to the whole more the appearance of a permanent residence, than of a caravan of adventurers seeking a home. A respectable looking old lady, with *spectacles on nose*, was seated on a chair at the door of one of the cabins, employed in knitting; another female was at the wash-tub; the men were chewing their tobacco, with as much complacency as if they had been in "the land of steady habits," [Connecticut] and the various family avocations seemed to go on like clock-work. In this manner these people travel at a slight expense. They bring their own provisions; their raft floats with the current; and honest Jonathan, surrounded with his scolding, grunting, squalling, and neighing dependants, floats to the *point proposed* without leaving his own fire-side; and on his arrival there, may step on shore with his house, and commence business, like a certain grave personage, who, on his marriage with a rich widow, said he had "nothing to do but to walk in and hang up his hat." . . .

Before the introduction of steam-boats upon this river, its immense commerce was chiefly carried on by means of *barges*—large boats, calculated to descend as well as to ascend the stream, and which required many hands to navigate them. Each barge carried from thirty to forty boatmen, and a number of these boats frequently sailed in company. The arrival of such a squadron at a small town was the certain forerunner of riot. The boatmen, proverbially lawless and dissolute, were often more numerous than the citizens, and indulged, without restraint, in every species of debauchery, outrage, and mischief. Wherever vice exists will be found many to abet and to take advantage of its excesses; and these towns were filled with the wretched ministers of crime. Sometimes, the citizens, roused to indignation, attempted to enforce the laws; but the attempt was regarded as a declaration of war, which arrayed the offenders and their allies in hostility; the inhabitants were obliged to unite in the defence of each other, and the contest usually terminated in the success of that party which had least to lose, and were most prodigal of life and careless of consequences. The rapid emigration to this country was beginning to afford these towns such an increase of population as would have ensured their ascendancy over the despots of the river, when the introduction of steam-boats at once effected a revolution.

The substitution of machinery for manual labour, occasioned a vast diminution in the number of men required for the river navigation. A steam-boat, with the same crew as a barge, will carry ten times the burthen, and perform her voyage in a fifth part of the time required by the latter. The bargemen infested the whole country, by stopping frequently, and often spending their nights on shore; while the steam-boats pass rapidly from one large port to another, making no halt but to receive or discharge merchandise, at intermediate places. The commanders of steam-boats are men of character; property to an immense amount is intrusted to their care; their responsibility is great; and they are careful of their own department, and of the conduct of those under their controul. The number of boatmen is therefore not only greatly reduced, in proportion to the amount of trade, but a sort of discipline is introduced among them, while the increase of population has enabled the towns to maintain their police. . . .

In descending the river, three different descriptions of boats are at the service of the voyager—the steam-boat, the keel, and the flat bottom. The steam-boats, which are numerous, are strong, beautiful, and swift, and are provided with excellent accommodations; but these can only run when the water is high, and this mode of conveyance is in some cases too expensive for the circumstances of the emigrant. In either of these events, the other boats are resorted to. The keel is a long, sharp vessel, drawing but little water; when loaded, the hull is nearly all immersed, but there is a deck or roof, about six feet high, covered on all sides so as to exclude the weather, and leaving only a passage of about a foot wide, which is called the running board, along the gun-wale, and a small space at the stem and stern. This deck, or roof, affords an admirable lounge in pleasant weather, but at other times the passenger is limited to very narrow bounds below; the oars, which are placed at the bow, are from eight to twelve in number, and are used only in descending the river. By means of these the boat is propelled at the rate of two or three miles an hour faster than the current, which has an average velocity of about three miles. The oars are plied during the day, and at night the boat is suffered to float, with a man at the helm, and one at the bow to look out, except in those parts of the river where the navigation is difficult, and where they always lay by for daylight. A hundred miles in twenty-four hours is accomplished with ease. In ascending the stream these boats are propelled with poles, and the passage is very tedious, seldom averaging more than from ten to twenty miles per day.

The flat-bottom boat is a mere raft, with sides and a roof; but it is more roomy and convenient than the keel, if well built and tight, as indeed they mostly are. An immense oar is placed on the roof on each side near the bow, (which has given these boats the nick-name of "broad horns,") and another at the stern. These are used only to direct the course of the flat, which is allowed to float with the current, and thus she pursues her voyage, like man on his earthly pilgrimage, to that undiscovered country from whose bourne no traveller of her species ever returns; for, being calculated to stem the current, she is useless after she has reached her destination, except as so much lumber.

William Cooper Howells

WILLIAM COOPER HOWELLS *in his* Recollections of Life in Ohio From 1813 to 1840 *(Cincinnati, Ohio, 1895), pp. 73–75, tells of the steamboats and their arrival at a river town.*

This was the period when steamboats were beginning to take their place in the navigation of the Ohio, and when the stream was full they made occasional trips up and down the river. Their appearance would create a great excitement along the banks, and at the towns and villages their arrival and landing were great occasions. The citizens turned out, and civic ceremonies were observed between those in command of the boat and those in command of the town. At Steubenville they had a . . . little cannon, with which they always fired salutes on these occasions; and the steamboats also carried a gun, with which they announced their arrivals and purpose landing. On the departure of a boat the like ceremony was observed. I remember, on one occasion, I was in town, in 1820 (in March, I suppose, from its being cold weather), when a steam-boat was said to be seen far down the river, and the people were gathered in groups to discuss the subject. At one tavern where there was a kind of lookout upon the roof, a man was stationed with a spy-glass to report progress. He announced the approach, which was very slow, as there was a strong current, with the opinion that there was something wrong with the machinery, as she was about to land. This cast dismay over the crowd, and there was a general rush for the river bank, to see what could be learned there. But she crept along up the shore till about a mile and a half below town, where she stopped; when there was a grand rush of men and big boys through the mud down the river bank to see the steamer, as if there never had been and never would be another. From the landing several salutes were fired, but received no answer. The engine was out of order, and when the curious crowd arrived the steamboatmen threw out a cable, by which the people towed the boat into port.

These steamboats were a queer style of water-craft, as they had not assumed the forms that were afterward found to be suited to the river navigation. Their builders copied the models of ships adapted to deep water, and the boats all drew too much water to be available in the dry season, so that they really could not be used on the upper Ohio more than about three months in the year. They looked just like a small ship without masts. Some of them were of peculiar models, and all had very little power in comparison with later boats. Very few of them could make over two or three miles against the stream when it was strong. When Fulton commenced steamboat building, he patented the side paddle-wheels, and held a monopoly of that form of boat. This led to an evasion in many of the western boats, which consisted of placing a wheel on each side of the keel at the stern of the vessel, so that the wheels were out of sight except from behind. The present stern wheels on river boats are a later and very different invention, and served a different purpose, being designed to place the wheel out of the current and clear the boat of the drag of its eddy. The first boats had no more decking than a common sailing vessel.

The business of the country was then very small, and few boats served the purpose. The habit of carrying off the produce of the country to New Orleans in flat-boats continued for a long time after the steamers were introduced, as being cheaper and better adapted to the seasons of shipping. It was only after steamers had become very common, growing in numbers with the country, that they took the business. It was some time before boats could obtain a proper supply of fuel. They all burned wood, and it took time to establish wood-yards. It often happened that crews of boats would have to land and cut wood, and it was very common for them to buy a piece of fence on the banks and use the rails for fuel.

15. Western Farming

THE "BUSINESS" of the western country was not in fact—as "small" as Howells remembered, as this account given in 1822 by François André Michaux, Travels to the West of the Alleghany Mountains reveals. The following extract is from the reprint in Thwaites (ed.) Early Western Travels, III, 239–241.

The harvest of 1802 was so plentiful in Kentucky, that in the month of August, the time that I was at Lexin[g]ton, corn did not bring more than eighteen pence per bushel, (about two shillings per hundred weight). It had never been known at so low a price. Still this fall was not only attributed to the abundance of the harvest, but also on account of the return of peace in Europe. They are convinced, in the country, that at this price the culture of corn cannot support itself as an object of commerce; and that in order for the inhabitants to cover their expense the barrel of flour ought not to be sold at New Orleans for less than four or five dollars.

In all the United States the flour that they export is put into slight barrels made of oak, and of an uniform size. In Kentucky the price of them is about three-eighths of a dollar, (fifteen pence). They ought to contain ninety-six pounds of flour, which takes five bushels of corn, including the expenses of grinding.

The freightage of a boat to convey the flour to Low Louisiana costs about a hundred dollars. They contain from two hundred and fifty to three hundred barrels, and are navigated by five men, of whom the chief receives a hundred dollars for the voyage, and the others fifty each. They take, from Louisville, where nearly the whole embarkations are made, from thirty to thirty-five days to go to New Orleans. They reckon it four hundred and thirty-five miles from Louisville to the *embouchure* of the Ohio, and about a thousand miles thence to New Orleans, which makes it, upon the whole, a passage of fourteen hundred and thirty-five miles; and these boats have to navigate upon the river a space of eight or nine hundred miles without meeting with any plantations. A part of the crew return to Lexin[g]ton by land, which is about eleven hundred miles, in forty or forty-five days. This journey is extremely unpleasant, and those who dread the fatigues of it return by sea. They embark at New Orleans for New York and Philadelphia, whence they return to Pittsburgh, and thence go down the Ohio as far as Kentucky.

An inspector belonging to the port of Louisville inserted in the Kentucky Gazette of the 6th of August 1802, that 85,570 barrels of flour, from the 1st of January to the 30th of June following, went out of that port to Low Louisiana. More than two thirds of this quantity may be considered as coming from the state of Kentucky, and the rest from Ohio and the settlements situated upon the rivers Monongahela and Alleghany. The spring and autumn are principally the seasons in which this exportation is made. It is almost null in summer, an epoch at which almost all the mills are stopped for the want of water. Rye and oats come up also extremely well in Kentucky. The rye is nearly all made use of in the distilling of whiskey, and the oats as food for horses, to which they give it frequently in little bunches from two to three pounds, without being threshed.

The culture of tobacco has been greatly extended within these few years. The temperature of the climate, and the extraordinary fertility of the soil gives, in that respect, to this state, a very great advantage over that of Virginia; in consequence of which tobacco and corn form the principal branch of its commerce. It exports annually several thousand hogsheads, from a thousand to twelve hundred pounds each. The price of it is from two to three dollars per hundred weight.

Hemp, both raw and manufactured, is also an article of exportation. In the same year, 1802, there has been sent out of the country, raw 42,048 pounds, and 2402 hundred weight, converted into cables and various sorts of cordage.

Many of the inhabitants cultivate flax. The women manufacture linen of it for their families, and exchange the surplus with the trades-people for articles imported from Europe. These linens, though coarse, are of a good quality; yet none but the inferior inhabitants use them, the others giving a preference to Irish linens, which comprise a considerable share of their commerce. Although whiter, they are not so good as our linens of Bretagne. The latter would have found a great sale in the western states, had it not been for yielding Louisiana; since it is now clearly demonstrated that the expense of conveying goods which go up the river again from New Orleans to Louisville is not so great as that from Philadelphia to Limestone.

A Northwest Farm

HOWELLS, Recollections of Life in Ohio From 1813 to 1840, pp. 115–116, 136–139, 154–157, has a detailed account of the small family-sized farm in the Northwest.

In that part of the country where the oak—mostly white oak—prevailed, the land was all cleared by the process of "deadening": that is, the small stuff was grubbed out by the roots; that too large to grub, and less than a foot in diameter, was cut down and burned up on the spot; and the larger trees were girdled by chopping them round with an axe, cutting through the bark and sap-wood (which killed them so that they put forth no leaves, or if in leaf, withered), and left standing. This was an easy way to clear the land and get in a crop of almost any grain. To have cut down the trees and cleared them off the ground, would have cost more labor than the new settlers could have afforded, and with their means it could not be done. After they had grubbed the bushes, chopped off the small trees and deadened the large ones and burned off the brush, they plowed and put in the crop. From that time forward there was a continual dropping from the deadened trees, first of leaves, twigs and bark, then of the larger limbs, and lastly the trunk, which would fall in any way the wind or its weight threw it.

These dead trees would not all disappear from a field in less than fifteen or twenty years. . . . The clearing-up consisted of gathering the limbs and chunks and laying them at intervals across the fallen trunks, so as to burn them off. This was easier and quicker than chopping the trunks into lengths, as by attending to them well two or three boys could burn off more logs in a day than a man could chop in a month. The burnt-off logs were afterward rolled

together and with the rubbish of other kinds burned up. The burn-
ing had to be done when the logs were dry, and it required care
to keep the fire under control. If it was windy it was liable to get
into the fences or the dry leaves of the adjoining woods, on the
grass or stubble of fields, and do great mischief. . . .

The farmers lived simply. . . . Most of them owned the land
they lived upon and all worked with their own hands, whether they
hired help or not. The houses and improvements depended upon
the length of time they had been on the place. A man who had
just settled was not expected to have much of a house, or other
buildings. The first care was to get up what would do, and this was
usually a good sized log cabin of round logs, covered with clap-
boards; that is, split pieces, four feet long and six inches wide, and
weighted down on the roof with logs. A barn of the same materials
was built, as soon as possible, for the protection of the crops and
animals. Such barns . . . were mostly made by putting up two log
pens—say eighteen feet square, that is, all the logs eighteen feet
long—at a distance of about eighteen feet apart; the pens were
carried up to about twelve feet high, when logs were placed so as
to connect the two pens under one roof, which would cover a
building of eighteen by fifty-four feet on the ground. The inter-
vening space served for the barn, or thrashing-floor, and was usually
closed, as soon as it could be done, with large double doors at front
and back.

The barns were, of course, very open, which, for stowing grain,
was no inconvenience, since the openings afforded ventilation and
prevented the grain or hay from being mow-burnt. In the intermediate space the grain was usually thrashed by hand with a flail,
until the farm was large enough to make it necessary to use horses
to tread it out. It was the custom, also, for laboring men to thrash
grain for the tenth bushel, as their compensation; and it was pretty
hard-earned grain at that. Ten bushels of wheat was a hard days'
thrashing, though rye, barley and oats were easier done; and a
good hand would knock out twenty to twenty-five bushels of oats.

The *flail* was a peculiarly made instrument, and very hard to get
the hang of. It was formed of two sticks, one about like a broom-
handle, and four feet long, the other near three feet long, with a
hole in the end of it, round, and an inch and a half in diameter.
The handle was very smooth and made with a button-like knob

on the end, away from the hand, and a groove around it to receive a cord, which was tied around the handle so that the handle would turn in it. The thrashing part, or blade, as they sometimes called it, having a hole in the end was tied to the handle by a link of cord. This made a loose and changeable joint, which allowed the whole length of the blade to strike the grain at once. It might be compared to a whip with a club for a lash. The handling of it required skill, and to hit yourself on the top of the head with it was the easiest thing imaginable.

The lower part of the two ends of the barn were usually fitted up for horse and cow stables, and the upper part as well as the space over the thrashing-floor was used for mowing away hay and grain. When the farms were small, this room would suffice. If not the surplus would be stacked up in the barnyard. The thrashing was mostly done in the winter, and, if possible, on cold, dry days. In wet weather the grain was hard to beat out of the straw. Thrashing was good, hearty winter work, and it had to be very cold, indeed, if you could not keep warm at it. The winnowing of the grain from the chaff was mostly done in a primitive manner, for it was only a well-to-do farmer who could afford a fanning mill. A very common method of clearing grain was to rake out all the short straw and lighter chaff after thrashing; then two persons would take a sheet, which they doubled into an oblong shape, and each standing opposite to the other, they took hold, one with the right hand uppermost and the other with the left up, and with the other hands they clutched the edge of the sheet about two-thirds of the width from the top as it hung from the upper hands. They would then give it a motion a little like the blade of an oar in rowing. This produced a good blast, before which the grain and chaff was shaken down from a coarse sieve, when the chaff was blown away, and the clean wheat fell on the floor. This winnowing with the sheet was hard work, and if there was much to be done, hands were changed; the women of the family would be called on to assist, and if, as was often the case, there were two or three lusty girls about the house, and big boys, they would soon do up a thrashing of grain, and have a jolly time besides.

Where the country had only been a few years settled, and where the farms were still being opened up, the families were mostly young; that is, the children nearly all in their minority, so that the farmer himself and one or two big boys made up the laboring strength of the farm; and for an extra lift at any time, the wife or older daughter would be called on to help, and sometimes they would assist in planting and hoeing the corn, raking the grain or hay in harvest. The rule was, that whoever had the strength to work, took hold and helped. If the family was mostly girls, they regularly helped their father in all the lighter farm work. . . . In all that country there were small streams, which though they had some kind of mills upon them, were sure to go dry or freeze up when grinding was wanted. One of the difficulties was that the new farmers generally ran out of grain, just before harvest, when there was plenty of water; and as soon as the wheat ripened grinding had to be done, by which time the water was dried up. Steam-power had not been introduced in a small way, and there was no sub-stitute for water but horse-power. Accordingly they used it for mills, and every here and there some thrifty fellow built a horse-mill. A big shed was put up, and covered in, to protect a single pair of very light and cheap mill-stones—sometimes second-hand, from a water-mill—and a great wheel on an upright shaft, to which four sweeps were fixed, for the attachment of horses. The wheel was overhead and armed with cogs to transmit the power to the mill. Sometimes they would have a cheap bolting apparatus, extem-porized from book-muslin, and sometimes they had none, and if you ground corn it had to be sifted at home. And these mills, though they punctually took toll, did not furnish their own power. Each customer took a couple of horses with harness on, and hitched them on to the mill to make the power. Sometimes they would meet others at mill, when they would unite their teams, putting on six to eight horses, and then it would go pretty merrily. But it took about so much power, either in time or teams to run the mill, and if you joined you had to wait till the united grists were ground. . . . Two horses could turn a mill if the horses were stout and the mill was light, but if it was otherwise, it was of no use to talk of the mills of the gods grinding slowly—these were slower still, and they ground exceedingly coarse. But the mills were a wonderful place to gossip, for you had to be there all day to get a moderate grist done; and there was time to hear and tell a great deal. . . .

When I look back to those times I am struck with the scarcity of money, and the difficulty of getting it, and the expedients of barter that were resorted to. For instance, at the stores there were articles that they called cash articles, that you could not buy without money. These were mostly tea, coffee, etc. Leather, iron, powder, lead, and like articles were also of this class. These things could not be bartered for with the produce of the country, except a few products that were treated as of cash value. Among them were linen, cloth, feathers, beeswax, deerskins, and furs, which were not too heavy to transport, and would be taken by wholesale dealers in payment for goods. Among the people in the country trade was conducted on a grain basis. Thus, a day's work in harvest was paid with a bushel of wheat or a bushel and a half of corn or rye or buckwheat. The shoemakers, tailors, blacksmiths, etc., took their pay in grain—the customer always finding the leather, cloth, or iron, and the mechanic doing the work.

We were thirty-five miles from the Ohio, the nearest point where there were merchant mills, and cash was paid for wheat. Consequently, the price of wheat with us was the cost of transportation less than the price of the river. Fifty cents a bushel was a great price for it at the river; and, as two horses and a man were required for four days to make the journey, in good weather, with thirty-five or forty bushels of wheat, and a great deal longer if the roads were bad, it was not to be expected that we could realize more than twenty-five cents in cash for it. But there was no sale for it in cash. The nominal price for it in trade was usually thirty cents, and the storekeepers took it at that rate, putting enough on the goods to make it up. I remember once taking a load of wheat to the store, in our wagon, for a man who had worked for it, which he sold for twenty-five cents, and took his pay in iron at twelve and one-half cents a pound.

We were situated half way between the Ohio river and the Ohio canal, when it came to be made, which was in 1825-6-7-8. That part of it nearest to us was in process of building in 1826-7, and this afforded work and money to the men who could do it during the winter, at prices they seemed glad to get and thought they were doing well to take. Hands were paid eight to ten dollars a month for chopping, digging, etc., receiving board and lodgings in addition; but every wet day was counted out, the laborer losing his time and the contractor the board. In this way, it would take all winter to make about two months time. It was hard earned money, but it was esteemed worth the labor. There were certain things for which money was required to be raised, the chief of which were taxes; and to these the ready money was applied.

16. Merchants and Merchandising

THE FOLLOWING *selection from Dwight L. Smith* (ed.), The Western Journals of John May, Ohio Company Agent and Business Venturer *(Cincinnati ,Ohio, 1961), pp. 137–141, relates the venture of an early merchant in the western country. A native of Massachusetts, May had a difficult time getting his store goods shipped to Baltimore and then 247 miles overland to Pittsburgh. The tenuous nature of early commerce in the region is well illustrated here. This version is from a manuscript in the Historical and Philosophical Society of Ohio.*

Thursday, September 10: Remarks on my expedition the season of 1789. Sett out from Boston 23rd of April/ had an agreable time to Baltimore where I found the Goods in good order. here an unluckey matter took place. I was obliged to pay better than thirty pounds Dutey [freight and storage costs] on merchandise or leave them behind. I thought this was hard luck whether it really was so or nott I am not at this time able to determine/ at any rate it deprived me of my travelling money. flour at Baltimore was Quick Market and so high prices the Waggoner Chose to Bring flour to Markett rather than Ingage to go over the Mountains. this made it impossable to procure Waggons to answer our purpose. I however engaged them to Carry our goods about 90 miles to Shippensberge where we stored them. Rode severall miles round and finally made a bargain with one Daniel Elliott to Carry the good[s] to Fort pitt or Redston[e] but when the time came he Did Not appear but sent word he Could not perform agreeable to his promise. Mr Breck and my self was at that time upwards of one hundred mil[e]s ahead and Downer was oblige to Contract anew/ this made a delay of 10 Days but finally the Waggons came on and we made out to gitt within 4 miles of Redstone, when a Terrible Tornado had laid prostrate all the forrests round that place as much as four miles Wide. this was an impenetrable Barrier which we could not pass. after reconoitering near a Whole Day we ordered the Waggons to go Down Little redstone, a small Creek that em[p]ties into the

manongohala 5 Miles below Redston Old fort [Brownsville, Pa.]/
here we put our goods into a Deserted Cabbin, within ¼ mile
of the River. next Day the Doctor and I went thro' the fields of
Devastation, to Sam Jacksons a Distance of 4 miles. here I bough[t]
a Kentuc Boat which was brought Down the next Monday and
tuesday putt our goods on Board. open[e]d store and did buisness
all this while the River was falling amazeingly/ we Dropt out at the
mouth of the Creek and the next Day hered [heard] the Downfall
[in the price] of gensang [gensing root]/ this was totall Confusion
to my former plans; thought it absolutely necessary to wait for a
Confermation of the affair. this I did under pretence that the river
was to Low to go Down for I did not want the inhabitants, who are
Verry Inquisitive, to know my Drift—however, the river did in fact
gitt so Low in a few Days that it was impossable for a boat as bigg
as ours to go over the Riffles/ this Continued a long time. and after
being confined upward of 30 Days on the Manongahola River, and
having the disagreeable Intelligence about sang Confirm'd I form'd
a plan of reconoitering the Countrey that Lay betwixt me and
Muskingim—and leaving direction for the Boat to come Down the
River should the waters rise in my Absence. On Wedness the 8th
July I set out by Land and afoot/ reach'd Washington at 2 oClock.
here spent the afternoon and night/ there are a number of stores
in this little place/ it is a County Town, and Conterall [central]
between a number of Rivers. I crittically obberv'd there manner of
Trade here and found it would not answer to Bring our goods to
this place. the next morning I stood for the mouth of Buffalow,
and reach'd it by Sunsett. here is a Little Town a building right at
the Confluance of this creek with the Ohio—they begun to build
only this spring and there is Nine Midling houses erected, and will
in a short time be a good place for Trade. here I stayd severall days
waiting for a passage Down the River. got acquainted with a Number of stout Wealthey farmer that Live back sum 7 or 8. miles/
these men raise a vast Deal of produce and will be of grate Consequence to the little Town. I had strong thoughts of bringing sum
or all of my goods to this place, however at Lenth I got a passage
Down to Muskingum, wher I found them poor and proud. they
wanted every thing but had nothing to pay with so that I durst
not Venture my self with Merchandize to this place, thro fearing
that they would prevail on me to lett them have good[s] without
pay—Kentuckey, is fill'd with Merchant[s], that know not what to

Do with there goods. there darling Gensang being Done; I am Tould by them that know, that there is 10 traders gone to that place this summer where ther was one last year, and it is the opinion of People in generall that more than two thirds of them will be ruin'd by this summers buisness

my situation was Verry disagreeable/ to stay with my effects in the Mongoho or take a store on Ither of its banks it wood not do/ I could not vend my goods and receive pay, until winter, and then it would be in produce which I could Not dispose of until spring or summer or perhaps go to New Orliens/ to go to Kentuckey was going further from home and no better prospect besides a grate probability of an Indian war to go to Muskingum afraied of being cosin'd out of the whole. therefore I bent my mind seriously on Wheeling. . . .

. . . at noon of ye 11th of august arived safely at Wheeling/ the next day unloaded the Bigg Boat and put up the goods in the store. I was induced to take this position from three motivs Vizt it is a pleasant and agreeable situation, a good New Store on a high bank of ye River Ohio, with a beautifull Island in front three Miles in Len[g]th/ from my store I have a delightfull prospect of this Island and Two miles down the river. I am 96 miles from Pitt and 84 from Marietta and 31 from Washington [Pa.]. here all the boats going too or from any of the settlements ither above or below allway stop here/ I am handy to the farmers and can watch the marketts of Marietta and send them suplies of provisions when wanted which is often the case.

Marketing and Credit Arrangements

WESTERN merchants were dependent on New Orleans and eastern houses for marketing and credit. The arrangements were often haphazard, as the following extracts from the Draper Collection (21CC4–5 and 16), The State Historical Society of Wisconsin, show.

J[AMES] W[IER] TO JOHN CLAY AT NEW ORLEANS

Lexington, 7 June [1805]

SIR

I have shipped on board Taylor & Lynns boat and consigned to you sixty six bales and five Hogsheads spun yarn and sixty cords baling rope. . . .

The yarns I wish ship'd on board some vessel and forwarded to the care of Alexander Henry[,] Philadelphia[,] and advise him thereof as soon as possible that he may affect an Insurance thereon. You will (no doubt) ship the yarns on the best possible terms (say from Nine to thirteen dollars prece). The baling rope I wish sold at N. Orleans for cash, or bartered for some other articles what may suit this Market, say half a ton of Logwood[,] the balance brown sugar and Coffee, and if practicable sent to Louisville. You may reasonably expect the boat in all next month. The bills of landing &c. will accompany her, [I] should be glad to hear from you as soon as convenient, what articles of our produce would pay well at New Orleans and what articles could be obtained in exch[ange] therefore and what probable chance there is generally of sending them up to Louisville. If Tar'd Cordage or Rigging of any description would answer please to give the dimenstion [sic].

WIER TO MESSER. ALEXANDER HENRY & CO.

Lexington, 12th October, 1805

GENT[LEME]N

Your favor of 5th. Ultimo, is to hand, and that of 16th is arrived p[er] this day's mail. I am much disappointed in finding the yarns shipped by Mr. Clay from New Orleans did not arrive in perfect good order, as I had taken every precaution (save that of packing in hhds) to insure its safety, in the first place, by imploying a Gent. of the first respect, ability and experience in that line to ship it to N. Orleans—Certificates of several respectable characters at Louisville testify that the Boat was a superior one, well furnished and in every respect fit for the voyage, and the Master and hands experienced and uncommonaly careful. Altho Mr. Clay signifies that all the reels were damaged except thirteen, he has certainly committed himself by shipping in that condition, for by so doing he has undoubtedly received it from the master of the Boat. I do not know what Kind of acquittal he has given the master of the Boat, not yet having seen him. If the yarns were not damaged on board the Brig I have no doubt but Certificates of proper disinterested persons could be procured to that effect—which would enable me to know when to apply for redress. As soon as it can be done with safety and convenience, I wish the damage of those yearns acertain'd—after w[ch]. you will dispose of them in the manner you may think most advantageous. I am fully sensible of the many obligations I am under to you for the frequent advances you have made on my account—be assured such favors will not be forgotten.

Andrew Jackson to John Hutchings

ANDREW JACKSON was a merchant in Tennessee as early as 1795. By selling lands he was able to import merchandise from Philadelphia. The letter printed below from Bassett (ed.), Correspondence of Andrew Jackson, I, 84–86, illustrates the diverse nature of his western trade.

Knoxville, March 17, 1804

DEAR JACK

On yesterday I reached this place from Jonesborough and found your letter of the 13th. Instant in the post office inclosing the price current at new orleans of all kind of groceries, from which I am certain that we will find a great advantage and saving in laying in all our Groceries, nails, and steel at that place, and perhaps Nankeens. I wish you to make the arangement with Mr Davidson, and I think the boat can reach Nashville from Neworleans against the first of July. this plan will enable us always to convert our cash to beneficial purposes in cumberland, and in case the Boat can reach Nashville against the 10th. or 20th of July it will be as early as our goods can reach there from Philadelphia. I therefore think that the better plan to adopt, is to bring our groceries, nails and steele from Neworleans. From the prices of Deer and Bear skins I think it will be well to sell at Neworleans, the small furs in Nashville. Bear skins sells well in Baltimore, but as our object is to get clear of Debt I think it best not to risque much, and to sell at any market where we can sell to save ourselves.

I am sorry Mr Fisher did not buy the Bear skins, but it may happen that we will receive a better price for them at Neworleans. The iron is delivered at the north fork of Holston, I saw colo. Preston, and also Mr Baker who I had the contract with to carry it to Nashville. he as soon as the iron was delivered declined taking Mr Kings load, in short such was the situation of things I was obliged to agree to receive it, and from Mr Deaderick telling me he would not receive the half I have changed the contract in part, I have agreed to receive five ton of castings in lieu of that much iron, the castings at forty pounds pr ton, this in case the castings reaches the north fork before the water rises. Holston is now rising and I expect the Boat to descend the river in a few days—this expence will have to be met some how. I hope Mr Sewal has returned and has brought some cash and that Capt Campbell has remitted the cash on hand, and that the Debt of Thos Mitchel has been recovered, from this source I hope the amount of the freitage of the iron can be raised which will be $375. if it cannot write me immediately and I will remit what I can to that use, it must be had, and be there at the arival of the Boat. I have stated to Mr Deaderick that he may still have half, and requested him to say to you whether he will receive it or not, if he does only half the above sum will be [have] to be paid by us. write me on the receipt of this letter and inform me whether the sum can be raised or not there and I will in case it cannot send on my certificates for two hundred dollars, and the Ballance in cash. we can make money out of the iron and castings. we must sell for cash if Possible. you will place the money in the hand of Tatam if you can raise it, to whom I have directed Baker to apply. you will have to give Greer a particular charge about the iron to have it all weighed, and get Major Tatam to notify him on its arival. I shall expect you to send me a statement of the amount of cotton shipped to Neworleans by us— as soon as sold send on the Bills to me in Philadelphia, directed to the care of Meeker Denman and Co. . . . I am sorry I wrote Mr. Coffee to come to this place unless he comes on prepared to go on to Philadelphia. . . .

. . . Let me Just repeat, write me about the cash to pay the freightage of the iron, whether it can be raised or not, whether D[eadrick] and Tatam takes one half. send me the amount of our cotton, and a memorandom of goods to be Bot. and lastly, send on the Bills as soon as Possible to me at Philadelphia directed as before, and if Possible purchase they Groceries at Neworleans. You must state to me your determination on this subject and May heaven Preserve you farewell.

P S   Say to Mr Coffee if he is not started that he need not come on unless he intends [to go] on to Philadelphia. Would it not be well to sell as much of the iron at cost, say seven pence pr lb. as would pay the carriage, even at six pence. if Mr Deaderick does not receive half, I think some of the merchants would buy at this price. the ballance we would then have to raise the original cost out of. if cash can not be commanded in hand for it it will sell at

one shilling for cotton by retail and we will have to this time
twelve months to make the cash out of the produce we receive. if
we can have a general assortment of groceries iron salt and so forth
we must make money the ensuing season. resolution and industry with oeconomy will remove mountains. will it not be well to
get the Boat to deliver the iron at my landing instruct Greer accordingly. I wish a house prepared to receive the goods either the
long room of the new building [?] or a house at the lick as you
and Mrs Jackson may conclude.

Instructions to an Overseer

IN THE last decade of the eighteenth century the Austin family moved
to Illinois, where they engaged in extensive lead mining. The following
instructions from Moses Austin to his overseer are taken from Barker
(ed.), The Austin Papers, I, 247–249.

Mine a Burton, Feb[ruar]y the 22nd 1815

Mʳ JOHN S. BRICKEY

I give you the following Memorandum by which you will fully
understand, what I wish you to take under your Charge; and to
which your attention will be Directed.

1ˢᵗ You will make a mess Book in which you will enter this memorandum as a standing order and in which you will enter the names
of each Negroe, in the Mess. The Messes you will number. You
will see that provisions are delivered to each mess both of meat,
and meal, you will see that meal is procured—

2 The regular allowance to each hand is ¾ of a pound of meat
pʳ Day and at the rate of a peck of sifted Indian meal pʳ week. Or
half meal, and half Hominy. potatoes and beans will be given in
lieu of hominy—

3ʳᵈ You will take charge of the Keys of the Meat, and Corn
House, also, the waggon Yard, and see that the corn is properly
divided out, also see that the work oxen, and milk cows are properly
attended to and salted, and that all strange horses, and Cattle are
kept from the wagon and stable yards, and they secured.

4ᵗʰ You will examine each morning and see, that all the hands
not engaged at the mine hill, are at work by sun rise and that they
do their duty; and never suffer your orders to be neglected, or set
aside.

5ᵗʰ You will see that the Cook in the negroe Kitchen keeps it in proper order, and has her meals in due time, that Homony is made ready, and duly provided

6th It has been always my rule to have as much homony made ready the evening as may be wanted the next day—Each in turn to pound a motar of Homony. This must be the rule and the Homony delivered each morning.

7th You will each night before you go to rest examine and see that all strange negroes are ordered away, and the yards closed, and the Cooks Kitchen lock'd. The key may be lodged with Old Jack who will be accountable for the same

Furnace Regulations

8th When the Furnace is out of Blast you will see that the Lead is removed, and the house cleaned out, and made fast, both Doors and windows, and all the Tools collected and placed in a corner of the Furnace. Its the duty of the hands not in the Last Charge to clean up and secure the furnace

9th When the Furnace is in Blast you will see that no strange negroes are suffered to lounge about, but order them away, and make them off. The proper time to Smelt a charge is 18 hours and 20 hours the longest time and for each 2000 pounds of mineral ought to produce 30 to 31 & 32 bars of Lead of 42℔. each. You will observe that proper wood is of the first consequences to Smelt well. You will therefore cause the back door hand to bring in his wood, that is to furnish his Charge, and place it over the furnace, and at the furnace ash hole to be made as dry as possible, and this ought to [be] done as soon as the Charge goes into the furnace, and so remain untill the Charge is nearly finished when it may be used. You will also understand that dry wood is necessary for smelting Lead Ore, Negroes and Whites aught to be prevented, Visiting the furnace nor suffered to remain about the furnace, they draw off the attention of the hands, the furnace tools should be always kept in order and the master of each charge should and must be made accountable for any damage done the furnace and Tools to him you will give any orders you may receive respecting the furnace—

10th You will see that mineral is cleaned and Buckd down to charge the furnace in due time, and also that both the furnace and mineral house are kept clean and nothing wasted, the Charge for the furnace will be 2000^{lb} mineral and aught to be weighed up in time not to detain the work.

11th You will see that all the Tools, such as axes, hoes, plows, and every kind of Tools is taken good care of, and each person that uses them must account for them, and you will remember, that not a Tool can be lent out to any man, on any account whatever. The waggon and carts must be considered under your care, and each waggoner must be accountable for every thing belonging to his waggon. Every thing that may be wanting to keep the waggons in order, and horses also, you will consider under your charge.

12th If any are sick you will let me know, and you will at all times take the utmost care that they be provided for, and treated with Humanity.

13th You will suffer no Drinking or fighting among the negroes without letting me know of it, if you can not stop it yourself, report it to me.

14th You will report to me should it be necessary in time that I may provide such things as may be needed to carry the above regulations into Execution, which I request may be most strictly executed to the utmost of your power.

Plantations on the Lower Mississippi

THE VARIEGATED economy of the West also included plantation-produced staples. Estwick Evans in his Pedestrious Tour—reprinted in Thwaites (ed.), Early Western Travels, VIII, 325–327—left this account of the plantations on the lower Mississippi in 1818.

For about one hundred miles above New-Orleans, both banks of the river are under a high state of cultivation. The country continues thus cultivated for twenty miles below the city. The plantations within these limits are superb beyond description. Some of them resemble villages. The dwelling houses of the planters are not inferior to any in the United States, either with respect to size, architecture, or the manner in which they are furnished. The gardens, and yards contiguous to them, are formed and decorated with much taste. The cotton, sugar, and ware houses are very large, and the buildings for the slaves are well finished. The latter buildings are, in some cases, forty or fifty in number, and each of them will accommodate ten or twelve persons. The plantations are very extensive, and on some of them there are hundreds of negroes. The planters here derive immense profits from the cultivation of their estates. The yearly income from them is from 20,000 to 30,000 dollars. Their produce is sent down to the New-Orleans market, at which place prompt payment in specie is immediately realized. At Natches and New-Orleans, gold and silver are as plenty in the market as any other article. Some of the noted plantations above mentioned are those of Balay, Arnold, Baronge, and Forteus.

The plantations on the Mississippi produce vast quantities of sugar and cotton. The latter article grows in pods, upon a stalk; and the appearance of the latter is not much unlike that of the bean. These pods, when ripe, open; and the cotton is then gathered from the stalk, and separated from the seeds by a machine which will clean 1000 pounds in a day. An acre of land will yield about 800 pounds.

Cotton is sewed in drills about eight feet apart. The seed is thrown in thick; and after they spring, the stalks are thinned so as to make them eighteen inches apart. They are then weeded, and the earth taken from the upper roots, so as to leave them bare. A few weeks after this process, the earth is hoed up to the stalk, and the roots covered. Then there is a third hoeing like the second. If the ground is well prepared, and the growth favourable, the rows of cotton, when fully grown, will nearly meet each other.

The sugar cane is a jointed stalk, not unlike that of corn; and it grows from three to seven feet in length, and from one half inch to an inch in diameter. It is pithy, like the corn stalk, and affords a copious supply of juice. No sweet is less cloying, and no vegetable substance so nutritious as the sugar cane.

Sugar is cultivated by cuttings, set two inches from each other, in drills eight feet apart. Each cutting possesses one joint; and one setting answers for two years. In getting in the harvest the first year, the stalks are cut within about eight inches of the ground. In the production of sugar, the stalks are passed end ways through smooth brass nuts, and the juice thus extracted is boiled down to a thick syrup. It is then put into other vessels, and as it becomes cool, it forms into small grains, and thus becomes sugar. Molasses is produced from the drainings of the sugar; and after this process there is another by distillation; and here rum is obtained. The sugar and molasses of New-Orleans are celebrated for their excellence.

17. Western Industry

CITIES developed at an early date as centers of the western economy, both for marketing produce and for manufacturing. The accounts of Lexington and Pittsburgh in 1802 are from Michaux, Travels to the West of the Alleghany Mountains, reprinted in Thwaites (ed.), Early Western Travels, III, 199–204, 157–160. Pittsburgh twenty years later is from Hall, Letters from the West, pp. 32–35.

Lexington

This town founded in 1780, is the oldest and most wealthy of the three new western states; it contains about three thousand inhabitants.

There are two printing-offices at Lexinton, in each of which a newspaper is published twice a week. Part of the paper is manufactured in the country, and is dearer by one-third than in France. That which they use for writing, originally imported from England, comes by the way of Philadelphia and Baltimore. Two extensive rope walks, constantly in employ, supply the ships with rigging that are built upon the Ohio. On the borders of the little river that runs very near the town several tan-yards are established that supply the wants of the inhabitants. . . .

The want of hands excites the industry of the inhabitants of this country. When I was at Lexinton one of them had just obtained a patent for a nail machine, more complete and expeditious than the one made use of in the prisons at New York and Philadelphia; and a second announced one for the grinding and cleaning of hemp and sawing wood and stones. This machine, moved by a horse or a current of water, is capable, according to what the inventor said, to break and clean eight thousand weight of hemp per day.

The articles manufactured at Lexinton are very passable, and the speculators are ever said to make rapid fortunes, notwithstanding the extreme scarcity of hands. This scarcity proceeds from the inhabitants giving so decided a preference to agriculture, that there are very few of them who put their children to any trade, wanting their services in the field. The following comparison will more clearly prove this scarcity of artificers in the western states: At

Charleston in Carolina, and at Savannah in Georgia, a cabinet-maker, carpenter, mason, tinman, tailor, shoemaker, &c. earns two piastres a day, and cannot live for less than six per week; at New York and Philadelphia he has but one piaster, and it costs him four per week. At Marietta, Lexinton and Nashville, in Tenessea, these workmen earn from one piaster to one and a half a day, and can subsist a week with the produce of one day's labour. Another example may tend to give an idea of the low price of provisions in the western states. The boarding-house, where I lived during my stay at Lexinton, passes for one of the best in the town, and we were profusely served at the rate of two piastres per week. I am informed that living is equally cheap in the states of New England, which comprise Connecticut, Massachusets, and New Hampshire; but the price of labour is not so high, and therefore more proportionate to the price of provisions.

Independent of those manufactories which are established in Lexinton, there are several common potteries, and one or two powder-mills, the produce of which is consumed in the country or exported to Upper Carolina and Low Louisiana. The sulphur is obtained from Philadelphia and the saltpetre is manufactured in the country. . . .

. . . The majority of the inhabitants of Kentucky trade with Lexinton merchants; they receive their merchandize from Philadelphia and Baltimore in thirty-five or forty days, including the journey of two days and a half from Limestone, where they land all the goods destined for Kentucky. The price of carriage is from seven to eight piastres per hundred weight. Seven-tenths of the manufactured articles consumed in Kentucky, as well as in the other parts of the United States, are imported from England; they consist chiefly in coarse and fine jewellery, cutlery, ironmongery, and tin ware; in short, drapery, mercery, drugs, and fine earthenware, muslins, nankeens, tea, &c. are imported directly from India to the United States by the American vessels; and they get from the Carribbees coffee, and various kinds of raw sugar, as none but the poorer class of the inhabitants make use of maple sugar.

The French goods that are sent into this part of the country are reduced to a few articles in the silk line, such as taffetas, silk stockings, &c. also brandies and mill-stones, notwithstanding their enormous weight, and the distance from the sea ports.

From Lexinton the different kinds of merchandize are despatched into the interior of the state, and the overplus is sent by land into Tenessea. It is an easy thing for merchants to make their fortunes; in the first place, they usually have a twelvemonth's credit from the houses at Philadelphia and Baltimore, and in the next, as there are so few, they are always able to fix in their favour the course of colonial produce, which they take in exchange for their goods: as, through the extreme scarcity of specie, most of these transactions are done by way of barter; the merchants, however, use every exertion in their power to get into their possession the little specie in circulation; it is only particular articles that are sold for money, or in exchange for produce the sale of which is always certain, such as the linen of the country, or hemp. Payments in money always bear a difference of fifteen or twenty per cent to the merchant's profits. All the specie collected in the course of trade is sent by land to Philadelphia; I have seen convoys of this kind that consisted of fifteen or twenty horses. The trouble of conveyance is so great that they give the preference to Bank bills of the United States, which bear a discount of two per cent. The merchants in all parts take them, but the inhabitants of the country will not, through fear of their being forged. . . .

Pittsburgh

Pittsburgh has been long considered by the Americans as the key to the western country. . . . It serves as a staple for the different sorts of merchandise that Philadelphia and Baltimore send, in the beginning of spring and autumn, for supplying the states of Ohio, Kentucky, and the settlement of Natches.

The conveyance of merchandise from Philadelphia to Pittsburgh is made in large covered waggons, drawn by four horses two a-breast. The price of carrying goods varies according to the season; but in general it does not exceed six piastres the quintal. They reckon it to be three hundred miles from Philadelphia to Pittsburgh, and the carriers generally make it a journey of from twenty to twenty-four days. The price of conveyance would not be so high as it really is, were it not that the waggons frequently return empty; notwithstanding they sometimes bring back, on their return to Philadelphia or Baltimore, fur skins that come from Illinois or Ginseng, which is very common in that part of Pensylvania.

Pittsburgh is not only the staple of the Philadelphia and Baltimore trade with the western country, but of the numerous settlements that are formed upon the Monongahela and Alleghany. The territorial produce of that part of the country finds an easy and advantageous conveyance by the Ohio and Mississippi. Corn, hams and dried pork are the principal articles sent to New Orleans, whence they are re-exported into the Carribbees. They also export for the consumption of Louisiana, bar-iron, coarse linen, bottles manufactured at Pittsburgh, whiskey, and salt butter. A great part of these provisions come from Redstone, a small commercial town, situated upon the Monongahela, about fifty miles beyond Pittsburgh. All these advantages joined together have, within these ten years, increased ten-fold the population and price of articles in the town, and contribute to its improvements, which daily grow more and more rapid.

The major part of the merchants settled at Pittsburgh, or in the environs, are the partners, or else the factors, belonging to the houses at Philadelphia. Their brokers at New Orleans sell, as much as they can, for ready money; or rather, take in exchange cottons, indigo, raw sugar, the produce of Low Louisiana, which they send off by sea to the houses at Philadelphia and Baltimore, and thus cover their first advances. The bargemen return thus by sea to Philadelphia or Baltimore, whence they go by land to Pittsburgh and the environs, where the major part of them generally reside. Although the passage from New Orleans to one of these two ports is twenty or thirty days, and that they have to take a route by land of three hundred miles to return to Pittsburgh, they prefer this way, being not so difficult as the return by land from New Orleans to Pittsburgh, this last distance being fourteen or fifteen hundred miles. However, when the barges are only destined for Limeston[e] in Kentucky, or for Cincinnati, in the state of Ohio, the bargemen return by land, and by that means take a route of four or five hundred miles.

The navigation of the Ohio and Mississippi is so much improved of late that they can tell almost to a certainty the distance from Pittsburgh to New Orleans, which they compute to be two thousand one hundred miles. The barges in the spring season usually take forty or fifty days to make the passage, which two or three persons in a pirogue make in five and-twenty days.

What many, perhaps, are ignorant of . . . is, that they build large vessels on the Ohio, and at the town of Pittsburgh. One of the principal ship yards is upon the Monongahela, about two hundred fathoms beyond the last houses in the town. . . . The whole of this timber being near at hand, the expense of building is not so great as in the ports of the Atlantic states. The cordage is manufactured at Redstone and Lexinton, where there are two extensive rope-walks, which also supply ships with rigging that are built at Marietta and Louisville. On my journey to Pittsburgh in the month of July 1802, there was a three-mast vessel of two hundred and fifty tons, and a smaller one of ninety, which was on the point of being finished. These ships were to go, in the spring following, to New Orleans, loaded with the produce of the country, after having made a passage of two thousand two hundred miles before they got into the ocean.

Pittsburgh Twenty Years Later

It would require more room than I can afford, and more patience than I possess, to give you a detailed account of all the branches of commerce and manufactures which contribute to the prosperity of Pittsburgh. The latter have flourished here extensively, in consequence of the variety of raw materials indigenous to the country, the abundance of fuel, the salubrity of the climate, the cheapness of provisions, the convenience of the markets, and the enterprising spirit of the people. The most important branch includes articles manufactured of iron, a metal which is found in great abundance in the neighbouring mountains, whence it is brought in *pigs* and *bars* to this place, at a small expense, and here wrought for exportation. Most of the machinery for this and other purposes is propelled by steam, the management of which has been brought to great perfection; but the neighbourhood also affords many fine water-courses, some of which are occupied; cannon, of a very superior quality, have been cast here for the United States' Service. The manufacture of glass, which was introduced by the late General O'Hara, about the year 1798, has been carried on with great success; there are now a number of establishments in operation, which produce large quantities of window-glass, and other ware of the coarser sort, and one, at which flint glass is made and ornamented with great elegance. Messrs. Bakewell, Page, and Bakewell, have the credit of having introduced the latter branch of this manufacture; and their warehouse presents an endless variety of beautiful ware, designed and executed in a style which is highly creditable to their taste and perseverance. Manufactories of wool and cotton have been supported with some spirit, but, as yet, with little success. We have a foolish pride about us, which makes our gentlemen ashamed of wearing a coat which has not crossed the Atlantic; I hope we shall grow wiser as we grow older. Articles of tin and leather are fabricated at Pittsburgh to an astonishing amount. So long ago as 1809, boots and shoes were manufactured to the amount of seventy thousand dollars; saddlery to the amount of forty thousand, and tin ware to the amount of twenty-five thousand dollars, in one year. In the same year, hats were made to the amount of twenty-five thousand dollars, and cabinet ware to the amount of seventeen thousand. In addition to these, there have been tan-yards, rope-walks, manufactories of white lead and paper, and extensive ship-yards. . . .

The commerce and trade of Pittsburgh arise partly from her manufactories, and partly from having long been the place of deposit for goods destined for the western country; all of which, until very recently, passed from the Atlantic cities, through this place, to their respective points of destination. They are brought in waggons, carrying from thirty-five to fifty hundred pounds each, and embarked at this place in boats. Upwards of four thousand waggon loads of merchandize have been known to enter Pittsburgh in the course of one year, by the main road from Philadelphia alone, in which is not included the baggage and furniture of travellers and emigrants, nor is notice taken of arrivals by other routes. This business has brought an immense quantity of money into circulation at Pittsburgh; but it has lately been much injured by the competition of Wheeling, and the introduction of steam-boats upon the Ohio.

VII

Society and Culture

18. Classes and Manners

ELIAS PYM FORDHAM, who traveled in the West and for a time resided in Illinois, left the following sketch of classes and social distinctions in the region during the years 1817 to 1818. The extract below is from his Personal Narrative of Travels . . . , edited by Frederic Austin Ogg (Cleveland, Ohio, 1906), pp. 125–129.

The people who live on these frontiers may be divided into four classes,—not perfectly distinct yet easily distinguishable.

1st. The hunters, a daring, hardy, race of men, who live in miserable cabins, which they fortify in times of War with the Indians, whom they hate but much resemble in dress and manners. They are unpolished, but hospitable, kind to Strangers, honest and trustworthy. They raise a little Indian corn, pumpkins, hogs, and sometimes have a Cow or two, and two or three horses belonging to each family: But their rifle is their principal means of support. They are the best marksmen in the world, and such is their dexterity that they will shoot an apple off the head of a companion. Some few use the bow and arrow. I have spent 7 or 8 weeks with these men, have had opportunities of trying them, and believe they would sooner give me the last shirt off their backs, than rob me of a charge of powder. Their wars with the Indians have made them vindictive. This class cannot be called first Settlers, for they move every year or two.

2d. class. First settlers;—a mixed set of hunters and farmers. They possess more property and comforts than the first class; yet they are a half barbarous race. They follow the range pretty much; selling out when the Country begins to be well settled, and their cattle cannot be entirely kept in the woods.

3d. class.—is composed of enterprising men from Kentucky and the Atlantic States. This class consists of Young Doctors, Lawyers, Storekeepers, farmers, mechanics &c, who found towns, trade, speculate in land, and begin the fabric of Society. There is in this class every gradation of intellectual and moral character; but the general tone of Social manners is yet too much relaxed. There is too much reliance upon personal prowess, and the laws have not yet acquired sufficient energy to prevent violence.

Such are the Inhabitants of the Southern parts of Indiana, and of Shawanoe town, St. Louis, St. Geneviève, and the large settlements on the Mississippi.

4th. class—old settlers, rich, independent, farmers, wealthy merchants, possessing a good deal of information, a knowledge of the world, and an enterprising spirit. Such are the Ohio men, Western Pennsylvanians, Kentuckians and Tenessee men. The young men have a military taste, and most of them have served in the late war. They were great duellists, but now the laws against duelling are more strictly enforced; they carry dirks, and sometimes decide a dispute on the spot. Irritable and dissipated in youth, yet they are generally steady and active in Manhood. They undertake with facility, and carry on with unconquerable ardour, any business or speculation that promises great profit, and sustain the greatest losses with a firmness that resembles indifference.

You will perceive from this slight sketch, which I have made as impartially as I am able, that the Backwoods men, as they are called somewhat contemptuously by the Inhabitants of the Atlantic States, are admirably adapted by Nature and education for the scenes they live and act in. The prominent feature of their character is power. The young value themselves on their courage, the old on their shrewdness. The veriest villains have something grand about them. They expect no mercy and they shew no fear; "every man's hand is against them, and their hand is against every man's."

As social Comforts are less under the protection of the laws here, than in old countries, friendship and good neighbourhood are more valued. A man of good character is an acquisition; not that there is a small proportion of such men, but because the bad are as undisguisedly bad, as their opposites are professedly good. This is not the land of Hypocrisy. It would not here have its reward. Religion is not the road to worldly respectability, nor a possession of it the cloak to immorality.

I wish I could give you a correct idea of the perfect equality that exists among these republicans. A Judge leaves the Court house, shakes hands with his fellow citizens and retires to his log-house. The next day you will find him holding his own plough. The Lawyer has the title of Captain, and serves in his Military capacity under his neighbour, who is a farmer and a Colonel. The shop keeper sells a yard of tape, and sends shiploads of produce to Orleans; he travels 2000 miles in a year; he is a good hunter, and has been a soldier; he dresses and talks as well as a London Merchant, and probably has a more extensive range of ideas; at least he has fewer prejudices. One prejudice, however, nothing will induce him to give up—he thinks the Americans in general, and particularly those of his own state, are the best soldiers in the world. Such is the native Shopkeeper: the Eastern Emigrant is very different.

I have not seen an effeminate, or a feeble man, in mind or body, belonging to these Western Countries. The most ignorant, compared with men of the same standing in England, are well informed. Their manners are coarse; but they have amongst themselves a code of politeness, which they generally observe. Drinking whisky is the greatest pest, the most fertile source of disorders, amongst them. When intoxicated by it, they sometimes fight most furiously. In this they resemble the Lower Irish.

There is an universal spirit of enquiry amongst all classes of people. In the state of Indiana, in which there is but one town that is of six years standing, there are several Book-clubs. Newspapers and Reviews from Philadelphia, Baltimore, Kentucky, and S^t. Louis, are received weekly.

The "Lower Elements"

A LESS favorable view, at least of the lower elements, was left by the English observer William Faux in his Memorable Days in America . . . (London, 1823), reprinted in Thwaites (ed.), Early Western Travels, XI, 291–294.

Western labourers, some of whom are quarter-section farmers, very poor, dirty, and wretched, because idle and semi-barbarians, work about half the day and camp out all night, in all seasons and weathers. They surround a large fire, and lie on leaves under a clap-board tent, or wooden umbrella, wrapped in a blanket, with their clothes on. Their houses and families (if any) are perhaps, from 12 to 20 miles off, to whom they go when the job is done, or their shirts are rotting off their backs. They rarely shave, but clip off the beard, and their flesh is never washed; they look pale, wan, yellow, and smoke-dried. They live on the deer which they shoot. They are high-minded, not suffering their children to go to service, because it is disgraceful, but not so to live at home, in rags, idleness, and filth. The father is seldom at home, because of being sued. If he has land, he farms it not, because of bailiffs. He must then work out, until judgment is had against him; when he either pays or makes arrangements, or the property, real and personal, is sold. These labourers, though complete workmen when they like, are pests to the English farmers for whom they work, generally, at meals, haunting the fire-side, where they stand in pairs with their backs towards the fire, to the exclusion of the family, at whom they gaze, expecting to be asked to dinner, breakfast, or supper. They come too, for work, and brush in at meal times with their hats on, expecting to be fed; but they never invite themselves, nor express thanks if invited; and if requested to reach this or that to the host, they do it ungraciously, saying, "Why, I can, I guess." If the female of the family is in bed, they stand and see her get out and dress. They will not be affronted with impunity, and it is necessary to shew or threaten them with a pistol. When the English first came to Evansville settlement, these Rowdey labourers had nearly scared them out. Time is not property to these men; they are eternal triflers. . . .

The case of first settlers here [Illinois], particularly English, is hard, and their characteristic selfishness by no means tends to soften it. Nothing is to be had in the shape of necessaries but with great trouble, not even butter, cheese, or meat. They think that these are more trouble than they are worth, and that it is better to do without. The Americans make no trouble of it. If they can have money or credit, and can get good things, they have them. The English are too selfish to be provident; their boast is that they can do without such a thing, and the habit of doing without is esteemed a fine thing, and causes those who express dissatisfaction to be despised. Thus my countrymen barbarize. . . .

The Rowdies of Kentucky, and in thinly settled parts of Tenessee where they are farmers, frequently decoy travellers, supposed to have money, out of the road, and then shoot them. A traveller, some two or three years since, had taken money near Red Banks, and was waylaid in the above manner by two farmer Rowdies, who shot him and were detected in the act, bearing away the traveller's horse and carriage. One was hanged, and the other nearly whipped to death, and ordered out of the state by the regulators, without time to sell his property. At another time the regulators overtook and shot a murderer, and stuck his head on a pole in Tenessee.

These regulators are self-appointed ministers of justice, to punish or destroy those whom the law cannot touch, such as suspected persons, persons acquitted through false witnesses, or lack of good evidence, but whom public opinion deems guilty. Such individuals rarely benefit by a legal acquittal. Whipping, death, or banishment, is inflicted by these regulators. The law, in itself inefficient, permits or winks at such matters.

Judge Waggoner, who is a notorious hog-stealer, was recently accused, while sitting on the bench, by Major Hooker, the hunter, gouger, whipper, and nose-biter, of stealing many hogs, and being, although a judge, the greatest rogue in the United States. This was the Major's answer to the question *Guilty, or Not Guilty*, on an indictment presented against him. The court laughed, and the Judge raved, and bade Hooker go out and he would fight him. The Major agreed, but said, "Judge, you shall go six miles into the woods, and the longest liver shall come back to tell his tale!" The Judge would not go. The Major was now, in his turn, much enraged by the Judge ordering him into court to pay a fine of ten dollars for some former offence, the present indictment being suffered to drop.

An Amusing Episode

JOHN MATTHEWS, *a young Yankee surveyor and schoolteacher, recorded this amusing episode in his journal of the Ohio country in 1786. It is printed from the Hildred Collection, Marietta College Library, by Hulbert (ed.), Ohio in the Time of the Confederation, pp. 209–211.*

Saturday [November] 11th Cloud and cold the fore part of the day the after part clear and more moderate This morning I went to Mr Thomas Edgingtons who was The principal ingager with me before I went into the wood for to teach a School and Informed that I was ready to begin but I found their fickle Fancys had Started an objection which they had forgot before that was that I could not engage to teach a School for more than five months and they wanted for a year[.] this was a small disappointment for as I depended on Serving them I had not looked any further tho I expected to have erned but a small pittance yet I should have had and [sic] opportunity of studying (which I am determined to do however) and cleared myself of expences

From this I went to Mr Harmon Greathouses Father of my good friend Mr Wm Greathous where I found a number of the Neibors Seated in Social Glee round a heap of corn the inspiring Juce of rye had inlivened their Imaginations and given their Tongues such an exact ballance that they moved with the greatest alacrity while relating Scenes of Boxing, Wrestling, Hunting &c. at dusk of evening the Corn was finished and the Company retired to the House where many of them took shuch Hearty draughts of the generous liquor as quite deprived them of the use of their limbs Some quarreld some sung and others laughed and the whole display'd a Scene more diverting than edifying[.] at 10 o'clock in the evening all that could walk went home and left three or four round the fire hug[g]ing the Whiskey Bottle and arguing very obstanately on Religion at which I left them and went to bed

Sunday 12th Cloud and Cold the whole day[.] at 8 o'clock in the Morning rose from bed and found the neibors who had tary'd all night still with Raptures hug[g]ing the Whiskey Bottle and by 11 o'clock others had come in to help drink up the whiskey that was not drank last night[.] about 12 I left them and returned to Mr Wm Greathouses

A Duel

VIOLENCE *in many forms was prevalent in the West. Among the gentry it was codified and refined into the respectable code of the duel. The following letter appeared in the* Natchez Messenger, *December 9, 1806, and was reprinted in* Claiborne, Mississippi as a Province, Territory and State, *pp. 374–375.*

December 8, 1806

A variety of reports having been circulated relative to the affair of honor between Maj. Claiborne and Capt. Farar, I feel myself impelled as the friend of the former gentleman, to present the public with a brief narrative of the affair, and the manner in which it terminated.

The parties met on the western margin of the Mississippi, on Sunday morning the 30th ult. The arms on our part were a brace of pistols, on theirs two brace. The friend of Capt. Farar wore a dirk. Agreeable to arrangement the principals exchanged a shot at the distance of ten steps. While charging the pistols for a second fire, the friend of Capt. Farar suggested the propriety of a compromise. I informed him that I would receive propositions, but was not authorized to make any. Propositions were then made and reduced to writing. I deem it unnecessary minutely to detail, the various interviews and discussions between the friends of the parties. As to these propositions, it is sufficient to say, that after a long and deliberate discussion, Major Claiborne finally rejected them, unless Captain Farar would first give assurance that in his advertisement of Jett he had no intention to wound his private or public character, for that such was the general impression. Captain Farar's friend asked if this was our ultimatum? I answered in the affirmative. He then said the parties should take another shot. The principals took their posts for a second fire. The friend of Capt. Farar, with a pistol under his arm and one in his hand, stood nearer to Major Claiborne than to his friend—I was opposite to him. He observed, looking at Major Claiborne, that this business had become serious, and he would shoot the man who acted unfairly. Major Claiborne replied, "if I act unfairly you are at liberty to shoot me." I called to order and desired the friend of Capt. Farar to give the word. A second fire took place. Capt. Farar's ball passed through the cape of Major Claiborne's coat, and the Major's ball struck Capt. Farar under the right arm, and glanced without doing any material injury. My friend assured me that he was unhurt, and asked for the other pistol. Capt. Farar's friend desired me to give Major Claiborne a brace of pistols, as the affair should now take a course of which it appeared we were not aware. I was proceeding to charge my pistol, under an impression that it would be resolved to change the mode of combat, having been authorized by Major Claiborne to adopt any mode which might be proposed. In the interim, and before I reached the place of loading, Capt. Farar's friend advanced to Major Claiborne, with a brace of pistols in his hands, and one under his arm, apparently in a violent passion, said to him, "you must now fight me," repeatedly tendering one of the pistols, which Major Claiborne rejected, replying that he came there to fight Captain Farar, and that he would do so as long as Capt. Farar pleased. Capt. Bradish said, "Capt. Farar has a family, and he shall not fight any more." Major Claiborne remarked, "we both have families." I attempted to interrupt the friend of Capt. Farar, but in vain. Astonished at the novelty and unwarrantableness of such a proceeding, unable to divine the legitimate object of it, and knowing that no unfair practice had been used on our part, I was really at a loss how to act for a moment. By the rules of etiquette, and according to the proposition of the friend of Capt. Farar, I would have been warranted in shooting him on the spot. I had not the temper to pursue so sanguinary a conduct. Major Claiborne twice asked me if he should fight him. I peremptorally said, "you shall not, sir." He then advanced to Capt. Farar's friend, and said, "now if you are disposed to assassinate me, shoot."

This procedure was so unprecedented, unjustifiable, and violatory of every rule of etiquette, that I determined to take my friend from the ground, and we proceeded to recross the Mississippi.

Having given the preceding narrative, in which I have endeavored to be as accurate as possible, I think it proper to remark, that Major Claiborne, throughout the whole affair, acted with the firmness and intrepidity of a soldier and a man of honor. I must take the liberty to state that my conduct on this occasion, from the commencement to the close, was influenced by a disposition to preserve unsullied the honor of my friend, to adjust the matter amicably, if practicable, to the satisfaction of both parties, and that in every attempt to effect that desirable object, I was governed by motives of humanity.

W. B. Shields

Independence Day in Marietta

Mannerisms *often were as formalized in western society as elsewhere. In the following account, Enoch Parsons informs his mother of the manner in which the gentry of pioneer Marietta celebrated the anniversary of the Declaration of Independence. The letter was printed in Hall,* Life and Letters of Samuel Holden Parsons, *pp. 560–561.*

[July 21, 1789]

The 2d instant I wrote to you by Mr. McFarley, that we were

making preparations to solemnize the 13th anniversary of the Independence of the United States. I shall now, having nothing else to write, give you the particulars of our proceedings on that day.

In the afternoon we assembled at the northwest block house, where a short oration was pronounced, after which the militia paraded, discharged fourteen cannons, fired their muskets fourteen times, performed various evolutions, etc and were dispersed. The officers of the Government, together with a few other gentlemen, then repaired to Fort Harmar where we partook of an excellent dinner, and with good wine and under the discharge of cannons, we drank the following toasts:

1. The United States.
2. The President of the United States.
3. The Senate and House of Representatives.
4. The Secretary of War.
5. His most Christian Majesty [the King of France].
6. Perpetual union between France, Spain and America.
7. In memory of those heroes who fell in America in defense of the liberty of their country.
8. The Marquis de LaFayette.
9. The friendly powers of Europe.
10. The day.
11. Governor St. Clair and the Western Territory.
12. Agriculture, commerce and sciences.
13. Dr. Franklin.
14. The citizens of Marietta.

By this time our spirits were not a little exhilarated, however, the greatest order and decency was observed by every person throughout the day, which was closed by the beautiful illumination of Fort Harmar.

On Monday evening following, we had a splendid ball which was opened by a minuet walked by Mrs. Battle and Baron Tilas from Sweden, after which we had several country dances and closed with a minuet by Mr. Le Luce, a native of this country, a Chief among the Wyandots and one of the leaders. Twenty-four ladies attended this ball and between sixty and seventy gentlemen.

Affectionately yours,
ENOCH PARSONS

19. Rural Life

Pioneer Life in the Northwest

WILLIAM COOPER HOWELLS *in his* Recollections of Life in Ohio from 1813 to 1840 *offers a rich, detailed account of rural pioneer life in the Northwest. The following extracts are from pp. 122–126, 145–151, 157–158.*

The social condition of the people was rather primitive and very simple. None of them were wealthy. The possession of a quarter section or two of land, pretty well cleared up—that is, about a third or half of it under culture—with a log-house and barn, was thought to make a man well off. . . . Nearly every man lived on a piece of land of his own, and this was usually in eighty or one hundred and sixty acre tracts. Their stock was small, and mostly their families were large. Almost every man was the son of a farmer in an older settlement who had come in to this to have a farm of his own, out of what his father could spare; or some man who had been a farm laborer or renter in an older place, had bought land and was opening out a home. Among such a people there were no rich, and none very poor. Most of them lived very plainly. They usually had enough to eat, though they were liable to run short a while before harvest. All that would bring money was sold to provide for taxes and such payments as only money would make; and those who had payments to make on their land were pretty sure to sell themselves bare, and were often hard put to it to maintain themselves in provisions.

As for dress, that was very plain, and fortunately, there was but little temptation to extravagance in this way. The women of the family, in almost every instance, produced something to wear. Besides the knitting and sewing, which was the work of the older women, the wool of the few sheep each farmer kept was spun in the family. So also was the flax that grew on the flax-patch, which was regularly cleared off in the winter, sowed with flax in March, harvested in June, and immediately planted with potatoes—yielding two important Irish crops in one year. The wool was sometimes carded at home, but usually it was sent off to one of the carding machines that would be put up in a mill, for the purpose of preparing the wool for spinning by carding and making it into rolls, that were about a yard long and three-fourths of an inch in diameter, light and soft, and from which an even thread was easily spun, either on a large spinning-wheel or the little treadle-wheel used also for flax. The quarter acre flax patch and the few sheep would, almost without noticing the expense or labor, produce the material for clothing a large family. The women pulled the flax, or at least helped to pull it, and helped in dressing it, and always spun it up. One or two grown up daughters would dispose of a large supply of flax and wool. . . .

The wool was spun into an average grade for cloth and flannel. A mixed cloth was made with a linen warp and woolen filling, which they called *linsey*, that was worn mostly by the women and children. . . . Fulled cloth was made at home till it was woven, when it would be taken to the fulling-mill to be finished. This was worn by the men and big boys, and made excellent clothing, though it was not fine, and the color was apt to fade. There was hardly a family of girls where one of them did have a loom and weave all the plainer kinds of stuff for themselves and for others, so that the spinning and weaving was practically done at home. . . .

Another manufacture of these times, and which flourished through all changes, was whiskey. No difference if grain was scarce or dear, or times hard, or the people poor, they would make and drink whiskey. And the number of little distilleries was wonderful. Within two miles of where we lived there were three of them. They were small concerns, but they produced enough. They were commonly fitted up with a twenty-five or forty-gallon still and half a dozen tubs. They might, perhaps, have produced a barrel a day, if pushed to their capacity. The distillers would exchange a gallon of whiskey for a bushel of corn or rye, and when the whiskey-jug was empty, a boy would be sent on a bag of grain, perched on an old horse, to the still-house to make the exchange and renew the supply. People were not particular about the age of their liquor, and it was often drank on the day it was made. The custom was for every man to drink it, on all occasions that offered; and the women would take it sweetened and reduced to toddy. At raisings, huskings, log-rollings, and all manner of social gatherings, it was used as an invigorator and a sign of hospitality; and the manner of taking it was from the neck of the jug, each man swallowing as much as he wanted. . . .

Particularly remarkable was the general equality and the general dependence of all upon the neighborly kindness and good offices of others. Their houses and barns were built of logs, and were raised by the collection of many neighbors together on one day, whose united strength was necessary to the handling of the logs. As every man was ready with the ax and understood this work, all came together within the circle where the raising was to be done, and all worked together with about equal skill. . . . The men understood handling timber, and accidents seldom happened, unless the logs were icy or wet, or the whiskey had gone round too often. I was often at these raisings, because we had raisings of the kind to do, and it was the custom always to send one from a family to help, so that you could claim like assistance in return. . . .

This kind of mutual help of the neighbors was extended to many kinds of work, such as rolling up the logs in a clearing, grubbing out the underbrush, splitting rails, cutting logs for a house and the like. When a gathering of men for such a purpose took place there was commonly some sort of mutual job laid out for women, such as quilting, sewing, or spinning up a lot of thread for some poor neighbor. This would bring together a mixed party, and it was usually arranged that after supper there should be a dance or, at least, plays, which would occupy a good part of the night, and wind up with the young fellows seeing the girls home in the short hours; or, if they went home early, sitting with them by the fire in that kind of interesting chat known as sparking.

The flax crops required a good deal of handling, in weeding, pulling and dressing, and each of these processes was made the occasion of a joint gathering of boys and girls and a good time. . . . They found room to dance in an apartment of perhaps eighteen feet square, in which there would be two large beds and a trundle-bed, besides the furniture, which though not of great quantity, took some room. And then, if these were small houses, they often contained large families. . . .

One of the gatherings for joint work . . . and one that was always a jolly kind of affair, was the corn husking. It was a sort of harvest home in its department, and it was the more jolly because it was a gathering with very little respect to persons, and embraced in the invitation men and big boys, with the understanding that no one would be unwelcome. There was always a good supper served at the husking, and as certainly a good appetite to eat it with. It came at a plentiful season, when the turkeys and chickens were fat, and a fat pig was at hand, to be flanked on the table with good bread in various forms, turnips and potatoes from the autumn stores, apple and pumpkin pies, good coffee and the like. And the cooking was always well done, and all in such bountiful abundance, that no one feared to eat, while many a poor fellow was certain of a "square meal" by being present at a husking. You were sure to see the laboring men of the vicinity out; and the wives of a goodly number of farm hands would be on hand to help in the cooking and serving at the table. . . .

When the husking party had assembled they were all called out into line, and two fellows, mostly ambitious boys, were chosen captains. These then chose their men, each calling out one of the crowd alternately, till all were chosen. Then the heap was divided, by two judicious chaps walking solemnly along the ridge of the heap of corn, and deciding where the dividing rail was to be laid, and, as this had to be done by starlight or moonlight at best, it took considerable deliberation, as the comparative solidity of the ends of the heap and the evenness of it had to be taken into account. This done, the captains placed a good steady man at each side of the rail, who made it a point to work through and cut the heap in two as soon as possible; and then the two parties fell to husking, all standing with the heap in front of them, and throwing the husked corn onto a clear place over the heap, and the husks behind them. From the time they began till the corn was all husked at one end, there would be steady work, each man husking all the corn he could, never stopping except to take a pull at the stone jug of inspiration that passed occasionally along the line; weak lovers of the stuff were sometimes overcome, though it was held to be a disgraceful thing to take too much. The captains would go up and down their lines, and rally their men as if in a battle, and the whole was an exciting affair. As soon as one party got done, they raised a shout, and hoisting their captain on their shoulders, carried him over to the other side with general cheering. Then would come a little bantering talk and explanation why the defeated party lost, and all would turn to and husk up the remnants of the heap. All hands would then join to carry the husks into the fodder-house. The shout at hoisting the captain was the signal for bringing the supper on the table, and the huskers and supper met soon after. These gatherings often embraced forty or fifty men. If the farm house was small, it would be crowded, and the supper would be managed by repeated sittings at the table. At a large house there was less crowding and more fun, and if, as was often the case, some occasion had been given for an assemblage of the girls of the neighborhood, and particularly if the man that played the fiddle should attend, after the older men had gone, there was very apt to be a good time. There was a tradition that the boys who accidentally husked a red ear, and saved it, would be entitled to a kiss from somebody. . . .

It was a fault of people in that region that they were intolerably fond of lawsuits. The obstinacy of the Scotch in them, combined with the Irish irritability, seemed to fit them for constant quarrels. The justices of the peace and the higher courts were kept busy with suits, and the churches always had some case in the secular departments. These offered a way of going to law that was inexpensive, and on the whole about as satisfactory as the courts to the litigants, perhaps more so, as it left them to stick to their side of the question. But the costs of lawsuits were not so great as they are now, and the lawyers charged less; so the luxury of a suit was more within the reach of men of small means. A leading cause of lawsuits was slander. There was a great disposition [to] talk freely, and some one was sure to think he was slandered to the extent of great damages, for which he would go to law; or, he would seek redress in the church if the offender happened to belong to a church. If he got the offender turned out of the church and pretty thoroughly disgraced, he might be mollified; but if the church authorities were not fully convinced, and did not punish the accused brother or sister, he was as ready for a lawsuit as ever. The trials served to break the monotony of the country life, and sometimes spiced it to a high degree.

20. Religion on the Frontier

MANY OF the Protestant churches in the West imposed social discipline and restraint on their members. They were, of course, voluntary organizations. The following minutes are from the Baptist South Elkhorn Church, Kentucky, and the Mount Tabor Church, Kentucky. The

*Constitution and Rules are from the Baptist Church on Beaver Creek,
Kentucky. All are reprinted in William Warren Sweet (ed.), Religion
on the American Frontier, The Baptists 1783–1850 (New York, 1931),
pp. 50–51, 258–261.*

South Elkhorn Church

The 2nd Saturday in November 1804

excluded Charles, a Negroe man belonging to Bro Majors,
for abusing Winney a black member belonging to Sister Boulware

Also excluded Molly a black member formerly belonging to
Mr. Fitzgerald for telling lies

Excluded Hannah Davy's wife for swearing & keeping another
Man besides her Husband

Condorus a black member belonging to Jas Sanders was
also Excluded for lying, & taking another Wife contrary to the
Gospel

The 2nd Saturday in December 1804 the Church met and after
Divine Worship proceeded to business.

James Major was Excluded from the Church for Intoxication
and for Shooting for Liquor

Bro Red Major Came before the Church and was dealt with
for Shooting for Liquor, and the Church directed the Moderator
to give him a word of Admonition and was acquitted . . .

Roberts Hicklin was excluded from the Church for Horse
Raceing

WILLIAM HICKMAN
[Moderator]

2nd Saturday in March 1805 the Church met and after Divine
Worship proceeded to business

A Charge was brought against Sister Polly Edrington for frequently giving her Mother the lie, & calling her a fool and for
Indeavouring by tattleing to set several of the Neighbours at
strife with each other She was excluded for the same

The 2nd Saturday in December 1805 the Church met and after
Divine Worship proceeded to business

Bro Haydon Complains against Bro James Major for threatening a Man's life and saying that his conduct had been so bad that
he never would tell it. The Church after full Examination into
the Charges agreed to bear with him.

At the request of Bro James Haydon & Bro Samuel Price the
Church appointed the following Brethren William Hubbel

Daniel Peak William Samuel Abraham Gregory and Carter
Blanton to settle some difficulties between them

Bro John Price's Annaca is Excluded from this Church for
Stealing.

At the meeting the second Saturday in January, 1806

WILLIAM HICKMAN
Mod.

Brother Palmer complains against Bro Stephens and his wife
for not dealing with Nancy their Negroe Woman & bringing
her before the Church and for putting her in Irons Bro Stephens
was acquitted. . . . A second Charge against Sister Stephens
for giving their negroe Woman the lye—She was Acquitted from
both Charges

Charges brought against Bro Jas Major for saying that John
Dupey slapt him in the face & he draw'd himself up in the Chair
and bore it, and that Mr. Pulliam said he was the patientest Man
he ever see in his life . . .

Charge the 2nd for saying he gave Dupey no cause to treat
him in the manner he did and for going repeatedly to where
Dupey was and Quarreling with him

The above Charges was Substanchiated but when taking a
vote who can bear with Bro Major, the Church agreed to bear
with him

Bro Ramsey Boulware said he cou'd not fellowship Bro Major
and withdrew from the Church.

Constitution and Rules of a Church Formed on
Beaver Creek, Kentucky, 1798

A Covenant of a Baptist Church on Beaver Creek entered into
the 5th of November 1798 (with seven members)

And Constituted by Elders, William Hickman, Carter Tarrant,
and Alexander Davidson.

Agreed to be constituted on the essential doctrines of the Gospel
viz.

first,   We believe in one only true and living God and that their
are three persons in the God-head. the Father Son and Holy
Spirit.

2nd.   We believe that the Scriptures of the old and new Testaments, are the word of God, and the only rule of faith and practice.

3rd   We believe that we are saved by grace thro faith and that not of ourselves it is the gift of God.

4th   We believe in the doctrine of original sin.

5th   We believe in mans impotency to recover himself from the fallen state he is in by nature.

6th   We believe that sinners are justiyd in the sight of God, only by the imputed righteousness of Christ.

7th,   We believe that the saints shall persevere and never finally fall away.

8th   We believe that baptism and the Lord's Supper are ordinances of Jesus Christ, and that true believers and them only are the fit subjects of these ordinances, and we believe that the true mode of baptism is by immersion.

9th   We believe in the resurrection of the Lord and universal Judgement,

10th   We believe the punishment of the wicked will be everlasting and the Joys of the righteous will be eternal.

Rules and Regulations to be Observed in Church Deciplin

First, In all Church meetings, it is the duty and place of the Minister or Elder to keep good order, and be forward in carrying on business, and that no member leave their seat without leave,

Second, In all cases touching fellowship the Church shall act by a majority of two thirds, and in case a majority cannot be had the member shall be debar,d from Church privileges untill a majority of 2 thirds can be had, and should any individual shew obstinacy the Church may deal with him or her, as appears right on the case,

Third, In Temporal matters, or such as do not immediately touch fellowship they may decide by a majority.

Fourth, Any motion made and seconded shall be put to the Church and no motion, or question shall be put without a second,

Fifth, Any member making a motion, or speaking in the Church

shall rise from his seat, and stand and address the Elder and
direct his discourse to him,

Sixth, In all debates the members shall direct their discourse to the
elder and not to the contending party,

Seventh, No member shall speak more than three times upon the
same subject without leave from the Church,

Eighth, If two shall rise at once to speak the Elder shall determine
which rose first, and give him leave to speak first, and afterwards the other may speak,

Ninth, All members shall be receiv'd by experience, letter, or information of a member of our union, or Recantation, the
member who may be receiv'd upon information shall be
bound to produce his or her letter within twelve months.

Tenth, All offences must be dealt with in gospel order, but publick
offences or such as does not come under the denomination
of trespass against an individual ought to be dealt with in a
publick manner in Church,

Eleventh, From Scripture authority we count it a duty for all
members to attend each Church meeting unless providen-
tially hinder'd and especially the Male members, therefore if
any member neglect this duty, we count it a breach of good
order and agree that all such must be dealt with as the
Church direct . . .

Mount Tabor Church

[Taken from MSS. Volume of Mount Tabor Church, 1798–
1870]

Third Saturday in July 1803,

The Church met and after worship, proceeded to business;

1st A report was bro^t against Sister Arnett, for drinking too much,
and it appears she is guilty, we therefore, appoint Sisters Baugh,
Philips and Clack, to cite her to our next meeting.

2nd. Rec'd a peitition from Concord requesting helps, to set with
them the first Saturday in August next, therefore we appoint and
sent Bren R. Hunt, G. Right, J. Baugh, and Wm Baugh.

3rd The Church agree that bren Ferguson, and G. Right, hire the
finishing of the meeting house, and that each free male member
pay an equal part thereof; dismist in order;—

Third Friday in August 1803

The Church met and after worship proceeded to business, 1st The committee appointed to labour with and cite sister Arnett to this meeting, Report they acted agreable to the order of the Church, and say she appear'd to be humble, and very sorry for what she had done, therefore the Church restore her to fellowship

Saturday, The Church set after preaching, &ct.

1st Opened a door for the reception of members, and rec'd James Bradsberry, be recantation, 2nd Sister Dinah Allin apply'd fro a letter of dismission, which was granted; dismist

Third Saturday in Septr 1803

The Church met, and after worship, proceeded to business,

1st, Rec'd Reports against bror John Claspill, for drinking too much and appoint bre'r Phil. Baugh, Jas Bradsberry, and G. White to labour with and cite to next meeting,

2nd Rec'd an accusation against bro's Wm Bradsberry, for fighting and using rough language, Agreed to refer it to next meeting

Protestant Sects in Tennessee

ALTHOUGH *a variety of Protestant sects were to be found in the West, religious enthusiasm was not maintained at a high level throughout. The following account of the sects in frontier Tennessee in 1799 by two Moravian ministers, Abraham Steiner and Friedrich Schweinitz, is in the archives of the Moravian Church, Bethlehem, Pa. The extract below, edited and translated by Adelaide L. Fries, is printed in the North Carolina Historical Review, XXI (October, 1944), 376–371.*

[November 28, 1799]

The town of Nashville lies in Davidson County, on high hills close to the Cumberland River, and is the leading place in Cumberland. It is regularly laid out, and has a number of good buildings. It has about fifty houses. There is also a large, stone Presbyterian church here, in which a Presbyterian minister, named Craighead, preaches every four weeks. This man has built a stone church on his plantation in the country, and has there an inn and a mill. He also preaches every four weeks on his plantation, but people say that attendance there is more for horse trading than for the preaching, for he is one of the best horse-traders.

Other demoninations have no services here. . . .

The 30th. Today we visited various plantations, accompanied by Casper Fischer and his son. We called on old Mr. Harvey, formerly our neighbor, and his son John, who was one of the first Methodists in this part of the world. Then we went to see Adam and Jacob Binkly, and it was agreed that the preaching tomorrow should be at the house of Fischer; the English, of whom many live hereabouts, had asked for it. . . .

Sunday, Dec. 1. Although there was rain, with glaze ice, so many came to the preaching that had been announced that they could hardly find place to sit down in the dwelling and the adjoining house. As most of them were English there was first English preaching at twelve o'clock. Br. Steiner spoke on I Tim. i, 15. . . . By request Mr. John Harvey had brought a hymn book, out of which Br. Steiner lined the hymns and Mr. Harvey led the singing. The singing of the English was good. Immediately after this there was a German sermon, in which Br. Steiner spoke on Heb. ii, 14, 15. . . .

Immediately after the preaching Jacob Binkly and his wife asked that a service might be held in their house this week, chiefly in order that the many children in their neighborhood might once have an opportunity to hear something about the Saviour, and this was gladly promised. . . .

The 3rd. Br. Steiner was told that John Harvey, who is a beloved preacher among the Methodists of this neighborhood, would like to talk with him but was too shy to come here, so this morning we went to visit him. He said that he was very glad that two Brethren had come here, and would rejoice the more if one or more would come here to stay. That would be very useful for this neighborhood, where nearly all had sunk into sleep and continued to sin quite calmly. It would therefore be good if somebody would come to look after them. Interest in the Methodists was about at an end, and they were now fewer in number than formerly. Once there had been a fire among the residents, and he had never seen the power and work of religion so great as in this land; but for some years hearts had been growing lukewarm, and the love of many had waxed cold. It was therefore necessary that the people should hear the Gospel from others, and he believed the Brethren would be the most suitable to preach here. He advised Br. Steiner to preach sternly, saying that the inhabitants were so godless that they must be awakened by threatening and calls to repentence. Br. Steiner answered: "We preach Christ the Crucified, and the

Atonement which He made. His death on the cross is the hammer which breaks the hardest heart; that we have experienced, and through it have been redeemed."

On the 4th we continued to visit, calling among the rest on Stump. He said among other things that people had many things to say about him, and yet he liked what was good. We would always be welcome to preach here, which was good for them and for others. The man promised that if a Brother would come here as a teacher he would give him fifty bushels of corn as a beginning. A sermon is preached in his house every four weeks by the Baptists, but his wife can hardly stand it that the Lord's Prayer is never prayed. The Baptists and Methodists are the only denomination on this side of the Cumberland River, and they are not numerous; most people have no religion, or at least no preachers. Some years ago there came a German preacher, Friedrich August von Prügel, and the Germans accepted him as preacher on favorable terms, but soon they had to dismiss him because his conduct and his preaching did not harmonize. Since then no German preacher has been here. . . .

[The 6th.] In Nashville we visited General Armstrong on business. He was glad to see us. Among other things he told us that in Nashville and the surrounding country, espically among the upper class, deism and irreligion were more than usually prevalent, that not only was the Saviour of the world not honored but that His story was discussed satirically in their companies, with shocking ridicule. He said that he had recently been in such a company, and after they had had their fun with religion they had turned on him, and had ridiculed him for his silly beliefs, as they called it. He could not defend himself, nor did he wish to, but he replied something like this: "Gentlemen! I do not make fun of such matters. I think that among you all I have the safest belief. If what I believe is true that is my gain and your loss. If what you claim to believe is true it does you no good, and mine cannot harm me." And with that he left the company.

Then he took us to the Reverend Mr. Boyd, a minister of the English Episcopal Church, who had heard of our arrival and wished to speak with us. . . . He is not stationed here, but is only passing through, though slowly. He really lives in Georgia. On his journeys he has preached here and there, and especially in Knoxville, where he was much attracted to a young Indian man who attended his preaching. Now his physical infirmities do not allow him to preach. On this side of the river only the Baptists hold services, with the exception of the Presbyterians at two places. There are no Methodists or other denominations.

The Congregationalists in Michigan

MUCH the same situation prevailed far to the North in territorial Michigan almost thirty years later for Congregationalist ministers. In the following letters, printed in Sweet (ed.), Religion on the American Frontier, 1783–1850, Vol. III, The Congregationalists (Chicago, 1939), 288–291, Isaac Ruggles reports to the corresponding secretary of the Congregationalist United Domestic Missionary Society. In 1826 this was replaced by the American Home Missionary Society.

Pontiac, Aug. 29—1825

REV. & DEAR SIR:

. . . My labors have been confined almost entirely to Oakland County. Having no fellow laborer of my own order in the County, I have been constrained to visit & to preach in a large circuit; & owing to the scattered condition of the church, it has been expedient to administer the Lord's Supper in 3 or 4 several places. 41 have been added to the church since the first of December; 22 from other churches, & 19 by profession. 5 or 6 have, we hope, passed from death unto life during the past season. A few days since, we have been called to mourn the loss of one much beloved & esteemed, who was a Deacon & Ruling Elder in this chh. The whole number now in the chh. is 55. Several others will soon be added. I have baptised 21; 7 adults & 14 children; I have dispensed the communion 8 times. I have ordained in this chh. 2 Ruling Elders & 1 Deacon. Pastoral visiting has been my employment almost every day; & in this duty, I have generally, met with a kind reception. The people have often expressed their thanks for my labors of love.

Three Sabbath schools are instituted in the County; 3 concerts of prayer; & 2 Female weekly prayer meetings. A Female Tract Society has been instituted, & a Bible Society is contemplated. Meetings are, in general, well attended.

. . . The Lord's people are desirous that the same means should be continued, & also that more missionaries of the cross should be sent over to help them. No one, Dear Brother, but those residing in this destitute region, can be adequately sensible of the need there is, that more heralds of salvation should be sent to this part of the Lord's heritage. . . . Two weeks since, I organized a church in the South part of this County, styled the 2nd. ch[urc]h. of Oakland County; consisting of 8 members. One was added the Sabbath following. . . . Here in the wilderness, where 18 months ago, no civilized man resided, the standards of the cross is now erected. . . .

Brother Foutis, a missionary recently sent out by the General Assembly is now laboring with good success at the River Raisin. Br. Wells who has, the summer past, been preaching at Detroit, is about to be settled there. One or 2 more laborers is needed in Oakland Co. One is needed at Macomb Co., another at Washtenaw County. . . .

ISAAC W. RUGGLES

REV. M. BRUEN [the addressee]

Pontiac, Jan. 17—1825[1826]

REVEREND & DEAR SIR,
 . . . The people have raised by subscription, a sum which together with 100 dollars from your Society, will make a sufficiency for my support. The church in the South Western part of the County is prospering; 4 have been added since my return. The township is now named Farmington. The people are anxiously hoping that the Rev. Mr. Crawford, whom I mentioned, will be sent to them. I hope it is in the power of your society to grant their request.

I have visited Ann Arbour the County Seat in Washtenaw County which commenced settling about 2 years since. I find the prospect of building up a church here very flattering. The influencial characters are professors of religion; & almost without exception, are of our own profession. There are about 20 in & near the village who are professors in the Presbyterian Church, & contemplate being organized soon.

Yours in the best of bonds,

ISAAC W. RUGGLES

REV. M. BRUEN

Pontiac, June 17—1826

REVEREND & DEAR SIR,
Since my last Report, spiritual affairs have continued much as they were then, in a low state. . . . Within the last 3 months, 6

have united with the church at Pontiac; 5 of them by letter, &
one by profession. . . .

No fellow servant yet, comes over to help me; duty therefore,
constrains me to visit & to preach in a kind of circuit throughout
the county. A Baptist Brother who moved into the Territory before
I did, preaches at Pontiac one half the time. He is a good man & a
helper. Methodist Circuit riders pass thro the County once in 2 or
3 weeks & I hope are doing some good. We are all harmonious, &
endeavor so to arrange our appointments that we may not interfere,
but accommodate the people with preaching as well as we are able.

Yours Affectionately
I. W. RUGGLES

REV. A. PETERS [the addressee]

Revivals

PERIODICALLY, *emotional revivalism or "awakenings" swept the isolated
rural areas of the West, dividing communities and churches. Peter Pel-
ham, a prominent Methodist of Xenia, Ohio, reveals the depth of the
religious experience in the following extracts of letters to Edward
Dromgoole. They are in the Dromgoole Papers in the Historical Manuscript Collection of the University of North Carolina Library and are
printed in Sweet (ed.), Religion on the American Frontier, 1783–1850.
Vol. IV, The Methodists (Chicago, 1946), 183–184, 187–188.*

[September 8, 1809]

MY DEAR BR[OTHER] DROMGOOLE,

. . . Last week we had a Camp Meeting about a mile from
Xenia [with] about 22 preachers, (Travelling and Local) [and] a
very large Congregation in general for our part of the Country,
and on Sunday about 1000 people attended, powerful times, and
in the Evening my Son Peter, blessed be God, got powerfully converted I believe. On Monday last 38 joined society, and 45 professed to get converted during the C[amp] Meeting—but I think
there were between 50 and 60 new Converts several having gone
away before the meeting broke up. My dear Children are all in
Society, and all profess religion but poor Sarah who still remains
as when you saw her last, but I am not without hopes for her. We
expect Mr. [Francis] Asbury, Br[other] [William] McKendree,
and Br[other] [Henry] Beahm in our Neighborhood next Week.
Appointments are made for Mr. A[sbury] to preach in Xenia to-

morrow week and at our M[eeting] House the next Day which is a little more than ½ mile from us. . . .

[April 16, 1810]

My Dear Br[other] Dromgoole,

We have had very happy times of late in waiting on God at the Meeting House, and our prayer meetings, which we keep up regularly twice a week; Every Sunday Evening at my House and Wednesday Evenings at Br[other] Sales'. Two Souls have profes'd to find the Lord at one of our me[e]tings at my House not long since. Neddy preached yesterday at our M[eeting] H[ouse] [and] had great liberty, and I think did justice to the subject, it was a time of great power, many Xtians [Christians] happy, and one poor Sinner pricked to the Heart, and roared out for mercy, and before we all left, profess'd to have some comfort, and said he loved God. Our Society has increas'd to somewhat about, or above 90 members and is divided into three Classes, for convenience of the preachers to examine them. . . .

O the blessed Religion of Jesus, may it spread its glorious influence speedily to Earth's remotest bounds till there shall not be a sinner left to blaspheme the God of Heaven. Thro' mercy I feel I am on my way to the New Jerusalem, my Soul is happy my God & Savior is with me, and I have taken a fresh start for the Kingdom, and if I never more see you & yours in this vale of tears & sorrow, I hope to meet you all in Bliss & Glory. Yet while I am here I must give God the praise and Glory, for that my joys as far exceed my troubles and sorrows, as the brightness of the Sun outshines that of the Moon.

The Methodists of Ohio

A SOMEWHAT unfavorable view of the Methodists in Ohio a few years later is contained in Howells, Recollections of Life in Ohio From 1813 to 1840, pp. 103–107, 119–121. Howells here suggests the psychological and social function of religion in the rural environment.

Among the Methodists at that time [1824] there was a very steady succession of meetings of one kind or another, and those who belonged to the church found abundant entertainment, if nothing else, in the continual round of preaching, class and prayer meetings. There were then very few public entertainments, and religious meetings took the place of these for nearly all the people. A consequence of this was, that meetings were carried to an extreme, and religious enthusiasm and extravagant experiences were cultivated at the expense of propriety. There was a class of people who really made a dissipation of their religion, and were never satisfied unless going through the most powerfully agitating experiences. The more *thinking* and less *feeling* of the Methodist Church came to see that it was neither orderly nor desirable to keep things at this state of high pressure all the time, and were disposed to moderate affairs and take it more calmly. These were soon denounced by the enthusiasts, who chafed under what they called "a prevailing coldness," and they warred upon their spirit as one of pride and worldliness. They complained that they could not enjoy religion when controlled, and insisted that their quieter brethren did not enjoy it at all.

There was a number of ambitious brethren fond of leading in the various meetings, who in this way found a gratification of their spiritual pride, as well as earthly vanity. They were always clamoring for authority to preach or exhort, holding that they had a spiritual call to exercise these functions, which, they contended, overrode all want of talent, education or intelligence. They said if a man was called to preach or exhort, words would be put into his mouth, and he would not be wanting because he lacked worldly education; and besides, they held that "grammar and dictionary words" were hard for the poor and ignorant to understand, and engendered pride and haughtiness. In fact, cultivated men were at a discount. The Methodist Church at Steubenville, which was the largest church there numerically, was rent and distracted with controversies between those who wanted to preach, and those who did not want them to do any thing of the kind.

This state of things was soon scented out by some preachers in the adjoining country who were known as Newlights, but who called themselves Christians. In the way of doctrines they had little to say, though, so far as I can gather, they taught a kind of Unitarianism. But those fellows that came down on Steubenville about 1824 were a most unpolished and uncultivated set. They ranted and roared and shouted to the entire satisfaction of the most enthusiastic of the meeting-goers; and, as a prime article of their faith, they taught that every man or woman who wanted to do so

had a right to preach, and was at liberty to preach, though I remember that two or three of them managed to do it all themselves;
and they got rid of the clamorous aspirants by conceding them the
privilege without insuring them a congregation.

It was not long after the Newlights made their appearance before they had large meetings, filling such rooms as they could get to
overflowing, and generally raising a noise that could be heard half
over the town. Of course they drew to them the Methodists who
desired to preach, or, at least to have shouting meetings. These
insisted that the Newlights had the "real heartfelt religion" among
them, and went to their meetings, to the scandalous thinning out
of the old congregations. And they did not fail to denounce their
former friends as "dead in the love of the world," as proud and up-
lifted. The brethren who took no interest in the new state of things
were soon affected by a spirit of jealousy, and they fell into the
indiscretion of persecuting the Newlights by denouncing the
preachers as ignorant and wanting in good standing before the
world—they were really a little shaky in this respect—and particularly as teaching false doctrines. The result, of course, was the
detachment of a large body of the Methodists, who went directly
over to the new-comers, making up at once quite a respectable society, as to numbers at least. The Methodists, who were the losers
in the conflict, were exasperated to such a degree that they expelled
the members who had left, and talked violently against their rivals,
the Newlight preachers, and treated them in a most unchristian
manner. This soon reacted in favor of the Newlights, and though
they were admitted to be a rough set, there was soon a strong sym-
pathy with them among outsiders. They rapidly increased, and
took in many from the class of "wicked sinners" whom the Methodists had failed to reach. . . .

These Newlights picked up and developed a number of queer
cases, and as they had frequent experience meetings, at which every
one present had the privilege of voluntarily saying all that he could
put into the shape of an experience, the speeches on these occasions were often very singular. . . .

The settlers were mainly from western Pennsylvania, though
many had come in from the western part of Maryland and Virginia, and the prevailing nationality was the Scotch-Irish of the

second generation. Their religious persuasion was the Presbyterian—that is, it was their ancestral faith, though the Methodists had recruited their membership almost wholly from this element of the population. There were three or four sects of Presbyterians, who had divided on minor matters, but the larger body was that known as the "General Assembly" church. They were all Calvinists, and their confession of faith was the same, and all used the "Longer and Shorter Catechisms" of the Scottish Church, and the Westminster Confession of Faith was accepted by all of them. A chief point of difference was the singing of hymns and the Psalms of David. A small portion of them adhered to the old Scotch Covenanters. The religious feeling pervaded the whole community intellectually, and all accepted the general orthodox standard of faith. Those who were regarded as *religious* had joined themselves to some of the communions. The rest were material for missionary effort of the several sects. The public mind was more largely employed with religious subjects than in later years, and it was the subject and object of nearly all public meetings to consider religion in some of its relations. Politics occupied the people much less, and they talked less about it than in after times. This, however, was before the great Jackson era, whose poison has so thoroughly permeated the practical politics of the country.

I speak of a locality removed from the county seat. There politics was always active, though now it occupies less general attention in the larger towns than in the country. The discussions at the time I speak of were nearly all religious, and there were sometimes fierce controversies that did any thing but promote charity. The leading question at issue was at all times the freedom of the will and the Calvinistic doctrine of predestination. The Presbyterian sects all accepted this doctrine in its strong sense, and qualified it with no conditions. They insisted that God is all powerful and can do as He sees fit; and as He knows all things, present and future, He of course determines the arrangement of every thing. The free will side of this question was taken by the Methodists and Quakers and their adherents. They usually admitted the premises of the other side—not knowing what else to do, and invariably had the logic and the conclusions against them. They maintained their position more by a conscious conviction that man has freedom of will, than by any argument. These controversies were unending, of course, and nearly as fruitless as unending.

21. Western Schools

REVIVALISM influenced the establishment of schools, as this letter from the Congregationalist Joseph Badger to the Reverend Nathan Strong demonstrates. "New Connecticut" refers to the Western Reserve of northern Ohio. The document is printed in Sweet (ed.), Religion on the American Frontier, 1813–1850, Vol. III, The Congregationalists, pp. 79–81.

REVᵈ AND DEAR SIR:

After a long and tedious journey, I arived . . . on the 30th of December. I went on foot and led my horse nearly two hundred miles [over] the worst road I ever saw, owing principally to the season of the year—had much rain, snow and cold.

After passing the mountains and ariving in Washington County, I passed through, and near, about twenty Presbyterian Congregations, where for two years past there has been in most of them a pretty general serious awakening. Being detained seven or eight days by bad weather at two places and by attending the meeting of the Presbytery, I formed considerable acquaintance with about sixteen of the ministers and many more of the pious people.

They appear sentimental. The doctrines of total depravity, of regeneration, election, sovereignty, and their kindred doctrines, are insisted on by the ministers, with great plainness. It is under the preaching of these doctrines, God has been pleased to carry on his work in convincing and hopefully converting many hundreds [of] souls in these parts. The awakening extended [n]early 80 miles from east to west. A number of new settlements northwest of the Ohio [River], extending nearly to the eastern bounds of New Connecticut, were visited in a special manner; and there yet remains many instances of serious awakening. By what I learn, both from ministers and people, the work has been generally free from inthusiasm but powerful in humbling the proud heart, and in bringing it to be swallowed up in God's will. God has done great things for his Church in this country. About six years past there were several young married men and others in single life, hopefully brought into Christ's kingdom. By the advice of a few pious and learned ministers, a number gave themselves to study. An Accademic School was established where the languages and the other arts and sciences are thoroughly taught. There had been sixteen or seventeen very worthy and pious ministers raised up in this school. It was thought by many when they saw such a number seting out for the ministry, there would be no places for them, but the late awakening has opened places enough. The settlements are [a]wakening with such rapidity and so many congregations forming, that they cannot be supplyed, but for a part of the time. There are now eight or ten young men who appear to be pious, preparing for the ministery.

The school I have mentioned is kept in Cannonsbourgh in Washington County, nearly 100 miles from this place [Youngs-town, Ohio]. There are two instructors. The principal is a Mr. John Watson, educated at Princeton College, a very worthy pious minister.

There were ordained three ministers in and near this county [Trumble] last September, by the Ohio Presbytery. One of them, Mr. Wil[lia]m Wick, has settled [and] built in No. 2d, 1 Range, preaches in three congregations, lives 8 miles from Youngstown, preaches there one-third of his time. He appears to be a truly pious man. . . .

. . . I am happy in having a brother so near. From what I can learn of the present situation of the settlements on this reserve, it will be highly necessary to send on another missionary next spring if possible. I am confident from the best information I can get, I shall not be able to visit all the settlements without making too rappid a progress, to answer the design of Missionary labours. This is the oppinion of several Gentlemen I have consulted here.

I would write more, but have not time, as I have to ride some distance today. . . .

I have to acknowledge the great goodness of God through all my journey. My health is good; have had an uncommon share of kindness and respect showed me, wherever my character was known. I was received by the ministers with great cordiality. I was much disappointed with the little books; one-half of them was the history of Lovezinsky [sic], I . . . [gave] them away fo[r] 18 Springs sermons to Children. Please to send me, directing them to Youngstown, all the numbers of the Magazines, next spring, if there should be opportunity by some movers.

I feal as though I was at home, in regard to my work. Under the

Divine directions, I may be useful, but without heavenly aid, there will be nothing done.

I earnestly beg the prayers of the Missionary Society for me that I may be found faithful—and that God would in this wilderness set up his banner and save his people.

From your cordial friend and humble servant,

JOSEPH BADGER

Youngstown, New Connecticut
January 8, 1801

A Methodist School

THE "LEARNING" process at a Methodist school is described by William Cooper Howells in his Recollections of Life in Ohio From 1813 to 1840, pp. 39–41. The incident took place in 1816.

As soon as the winter set in I started to school. The teacher, then called master (for we had no "principals" to schools then), was John Finley, a brother of Father James B. Finley, well known among the Methodists as a preacher of great zeal and piety, for which he was more distinguished than for learning. John Finley was also a Methodist preacher, and as such superior to his brother; but he had left the itinerant service of his church to devote himself to teaching, which he seemed to prefer. He was regarded as an excellent teacher, and his school was large—including the sons of the leading men of the place. . . .

. . . I committed to memory nearly all the poetry in Murray's English Reader, and many other pieces. For one of these tasks I learned and recited Gray's Elegy entire.

Our studies at this school were spelling, reading, arithmetic and writing. We used the United States Spelling Book, a Pittsburgh book, the Western Calculator, also a Pittsburgh work, Murray's series of reading lessons, the English Reader, and the "Introduction" and "Sequel" to the same. Grammar and geography were not taught in the common schools then, nor for many years after. The paper used in writing was a pretty good article of foolscap, made in the country, but unruled. So we had to rule it for ourselves; and each boy was armed with a wooden rule, furnished by some friendly carpenter, to which was tied a pencil made of crude lead. With these we ruled our paper to all desirable widths, by which we were guided in *learning* to write; for it was expected that any one who had *learned* to write would not need such a guide. Our pens were all made of quills; and making a good pen was part of the art of writing, and an indispensable one at that. Our ink was usually made from ink powders, or from oak and maple bark with copperas added to the boiled decoction of these.

One of the most efficient agencies in education in that day was thrashing; and every master scrupulously availed himself of it. Mr. Finley understood it, and it was reasonably well dispensed in his school. My negligence, or talking frequently brought me under this discipline; but I know that there never was any necessity for it. It was the custom, and it saved words. To me it was so mortifying that I took my books home the first time, resolved that I would not endure it. But I was sent back; and I well remember how my appearance in the afternoon was received by the other boys as a thing of course, of which they had had experience. My nice sense of honor and self-respect was broken down then, and I, like the others, learned to care but little about it—the main point afterward being to stand it without crying. The second quarter I made up my mind that I would so behave as to escape, which I did till near the end, when I caught it almost without cause. The house where this school was kept was a one story frame about eighteen or twenty feet square—a mere box with doors and windows. . . .

School Advertisements

SCHOOLTEACHERS reached the frontier at an early date. The following advertisements appeared in the Kentucky Gazette—transcripts in the Draper Collection (18CC130), The State Historical Society of Wisconsin.

EDUCATION

[January 5, 1788]

Notice is hereby given, that on Monday the 28th of January next, a school will be opened by Messes. Jones & Worley, at the royal spring, in Lebanon town, Fayette County, where a commodious house, sufficient to contain 50 or 60 scholars will be prepared. They will teach the Latin and greek languages, together with such branches of the sciences as are usually taught in public seminaries —at 25 shillings a quarter for each Scholar, one half to be paid in cash, the other in produce at cash price. There will be a vacation of a month in the spring, and another in the fall, at the close of each of which, it is expected that such payments as are due in cash, will be made. For out washing and house room, for a year, each scholar pays 3 pounds in cash or 500 weight of pork on entrance, and 3 pounds in cash on the beginning of the 3rd quarter. It is desired that as many as can would furnish themselves with beds. Such as cannot may be provided for here to the number of 8 or 10 boys at 35 shillings a year for each bed.

ELIJAH CRAIG

N.B. It would be proper for each boy to have his sheets, shirts, stockings, &c. marked to prevent mistakes.

LEXINGTON GRAMMAR SCHOOL

[January 12, 1788]

Is again opened, where Latin, Greek, and the difficult branches of science will be carefully taught by Isaac Wilson, formally [sic] professor in Philadelphia College. The price of tuition is 4 pounds payable in cash or produce, boarding may be had on as reasonable terms as any in the district.

Petition for a University

TERRITORIAL governments in the West were anxious to establish institutions of higher education. The following petition to Congress from the Trustees of Vincennes University is reprinted in Carter (ed.), Territorial Papers of the United States, VII, 492–493. It was referred to the House Committee on Commerce and Manufactures but was then rejected. The manuscript is in the House of Representatives Files, 10th Cong., 1 sess.

[1807]

To the Senate and House of Representatives in Congress assembled—

Your petitioners Humbly pray and Shew, That the Legislature of the Indiana Territory, in the year Eighteen hundred and six, passed an act incorporating an University in the district of Vincennes, styled the Vincennes University, and in the same act your petitioners were authorized, to dispose of a small part of the Township of Land, appropriated by an act of Congress, (for the use and support of a publick school in the said district), for the purpose of erecting the necessary buildings for said institution, and your petitioners being convinced that an enlightened and virtuous people, is the only depositary of publick liberty and wishing to carry the said institution into immediate effect, but not being in possession of any funds, which will at this time yeild [sic] an annual income, whereby your petitioners would be enabled to established the said institution, on a liberal plan, so as to be reached by all classes of citizens, without encroaching upon the capital of said institution, which your petitioners conceive was only placed in their hands to make use of the profits thereof; and the said Township of land being situate in a new Country and unimproved, where land is cheap, and therefore will not lease to advantage, and being the only capital which they possess; it will of course yield no annual profit, probably for fifteen or twenty years during which time the citizens of the Territory, will be subject to the inroads of ignorance superstition and faction, which are inevitable consequences, of the want of the benign influence of Education and the liberal sciences—Your Petitioners seeing that our excellent government (which was purchased at the expence of the lives of thousands of brave men) is liable to be assailed by the various arts of cunning and intrigue, of designing, ambitious and desperate Individuals, and also subject to the attacks of silly and often deadly arts of foreign Politicks, your petitioners therefore being convinced, that the only safeguard and secure shield, against the dark Cunning of individuals and of foreign governments, is the blaze of science which will reach the mind of the plowboy, as well as the most wealthy citizen, and wishing to secure to the citizen domestick happiness, and stamp the principles of our government upon their plastick minds; but not having the means to apply the remedy with a strong and steady hand, we therefore pray that you may pass a law, laying a small tax on salt made at publick works in this Territory, and also lay a tax on Indian traders, for the use of the said institution, until the other institutions to which Congress hath granted donations of land in this Territory are organized; then to give said institutions a proportion of said tax, and as in duty bound your petitioners will ever pray

A Teacher's Plight

THE FOLLOWING *letter in the* General Land Office, *printed in Carter (ed.),* Territorial Papers of the United States, *XI, 535–536, reveals the plight of John Farmer, a teacher hired by the University of Michigan.*

[March 16, 1824]

To EDWARD TIFFIN, Surveyor General,

. . . God in his providence saw best at an early age to deprive me of both Father & Mother and also to leave me in a state of entire dependance: But my own industry secured me a living untill by my own intense application I became qualified to teach a common school This employment would have enabled me to make a decent saveing; had not repeated and long fits of sickness exhausted my earnings. I at length acquired the Lancaster system of education and was offered a salary of $450 to take charge of a school of this description at Johnstown payable quarterly if necessary: But the Trustees of the University of Michigan had written to Mr. Dale, principal of the Albany Lancaster school and earnestly requested him to send them a Lancasterian instructor to whom they would allow a sallary of $500 and many other advantages—Mr. Dale selected me and earnestly solicited me to accept the invitation: placeing much confidence in Mr. Dale produced at length my compliance although such were my circumstances that I had to have recourse to the kindness of a friend for means in a great measure to defray the expence of the journey. When I reached Buffalo navigation had closed, I was therefore subjected to the unpleasant and expensive rout through canada—On my arrival at Detroit I was authorised to take immediate charge of the primary school by the Trustees of the University who voted me a salary of $500 per year—The building was in bad order, the cellar was entirely open, forty panes of glass were out of the room and some benches broken &c I suggested to the board the propriety of repairing these and other things to which they readily concured and authorized and requested me to have the repairs done immediately and to present the account at the next session of the board for adjustment. accordingly as I was destitute of money had to obtain on my own personal responsibility a credit of about $80 to make necessary repairs expecting to obtain a draft on the Treasury from whence I would receive the money as soon as the ac^t could be audited—But to my surprise and grief I found when too late that the Treasury was in debt about $2000 without a cent to pay with or the prospect of obtaining any that even the building had not been paid for. I therefore had to wait till perhaps I would be in my grave or assume demands (most of which were desperate) to the amount of my salary and the repairs I had made—I have already totally lost the half of my earnings by bad debts. What I have collected has not been sufficient to defray my expences although I have been very economical—What I have due is very doubtful I have a demand against two of the Trustees for schooling their own children for which I told their notes to the amount of $70. But I can not realise one cent from it and I expect to lose the same—I purchased a city Lot last summer at Detroit that would be valuable in time but for want of means to defray my other debts [MS. torn]pect it will have to be sold—I have really done much for the citizens of Detroit have Laboured hard two years and find myself $100 worse than when I arrived there—

22. Villages and Towns

THE CULTURAL centers of the West were the villages and cities. Daniel Drake, an early settler in the Ohio Valley and later a physician, describes rustic Mays Lick, Kentucky. His account was contained in a series of letters to his children now in the Drake Library, Cincinnati General Hospital. The following extracts are from Daniel Drake, Pioneer Life in Kentucky, 1785–1800, edited by Emmet Field Horne (New York, 1948), pp. 187–189.

This place, although scarcely a village, was once an emporium and capital for a tract of country 6 or 8 miles in diameter, embracing several hundred families. . . . It was the place for holding Regimental militia musters, when all the boys and old men of the surrounding country, not less than those who stood enrolled, would assemble. Before dispersing at night, the training was quite eclipsed by a heterogeneous drama of foot racing, pony racing, wrestling, fighting, drunkenness and general uproar.

It was also a place for political meetings and stump conflict by opposing candidates, & after intellectual performances there generally followed an epilogue of oaths, yells, loud blows, & gnashing of teeth.

Singing schools were likewise held at the same place in a room of Deacon Morris' tavern. . . .

The infant capital was, still further, the local seat of Justice; and Saturday was for many years, at all times I might say, the regular "term time." Instead of trying cases at home, two or three justices of the peace would come to the "Lick" on that day, and hold their separate courts. This, of course, brought thither all the litigants of the neighbourhood, with their friends and witnesses. All who wished to purchase at the store would postpone their visit to the same day. All who had to replenish their jugs of whiskey did the same thing. All who had business with others expected to meet them there, as our city merchants, at 12 M. expect to meet each other on "change." Finally, all who thirsted after drink, fun, frolic or fighting, of course, were present. Thus Saturday was a day of largely suspended field labour, but devoted to public business, social pleasure, dissipation, and beastly drunkenness. You might suppose that the presence of civil magistrates would have repressed some of these vices, but it was not so. Each day provided a bill of fare for the next. A new trade in horses, another horse race, a cock fight, or a dog fight, a wrestling match, or a "pitched" battle between two bullies, who in fierce rencontre, would lie on the ground scratching, pulling hair, choking, goughing out each others eyes, and biting off each others noses, in the manner of bull dogs, while a Roman circle of interested lookers on would encourage the respective gladiators with shouts which a passing demon might have mistaken for those of hell. In the afternoon the men & boys of business and sobriety would depart, and at nightfall the dissipated would follow them, often two on a horse, reeling and yelling. . . . But many would be too much intoxicated to mount their horses, and must, therefore, remain till Sunday morning.

Pittsburgh and Lexington

THE SMALL cities in the West at an early date developed not only as commercial and industrial, but also as cultural centers. Once the early frontier stage had passed, eastern and even European cultural forms— art, music, and theater—were introduced. The following descriptions of Pittsburgh and Lexington in the first decade of the nineteenth century are from Fortescue Cuming, Sketches of a Tour to the Western Country . . . (Pittsburgh, Pa., 1810), reprinted in Thwaites (ed.), Early Western Travels, IV, 81–83, 183–189.

Several musical amateurs are associated here under the title of the Apollonian Society. I visited it by invitation at the house of Mr. F. Amelung the acting President, and was most agreeably surprised to hear a concert of instrumental musick performed by about a dozen gentlemen of the town, with a degree of taste and execution, which I could not have expected in so remote a place. I was particularly astonished at the performance on the violin of Mr. Gabler, a German, employed at Gen. O'Hara's glass house, and who is one of the society. His natural talents for musick were so great, that he could not bear the trammels of a scientifick acquisition of it, and therefore never learned a note, yet he joins a correct extempore harmony, to the compositions of Hayden, Pleyel, Bach, Mozart and the other celebrated composers, particularly in their lively movements; he is not quite so happy in his accompaniments of Handel, or of grand or solemn musick generally. His execution of Waltz's is in a sweet and tasty style, and he has composed by ear and committed to memory several pieces, which impress the hearer with regret, that they must die with their author. Indeed he now (when too late) regrets himself, that he had not in his youth, and when he had great opportunities, added science to natural taste.

The Apollonian society is principally indebted for its formation to the labours of Mr. S. H. Dearborn, a New England man, who came here about a year ago, to exercise the profession of a portrait painter, and being a very versatile genius, and having some knowledge of, and taste for musick, he soon discovered all the respectable people who were harmoniously inclined, and succeeded in associating them into a regular society, which meets one evening every week, and consists not only of those who can take parts, but also of many of the most respectable inhabitants of the town, who do not play, but who become members, for the sake of admission for themselves and families to the periodical concerts.

There are also two dramatick societies in Pittsburgh, one composed of the students of law, and the other of respectable mechanicks. They occasionally unite with each other in order to cast the pieces to be performed with more effect. The theatre is in the great room of the upper story of the courthouse, which from its size, and having several other contiguous apartments which serve for green room, dressing rooms, &c. is very well adapted to that purpose. It is neatly fitted up under the direction of Mr. Dearborn, whose mechanical genius has rendered him a useful associate of the disciples of Thespis; whether as machinist, dresser, scene painter and shifter or actor; particularly in the part of the garrulous Mrs. Bulgruddery in John Bull, which he performs with much re-

spectability. Mr. W. Wilkins excels in genteel comedy; Mr. John-
ston does justice to the part of an Irishman; Mr. Haslet to that of a
Yorkshire farmer or country squire; Mr. Linton in low comedy is
the Edwin of Pittsburgh, and Mr. Van Baun would be an orna-
ment to any established theatre, either in the sock or the buskin,
he being equally excellent in Octavian as in Fribble. The female
characters being sustained by young men, are deficient of that grace
and modest vivacity, which are natural to the fair sex, and which
their grosser lords and masters vainly attempt to copy. On the
whole however, the dramatick societies, exhibit in a very respectable manner, a rational entertainment to the inhabitants of
Pittsburgh about once monthly through the winter. They have
hitherto confined themselves to the comick walk, but I have no
doubt, that if they appear in the buskin, they will do equal credit
to tragedy. . . .

I employed the forenoon in running over and viewing the town
[Lexington]. It contains three hundred and sixty-six dwelling
houses, besides barns, stables and other out offices. The streets
cross each other at right angles, and are from fifty to eighty feet
wide. . . .
There are societies of Presbyterians, Seceders, Episcopalians,
Anabaptists and Roman Catholicks, each of which has a church,
no way remarkable, except the Episcopalian, which is very neat
and convenient. There is also a society of Methodists, which has
not yet any regular house of worship. The court house now finishing, is a good, plain, brick building, of three stories, with a cupola,
rising from the middle of the square roof, containing a bell and a
town clock. The cupola is supported by four large brick columns
in the centre of the house, rising from the foundation, through the
hall of justice, and in my opinion adding nothing to its beauty or
convenience. The whole building when finished, will cost about
fifteen thousand dollars. The masonick hall, is a neat brick building, as is also the bank, where going for change for a Philadelphia
bank note, I received in specie one per cent. advance, which they
allow on the notes of the Atlantick cities for the convenience of
remitting. There is a publick library and a university, called Transylvania, which is incorporated and is under the government of
twenty-one trustees and the direction of a president, the Rev.
James Blythe, who is also professor of natural philosophy, mathe-

maticks, geography and English grammar. There are four professors besides: the Rev. Robert H. Bishop, professor of moral philosophy, belles lettres, logick and history; Mr. Ebenezer Sharpe, professor of the languages; Doctor James Fishback, professor of medicine, &c. and Henry Clay, Esq. professor of law. The funds of the university arise from the price of tuition, (which is lower than in any other seminary of learning in the United States) and from eight thousand acres of first rate land, granted to it by the state of Virginia; five thousand of which are in the neighbourhood of Lexington, and three thousand near Louisville at the falls of Ohio. The legislature of Kentucky have also granted to it six thousand acres of valuable land, south of Green river. Its yearly income from the lands, now amounts to about two thousand dollars, which will probably be soon much increased.

There are no fewer than three creditable boarding schools for female education, in which there are at present above a hundred pupils. An extract from Mrs. Beck's card, will convey some idea of the progress of polite education in this country.

"Boarders instructed in the following branches, at the rate of two hundred dollars per annum, viz. Reading, spelling, writing, arithmetick, grammar, epistolary correspondence, elocution and rhetorick; geography, with the use of maps, globes, and the armillary sphere; astronomy, with the advantage of an orrery; ancient and modern history; chronology, mythology, and natural history; natural and moral philosophy; musick, vocal and instrumental; drawing, painting, and embroidery of all kinds; artificial flowers, and any other fashionable fancy-work; plain sewing, marking, netting, &c."

The card designates a regular course of education, as it proceeds through the successional branches, all of which cannot be studied by any individual at the same time.

Mrs. Beck is an English lady, and is in high reputation as an instructress. She was now absent, having taken advantage of a vacation, to visit the Olympian Springs, about fifty miles from Lexington, much resorted, on account of their salubrious effects.

There is no regular academy for males, but there are several day schools.

The number of inhabitants in Lexington, in 1806, was 1655 free white inhabitants, and 1165 negro slaves, in all 2820. The whole number may now be safely estimated at 3000.

There are three nail manufacturies, which make about sixty tons of nails per annum; and there are ten blacksmith's shops, which find constant employment for a considerable number of hands.

There are two copper and tin manufacturies, one of which manufactures ware to the amount of ten thousand dollars yearly; the other is on a smaller scale.

There are four jewellers and silversmiths, whose business is very profitable.

Seven saddler's shops employ thirty hands, the proceeds of whose labour is annually from twenty-five to thirty thousand dollars.

There are four cabinet-maker's shops, where household furniture is manufactured in as handsome a style as in any part of America, and where the high finish which is given to the native walnut and cherry timber, precludes the regret that mahogany is not to be had but at an immense expense.

Three tan yards and five currying shops, manufacture about thirty thousand dollars worth of leather every year.

There is one excellent umbrella manufactury, one brush, one reed, four chair, and two tobacco manufacturies which make chewing tobacco, snuff and cigars. Three blue-dyers. Five hatters, who employ upwards of fifty hands, and manufacture about thirty thousand dollars worth of fur and wool hats annually. Ten tailors, who employ forty-seven journeymen and apprentices. Fifteen shoe and boot makers, who employ about sixty hands, and manufacture to the amount of about thirty thousand dollars yearly; and two stocking weavers.

Two brew-houses make as good beer as can be got in the United States. A carding machine for wool, is a great convenience to the manufacturers of that article. There is one manufacturer of baling cloth for cotton wool, who employs thirty-eight hands, and makes thirty-six thousand yards annually; and two cotton spinning machines, worked by horses, yield a handsome profit to the proprietors. An oil mill, worked by horses, makes fifteen hundred gallons of oil per year. Seven distilleries make near seven thousand gallons of spirits yearly. Four rope-walks employ about sixty hands, and make about three hundred tons of cordage annually, the tar for which is made on the banks of Sandy river, and is bought in Lexington at from eighteen to twenty-five cents per gallon. There are two apothecaries' shops, and five regular physicians. Twenty-two stores retail upwards of three hundred thousand dollars worth of imported, foreign merchandize annually; and there is one book and stationary store on a very large scale, and two printing offices, where gazettes are printed weekly.

In the neighbourhood are six powder mills, that make about twenty thousand pounds of powder yearly.

There are seven brick yards which employ sixty hands, and make annually two million five hundred thousand bricks; and there are fifty brick-layers, and as many attendants, who have built between thirty and forty good brick houses each of the last three years. The Presbyterian society is now finishing a church which will cost eight thousand dollars. . . .

There are four billiard tables in Lexington, and cards are a good deal played at taverns, where it is more customary to meet for that purpose than at private houses.

There is a coffee house here, where is a reading room for the benefit of subscribers and strangers, in which are forty-two files of different newspapers from various parts of the United States. It is supported by subscribers, who pay six dollars each annually, and of which there are now sixty. In the same house is a billiard table, and chess and back-gammon tables, and the guests may be accommodated with wine, porter, beer, spirituous liquors, cordials and confectionary. It is kept by a Mr. Terasse, formerly of the island of St. Bartholomew. He had been unfortunate in mercantile business in the West Indies, and coming to this country, and failing in the recovery of some property he had shipped to New York, he had no other resource left to gain a provision for his family, but the teaching of the French language and dancing, in Lexington. The trustees of Transylvania college (or university, as the Lexington people proudly call it) employed him in the former, but had it not been for the latter, he might have starved. . . . Disgusted at length with the little encouragement he received, he bethought himself of his present business, in which he has become useful to the town and seems to be reaping a plentiful harvest from his ingenuity. He has opened a little publick garden behind his house, which he calls Vauxhall. It has a most luxuriant grape arbour, and two or three summer houses, formed also of grape vines, all of which are illuminated with variegated lamps, every Wednesday evening, when the musick of two or three decent performers sometimes excites parties to dance on a small boarded platform in the middle of the arbour. It is becoming a place of fashionable resort.

Acknowledgments

The author wishes to thank the following for permission to reprint materials previously published:

Abelard-Schuman Limited, for permission to use extracts from Daniel Drake, *Pioneer Life in Kentucky* (New York, 1948), pp. 187–189.

The Carnegie Institution of Washington, for extracts from John Spencer Bassett (ed.), *Correspondence of Andrew Jackson* (Washington, D.C., 1924), I, 84–86, 490–492.

The Cincinnati Historical Society, for permission to quote extracts from Beverly W. Bond, Jr. (ed.), *The Correspondence of John Cleves Symmes* (New York, 1926), pp. 63–65, 281–284; and Dwight L. Smith (ed.), *The Western Journals of John May, Ohio Company Agent and Business Venturer* (Cincinnati, Ohio, 1961), pp. 137–141.

The Arthur H. Clark Company, for permission to quote extracts from Ulrich B. Phillips (ed.), *Documentary History of American Industrial Society, Plantation and Frontier* (Cleveland, Ohio, 1910), II, 208–211.

The Cornell University Press and the Wyoming Historical and Geological Society, for permission to quote extracts from Julian P. Boyd (ed.), *The Susquehanna Company Papers* (Wilkes-Barre, Pa., 1930–1933), III, 43–47; IV, 146, 264, 271–272, 276, 377–378.

William B. Hamilton and Duke University Press, for permission to quote material from William B. Hamilton (ed.), *Anglo-American Law on the Frontier: Thomas Rodney and His Territorial Cases* (Durham, N.C., 1953), pp. 360–362, 381–382.

The Historical Society of Pennsylvania, for permission to quote extracts from the letters of Thomas Rodney, printed in the *Pennsylvania Magazine of History and Biography*, XLV (1921), 182–183.

The Illinois State Historical Library, for permission to quote from Theodore C. Pease (ed.), *The Laws of the Northwest Ter-*

ritory, Vol. XVII of *The Collections of the Illinois State Historical Library* (Springfield, Ill., 1925), 377–379.

The Indiana Historical Society, for permission to quote from Gayle Thornbrough (ed.), *The Correspondence of John Badollet and Albert Gallatin*, Vol. XXII of *Indiana Historical Society Publications* (Indianapolis, Ind., 1963), 91–93, 97.

The editor of the *Journal of American History*, for permission to quote extracts from the journal of William Calk, published in the *Mississippi Valley Historical Review*, VII (March, 1921), 365–369.

The Dean and Librarian of Marietta College, Marietta, Ohio, for permission to use extracts from Archer Butler Hulbert (ed.), *Ohio in the Time of the Confederation*, Vol. III of *Marietta College Historical Collections* (Marietta, Ohio, 1918), 98, 99, 103–109, 137–140, 209–211.

The Office of State History, New York State Education Department, for permission to use extracts from Milton W. Hamilton (ed.), *The Papers of Sir William Johnson* (Albany, N.Y., 1951) X, 981–984.

The editor, North Carolina Department of Archives and History, for permission to quote extracts from the journal of Abraham Steiner, Adelaide L. Fries (ed. and trans.), *North Carolina Historical Review*, XXI (October, 1944), 334–371; and Alice B. Keith (ed.), *The John Gray Blount Papers* (Raleigh, N.C., 1952), I, 168–171.

William W. Sweet, Jr., of Dallas, Texas, for permission to use material from William W. Sweet, *Religion on the American Frontier* (New York and Chicago, 1931–1946), I, 50–51, 258–261; III, 79–81, 288–291; IV, 183–184, 187–188.

The Earl Gregg Swem Library of the College of William and Mary in Virginia, for permission to quote extracts from the Edward Coles letters, printed in *The William and Mary College Quarterly*, 2nd series, VII (April, 1927), 100–103.

The State Historical Society of Wisconsin, for permission to use the letters of John Floyd dated October 30 and November 26, 1779, Draper Collection (17CC184–186); extracts from Thomas Hanson's journal, Draper Collection (14J58–84); a transcript from the *Kentucky Gazette*, Draper Collection (18CC130); extracts of the letter from Evan Shelby to John Shelby dated January 3, 1774, Draper Collection (16DD4); and extracts from the letters of James Wier, Draper Collection (21CC4, 5 and 16).

The Tennessee Historical Commission, for permission to quote from Samuel Cole Williams, *Tennessee During the Revolutionary War* (Nashville, Tenn., 1944), pp. 19–21.

The University of Pittsburgh Press, for extracts from Richard C. Knopf (ed.), *Anthony Wayne . . . Correspondence . . .* (Pittsburgh, Pa., 1960), pp. 351–354; Paul A. W. Wallace (ed. and trans.), *Thirty Thousand Miles with John Heckewelder* (Pittsburgh, Pa., 1958), pp. 236–243; and Lois L. Mulkearn (ed.), *George Mercer Papers Relating to the Ohio Company of Virginia* (Pittsburgh, Pa., 1954), pp. 144–147.